IMAGES
of America

Surfing in Hawai'i 1778–1930

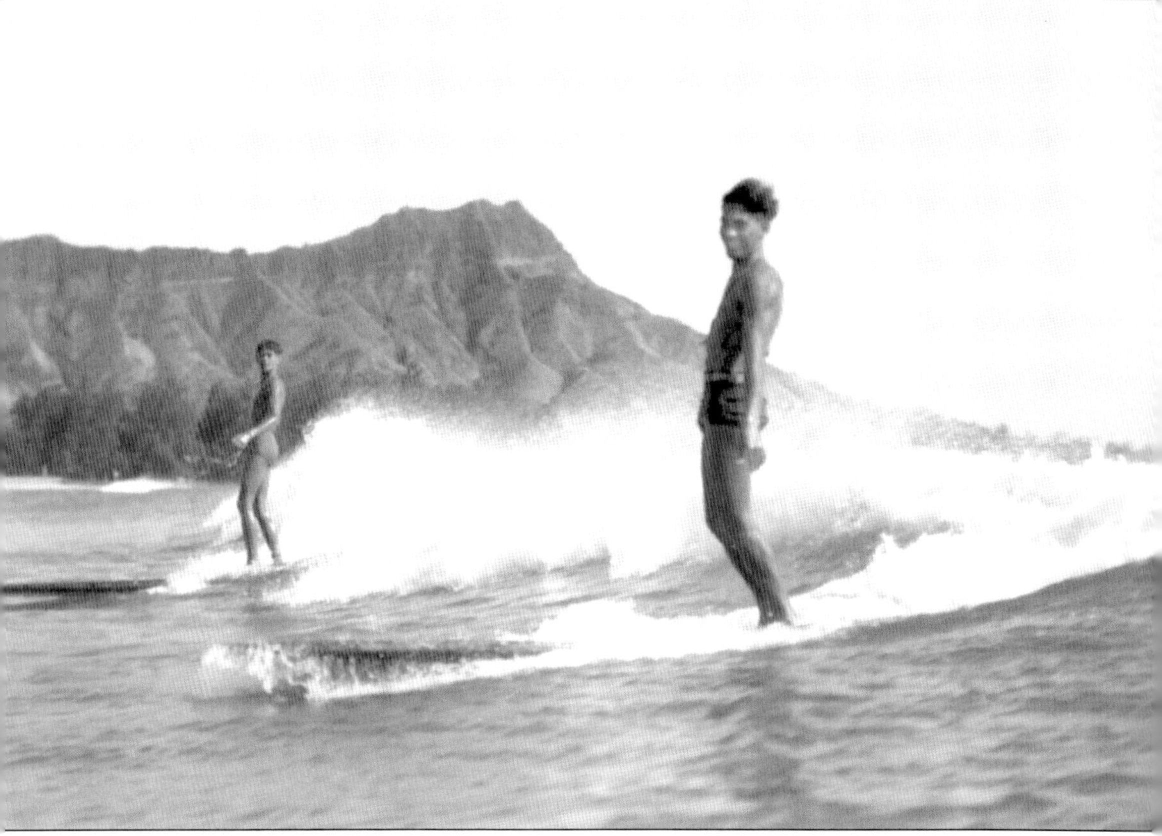

The "Pure Stoke" of a Beachboy Surfing off Waikiki Beach, c. 1929. During the rebirth of surfing from its near demise at the end of the 19th century, no place was more instrumental than the perfect arena for solid wood surfboards located at Waikiki Beach, nor was any group more influential than the beachboys, who established the surfing lifestyle of the 20th century. (Photograph by Post, Honolulu; courtesy Outrigger Canoe Club.)

On the Cover: A surfer in a *malo* (loincloth) poses with his surfboard around 1893. This iconic photograph was one of the most popular images published around the end of the 19th century. The surfer may be Charles Kauha, who also posed for the Frank Davey photograph on page 32. Waikiki at this time was a sleepy bay unprepared for the coming century of change. (Courtesy DeLaVega family archives.)

IMAGES
of America

SURFING IN HAWAI'I
1778–1930

Timothy Tovar DeLaVega

ARCADIA
PUBLISHING

ISBN 978-0-7385-7488-2

Published by Arcadia Publishing
Charleston, South Carolina

Printed in the United States of America

Library of Congress Control Number: 2010941636

For all general information, please contact Arcadia Publishing:
Telephone 843-853-2070
Fax 843-853-0044
E-mail sales@arcadiapublishing.com
For customer service and orders:
Toll-Free 1-888-313-2665

Visit us on the Internet at www.arcadiapublishing.com

To those surf riders of distant days
who rode the spirit of the mighty trees
speeding upon charging, steaming billows
to the beaches of Hawai'i nei

Contents

Acknowledgments		6
Foreword		7
Introduction		9
1.	‘Ikena He‘e Nalu (Visions of Surf Sliding) Ancient Hawai‘i: 300 AD–1778	11
2.	Western Etchings of Exploration: 1778–1900	15
3.	The Photographic Era Begins: 1888–1910	27
4.	The Outrigger Canoe Club: 1908	45
5.	Hui Nalu (Club of the Waves): 1908	53
6.	Surfing’s First Boom: 1910–1920	61
7.	Duke Paoa Kahanamoku: 1890–1968	83
8.	On Solid Ground: 1920–1930	95
Bibliography		127

ACKNOWLEDGMENTS

This project was done to properly identify the early photographers/artists as well as establish a proper timeline of early surfing images. We hope you enjoy our discoveries and that this will promote future research. This book could never have been accomplished without a worldwide TEAM (Together Everyone Achieves More) of dedicated surfing fanatics who have again combined energy to create our third project in 10 years. This book is an example of aloha (affection, love, and peace), as each door I knocked on was opened wide with warmth and love. *Mahalo nui loa* (gratitude) TEAM participants: Sandra Kimberley Hall, who was always there for fact checking and especially for prose that moved me to my soul; Cary Weiss, who got this project going and allowed use of his massive collection and the research on the George Freeth era; Dan Pincetich and his amazing collection, as well as the research and text he put in on the early postcards and advertisements; Edward Stasack, Diane Stasack, and John R.K. Clark for all their assistance in the Ancient Hawai'ian era; Prof. Patrick Moser, who reviewed and edited the book three times, checking for historical accuracy; DeSoto Brown for his help on the early images; Keao NeSmith and Mark Fragale for their wonderful prose; and to "Baby" Dave Rochelen and Barbara del Piano for their assistance and hospitality. Mahalo TEAM contributors: Al and Courtney Carpenter, Geoff Carter, Jamie Clark, Chris Cook, Keith "Maynard" Eshelman, Cindy Fragale, Al Hunt, Allen Kukel, Gary Lynch, MaryAnne Maigret, David Marsh, and Joel T. Smith. Mahalo TEAM supporters: Nick Galante, Jens Jensen, Joe Tabler, Bob Smith, Puuloa Teves, and Mark Thomson.

Mahalo to the following *ohanas* (families) for their cooperation and assistance: the A.R. Gurrey Jr./Walter G. Bayer families and the J.J. Williams family. Mahalo to the following organizations for allowing access to their archives: Outrigger Canoe Club and the State of Hawaii Archives. Mahalo to Sunset Publication Corporation for the use of a 1926 *Sunset* magazine cover. The Duke Kahanamoku imagery is published under permission from Malama Pono Ltd., with special thanks to Jim Fulton, Don Love, and the Outrigger Duke Kahanamoku Foundation for their support. Mahalo to the Surfing Heritage Foundation and the Bishop Museum; my favorite research site, www.soulsurfingimages.com; and, most importantly, my patient and understanding ohana that includes lovely wife Jan, Abby, Lisa, and Donna.

All images used in this book come from the DeLaVega family archives unless otherwise noted. Artists and photographers are noted only if known. All attempts have been made to track down the original artists.

FOREWORD

He hana ka he'e nalu i ho'okumu 'ia ma nā pae'āina o ka Pākīpika nei e like me Aotearoa, Polapola, a me Hawai'i nei he mau kenekulia i hala akula. No ka ma'a a me ka nui o ke akamai o ka po'e kānaka he'e nalu, ua laulā nā 'ano hana he'e nalu, he kū i luna, kulikuli i lalo, a moe pālaha nō. Nui nā 'ano papa e he'e ai a he he'e kino nō kekahi. 'A'ole 'o ka he'e nalu wale nō ka pā'ani kai, 'o ka hoehoe wa'a pū nō, ka pākākā nalu a me ka lele kawa nō ho'i kekahi o nā pā'ani kai i akamai ai nā lāhui 'ōiwi o ka Pākīpika. 'O ke ola nō ia o ka po'e ola i ke kai i 'ike i nā 'ale nui, nā 'ale iki, ke au kō a me ke au kā.

He kōkua nui ka heluhelu 'ana i nā palapala a ka po'e Hawai'i i ola i ka wā o nā Kamehameha i kākau no nā hana pā'ani a nā kūpuna e like me ko lākou 'ike maka a hana maoli. 'O 'Ī'ī, Kamakau, Malo, a me Kepilino kekahi o lākou no ka nui o kā lākou mau mea i kākau ai no nā pā'ani kai.

Eia kā, ua nui hewahewa pū ka 'ōlelo i loko o nā nūpepa 'ōlelo Hawai'i o ke kenekulia 'umi kumamāiwa a me ka hapa o mua o ke kenekulia iwakālua no nā pā'ani kai. He kumu waiwai nui palena 'ole ua mau palapala nei no ka ho'ākāka 'ana no ua mea nei he he'e nalu ma kona mau 'ano a pau a pēlā pū ka 'ōlelo wehewehe no nā 'ano 'oni o nā nalu, nā 'ale, nā au, nā makani, a me ka lewa. He mau mea ia e memele nui ai ka po'e aloha i ke kai a me nā pā'ani kai a he lehulehu pū nā mele like 'ole a nā kūpuna.

Ua ho'ololi 'ia nā 'ano papa he'e nalu o kēia wā nei ā kūpono no nā makemake o ka po'e he'e nalu o kēia wā a he he'e nalu nō nā lāhui like 'ole o ka honua nei mai 'ō a 'ō i kēia manawa. Akā, he hapa wale nō nā 'ano hana kai i hana 'ia i kēia wā ke ho'okūkū 'ia me nā 'ano hana a ka po'e kānaka o nā kenekulia i hala a he nui 'ino nō ka 'ike i koe ma ka nānā 'ana i nā palapala kahiko i nānā 'ole 'ia ā hiki i kēia manawa.

He hō'ike'ike nā ki'i o kēia puke e ho'omaopopo ai i ke 'ano o nā pā'ani kai i hiki ke hana 'ia e like me nā kūpuna o ka wā i hala. He mahalo ka makahehi 'ana i ke akamai o lākou i ka 'oni pū me ke kai i kona mau ea a emi 'ana, i kona pōpo'i a mimiki 'ana, a i kona 'ōkaikai a malino 'ana.

Surfing and sea sports have been a natural part of everyday life to Pacific islanders from New Zealand to Tahiti to Hawai'i for centuries. They were as important to the physical, mental, and spiritual well-being of the individual and society in times past as farming, fishing, industry, and spiritual devotion. Innovators of ocean sports in antiquity formulated numerous methods and equipment for taking advantage of the often unpredictable movements of the sea, including surfboards and specially designed canoes for riding waves. This seems to have come natural to societies that not only survive on the sea and the resources it provides but also love these things as sentimental gifts of nature.

Among the great Hawai'ian writers of the era of the Kamehameha dynasty (1810–1874) are Kamakau, Malo, and Kepelino. Although their contributions have been great regarding the description of traditional ocean sports of the Hawaiian Islands, the greatest treasury of language and lore regarding ocean sports lies in the immense volumes of Hawai'ian language newspapers of the 19th and early 20th centuries. Those who are able to read these texts are able to appreciate the language of ocean sports and the terms and idioms that do not translate into English easily or at all. Therefore, it is one thing to talk about these activities in Hawai'ian and quite another to talk about them in English.

The ocean, its movements and resources, are something to sing about, and this has been done among Hawai'ians and Polynesian peoples in general for centuries. In the lyrics lie a specially coded language that describes atmospheric phenomena, movements of nature and people, passions of all types, and philosophies that are often inexplicable in modern English terms. The images contained in this book facilitate meaning as they portray the activities and environments of times past that have brought us to this day and age as all people of the world continue to enjoy some of the numerous ocean sports that have been known for centuries in the Pacific. It is hoped that this book will assist the movement in this age towards awareness of the sanctity of the natural world and the need to protect ocean resources and our natural environment.

—R. Keao NeSmith
Instructor of Hawaiian Language
Kawaihuelani Center for Hawaiian Language
University of Hawai'i at Manoa

INTRODUCTION

Explorations into history are all too often fraught by revisionist speculation; the origins as to the sport of surfing are no exception. Historians delving into such disciplines often find themselves challenging declared key tenets, eventually wrangling towards an imprecise but otherwise marshaled consensus. Debates and further refinements of existing knowledge become an ongoing process.

Add to this assessment that few if any historians studying the source of surfing in Greater Oceania would take issue with the belief that the Hawaiian Islands were indeed the hallowed ground that brought the art of surf riding to its fullest realization and present-day fruition.

Of important note is the fact that primordial Hawai'ians were devoid of any written language or tangible visual imagery of consequence; the result was the collection of past events, traditions, culture, and histories being passed down through countless generations of progeny via the mediums of the spoken word, dance, and *meles* (song/chants/poems).

The verbal and storied histories advanced forward via trans-generational Ancient Hawai'ians by some measures eclipse the tangible records of Western civilization modes. One can convincingly argue, at least on a spiritual plain, that the very essence of Hawai'ian ancestral preservation of history via the storied mind fills the senses with a far richer imagery than material stores. Clearly, this practice allowed the early Hawai'ians a close and intimate harmony amidst the sea, the land, and the natural world surrounding them.

In keeping with the natural world, early Hawai'ians had no choice other than to utilize existing native materials in constructing their surfboards. Legend has it that surfboard and canoe building was a sacred affair. It is said that once a suitable tree was selected to build from, a prayer was said. Once the tree was felled, an offering of deep respect to the gods and nature was made by burying a fish or foodstuff at the base of where the tree once stood. In the absence of milled lumber and metal tools, the boards were crafted in one piece from the tree trunk. The finished surfboard was treated with great importance, as many early explorers have duly noted, and was often stored prominently in the *hale* (home) in a place of reverence.

Spiritually, these wooden surfboards were very much alive; once animate, living and respiring amidst an earthly terrain, their souls were reshaped, transformed, and then entombed in a slathering of indigenous oils, destined expressly to glide upon the billowing breakers in the watery world of the ocean. They were wings on the water if you will, vehicles for the Hawai'ians to surf upon, further communing with nature.

Yet the people of then isolated Ancient Hawaii were decimated by the scourges of disease and plague, introduced to the islands by Western voyagers, with the vast amount of the populace being overwhelmed by newly introduced sicknesses that the islanders were never before exposed to. Although diminished in number, the Hawai'ian spirit was carried on by the strong who survived, with many of their traditions intact.

It was at the end of the 1800s that the pastime of surfing found resurgence within the island chain. Nowhere was this more evident than at Waikiki Beach, where riders were becoming experts in the art of wave riding. Waikiki was the quintessential arena for the wooden plank boards. Blessed with plentiful and gentle wave fields, the surf there had an allure to both expert and novice participants alike. Further amplifying the popularity of surfing was the advent of a burgeoning tourism trade in the Hawaiian Islands.

The role of photography in documenting early Hawai'ian surfing is not to be underestimated. In 1901, the Moana Hotel opened, and Waikiki became a fabled destination synonymous with surf riding itself. Photographs and film clips made their way into far reaches of the globe and became a source of fascination and intrigue to audiences most everywhere. The photographs left behind today validate the Hawai'ian rebirth of postmodern surfing. Soon thereafter, both the Outrigger Canoe Club and Hui Nalu (Club of the Waves) provided a foundation to build upon the growth of surfing and outrigger canoeing.

Truly, the ambassadors of aloha ushering in this new era were the so-called beachboys, as they shared their carefree ways and island knowledge with visiting travelers and dignitaries. Little did the then beachboys realize the scope and reach of their sphere of influence. It is safe to say that the lifestyle of the Waikiki beachboys was the beginning of what is referred to today as surf culture. So profound was their sway that in years to come, vestiges of their way of life would be found in strongholds of visiting surfers and beyond celebrating the Hawai'ian ways of surfing and aloha.

As you peruse the pages of this book, keep in mind that this was a unique era, based on one simple fact: this was the time when surfing was done on solid wood—wood that had once grown high into the sky, wood that had once lived and breathed, wood that had a *'uhane* (soul). This was the era when surfers rode those billowing crests on the souls of trees. Soon it would all change: first waterproof glue, then fiberglass, and modern technology continued to march on. So those of us looking back are left to ponder the special beauty found in the simplicity of it all in the days when surfers rode souls.

—Mark Fragale
Curator of the Honolulu Surfing Museum

One

ʻIkena Heʻe Nalu (Visions of Surf Sliding) Ancient Hawaiʻi 300 AD–1778

by Timothy T. DeLaVega

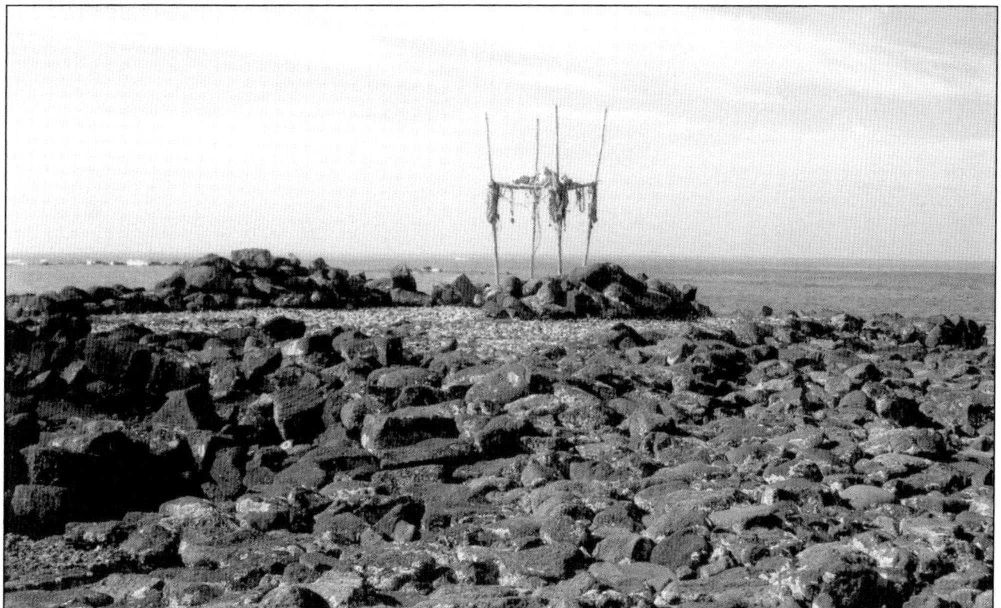

Kuʻemanu Heiau, Kona Coast. A *heiau* is an ancient Hawaiʻian place of worship or a shrine, built in connection with a certain activity, event, or individual deity. In the 1906–1907 publication *Heiau of the Island of Hawaiʻi: A Survey of Native Hawaiian Temple Sites*, John F.G. Stokes wrote, "The natives explained that it [Kuʻemanu Heiau] was a heiau for surf-riding, where they could pray for good surfing weather and consequently good sport." On-site is a stone called ʻOha that was tapped like a bell to call the surf and a pond, Waikuʻipunawai, to rinse off. (Courtesy MaryAnne Maigret.)

Mele Pohuehue

Pohuehue Chant

Ina a'ohe nalu, alaila, kahea aku i kai, penei e hea ai,
If there is no surf, invoke seaward in the following manner,

Ku mai! Ku mai! Ka nalu nui mai Kahiki mai,
Arise, arise you great surfs from Kahiki,

Alo poi pu! Ku mai ka pohuehue,
The powerful curling waves. Arise with the pohuehue,

Hu! Kaiko'o Loa.
Well up, long raging surf.

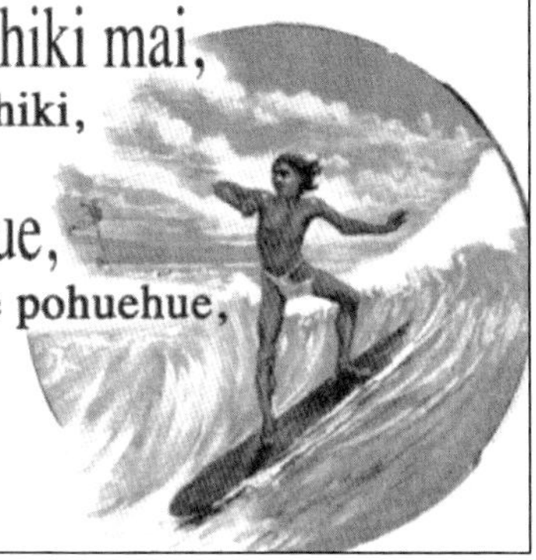

Ancient Hawai'ian Surfing Chant, Called a Mele Pohuehue, after the Beach Morning Glory. In *An Account of the Polynesian Race* (1878), Abraham Fornander stated, "If there was a serious dearth of surf in a particular area, the appointed *Kahuna* (priest) would take several strands of the *pohuehue* and, in unison with the 'swimming party' " swing the vines around and lash them "unitedly upon the water until the desired undulating waves were obtained."

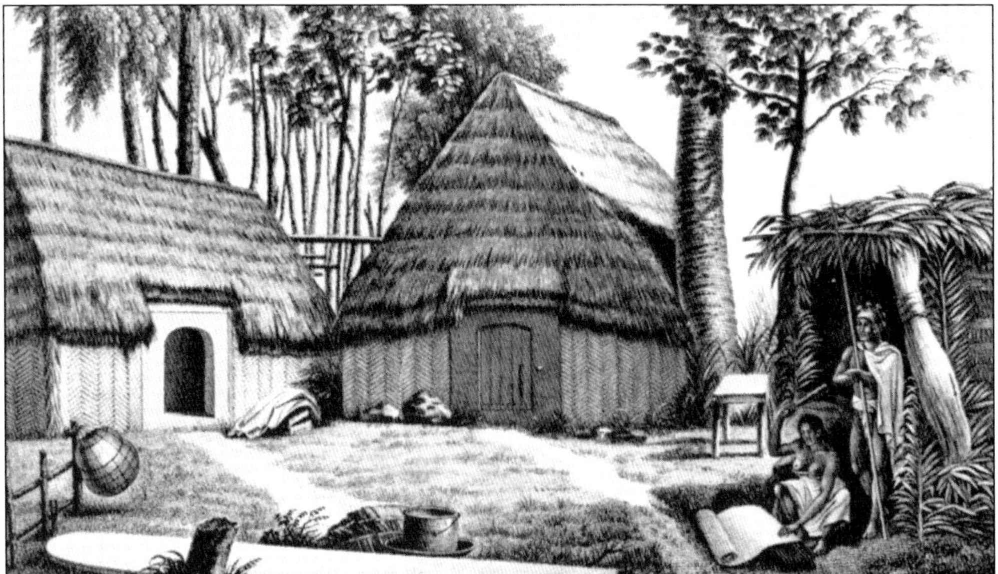

The Houses of Chief Kraimokou, Jacques Arago, c. 1819. The four types of surfboards in ancient Hawai'i were the *olo*, which was narrow, thick, and up to 16 feet long; the *kiko'o*, which was wide, thin, and between 9 to 16 feet long; the *alaia*, which was wide, thin, and from six to nine feet long; and the *papa li'ili'i*, which was narrow, thin, and less than six feet long. Note the olo in the etching.

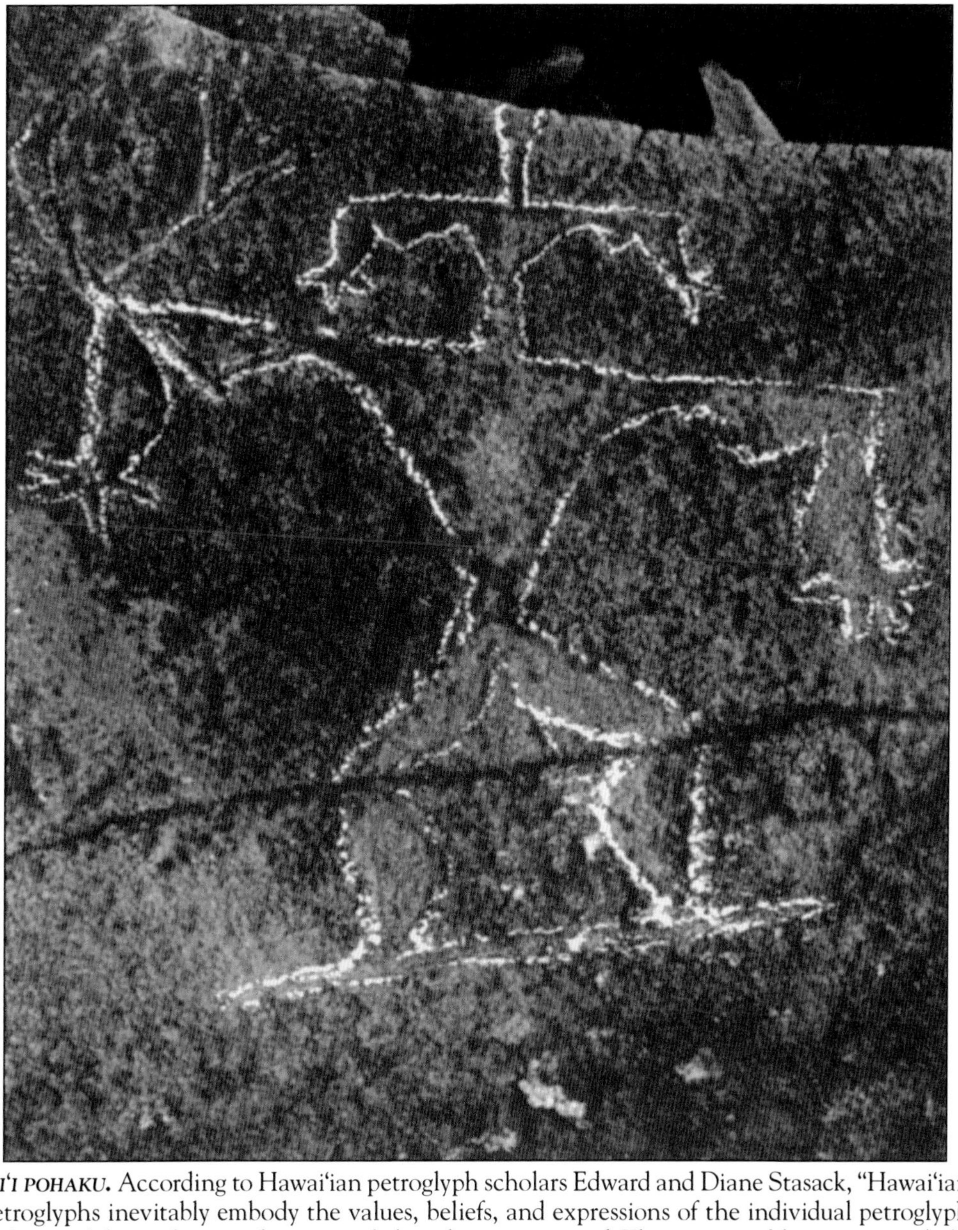

KI'I POHAKU. According to Hawai'ian petroglyph scholars Edward and Diane Stasack, "Hawai'ian petroglyphs inevitably embody the values, beliefs, and expressions of the individual petroglyph makers and their culture, at the time and place they were created. They consist of depictions, symbols, chronicles, records, and icons that were preserved in stone to insure that they would perdure *noho pa'a* (live forever and unchanged). They were almost never intended to be entertaining, and they are usually found assembled in sacred places called *wahi pana,* the Hawai'ian equivalent of monuments and just as sacred." The Lana'i petroglyph pictured here is located near a heiau. "In our extensive data there are only five possible surfer petroglyphs, four on Hawai'i Island, one on Lana'i. We have found no verifiable information that the 'tandem surfers' on Lana'i, are in fact 'tandem surfers.' Three of the five possible surfers are probably of 20th century origin. The fisherman standing on 'an object or platform' at Kona Village is a depiction of an authentic fisherman, but the object that some have suggested may be a surfboard, is apocryphal (doubtful authenticity)." (Courtesy Hawai'i State Archives.)

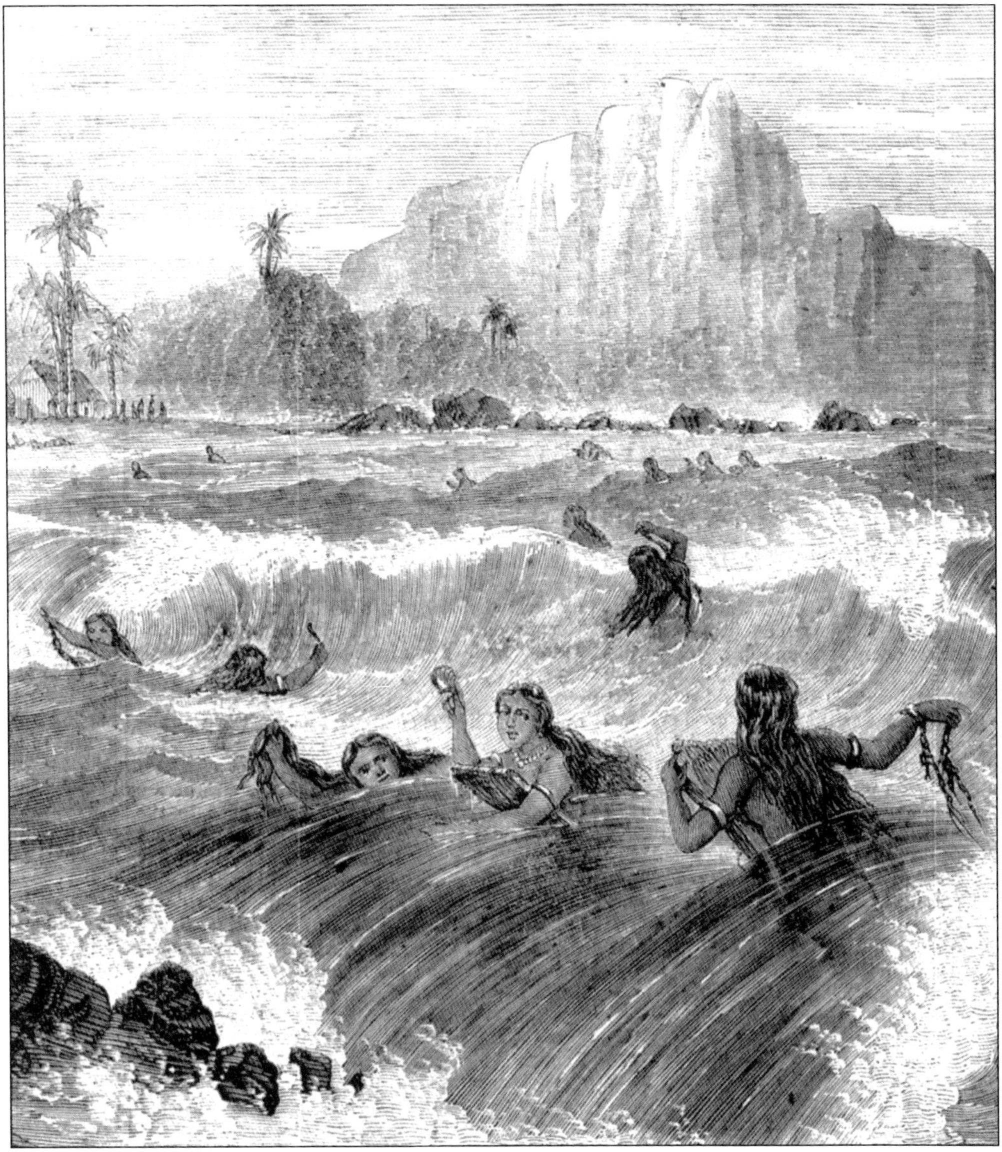

KELEA, THE SURF RIDER. The Hawai'ians had no written language. Their history, legends, and lineage were passed flawlessly from generation to generation through chants and mele. The story of Kelea was written down in 1881 by King Kalakaua, who was vitally concerned with the revival and preservation of Hawai'ian culture. Kelea was a princess from Maui. While visiting Waikiki on the island of O'ahu, "she found a large number of nobles and retainers of Kalamakua, the high chief of the district, amusing themselves in the surf . . . Kelea could not resist the temptation to indulge in her old pastime, and, borrowing a surf-board from one of the bathers, plunged into the sea, and soon joined the party of surf-riders beyond the breakers. . . . Soon a huge roller made its appearance, and all mounted it and started for the shore. The race was exciting, for the most expert swimmers in the district were among the contestants; but in grace, daring and skill Kelea very plainly excelled them all, and was loudly cheered as she touched the shore." (Etching detail from *Leslie's Illustrated Weekly*, 1866.)

Two

WESTERN ETCHINGS OF EXPLORATION 1778–1900

BY TIMOTHY T. DELAVEGA

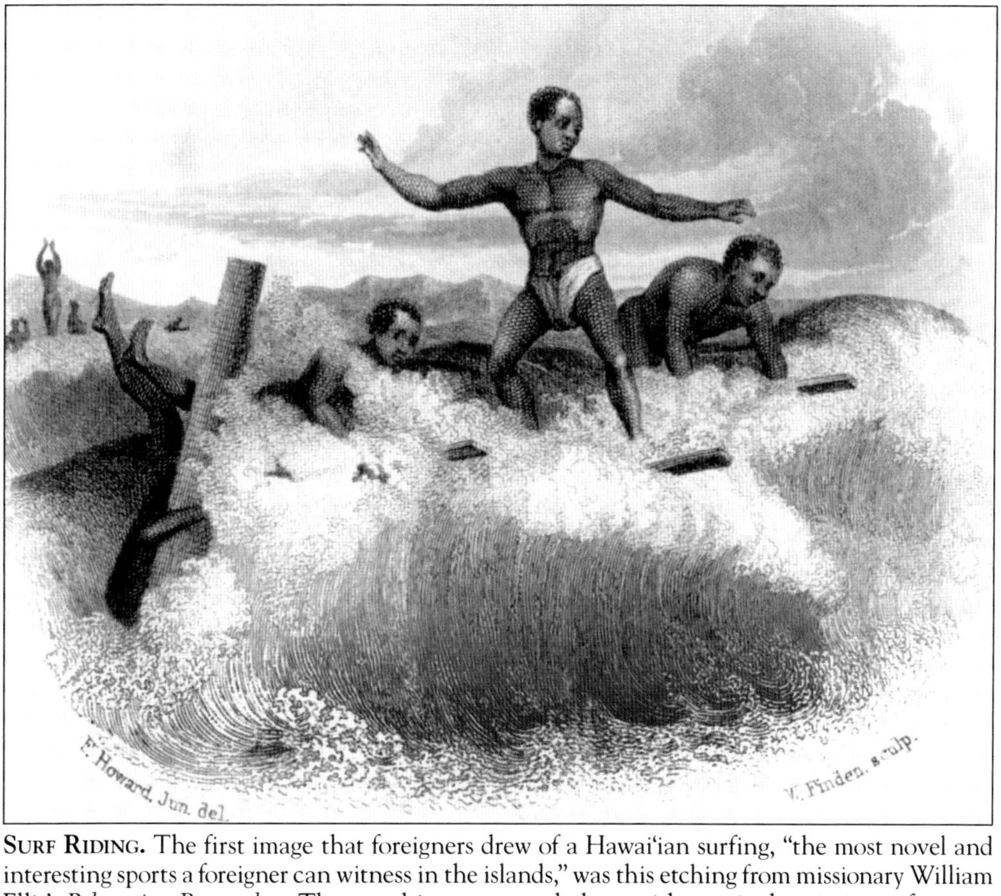

SURF RIDING. The first image that foreigners drew of a Hawai'ian surfing, "the most novel and interesting sports a foreigner can witness in the islands," was this etching from missionary William Ellis's *Polynesian Researches.* These etchings appeared along with poetic descriptions of a sport that was incomprehensible to Westerners, people who seldom swam in the ocean. These etchings supply a unique look at he'e nalu before photography. (Etching by F. Howard.)

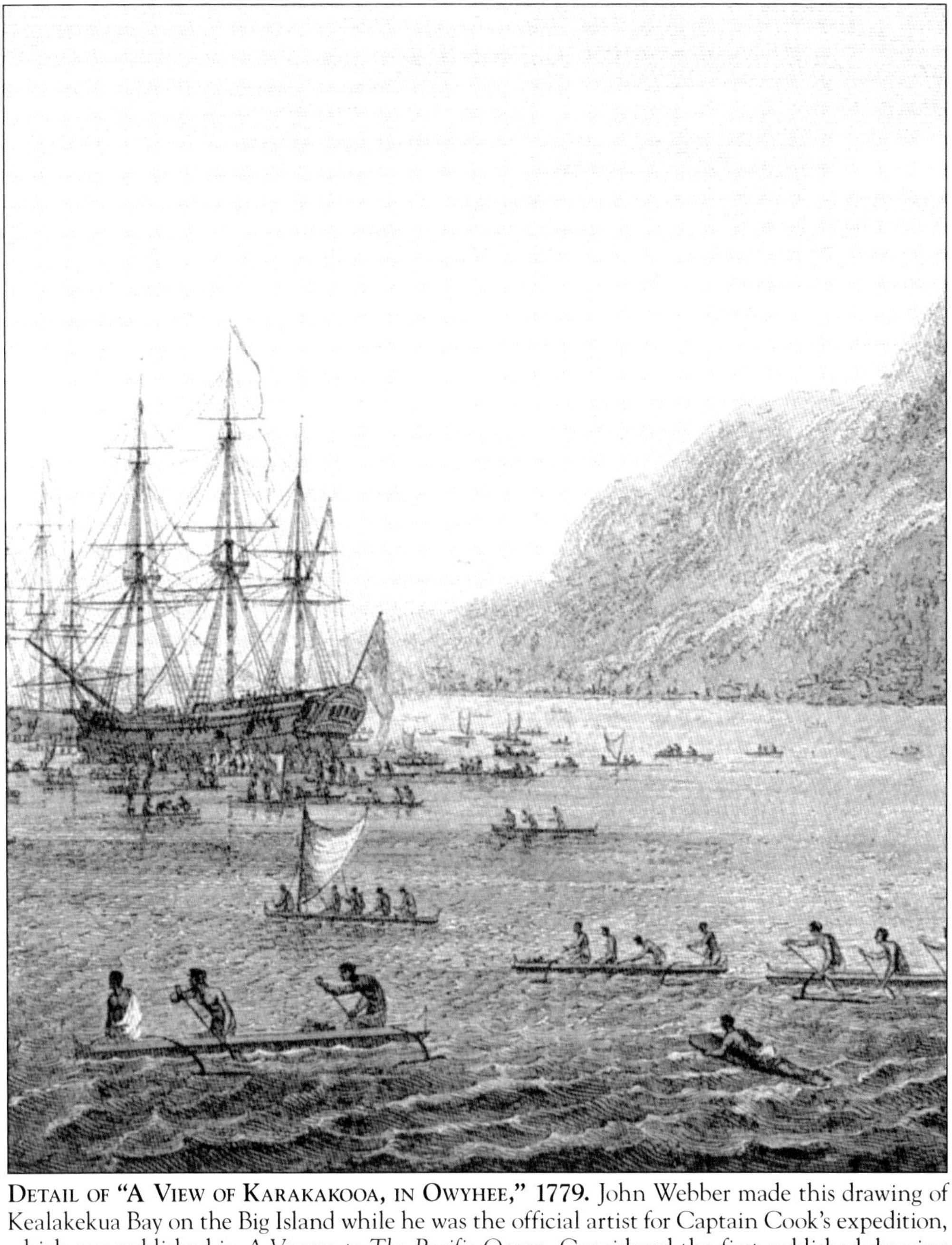

DETAIL OF "A VIEW OF KARAKAKOOA, IN OWYHEE," 1779. John Webber made this drawing of Kealakekua Bay on the Big Island while he was the official artist for Captain Cook's expedition, which was published in *A Voyage to The Pacific Ocean*. Considered the first published drawing of a surfboard, it is accompanied by the first Western description of Hawai'ians surfing by Lt. James King, who replaced Captain Cook after his death at Kealakekua: "Both sexes and all ranks unite in it [surfing], and even the very chiefs themselves. . . . Some of the performers attain to a wonderful degree of skill, and, not content with lying on the board, sit, kneel, and even stand on it as they are hurled shorewards by the giant waves." (Courtesy Dan Pincetich.)

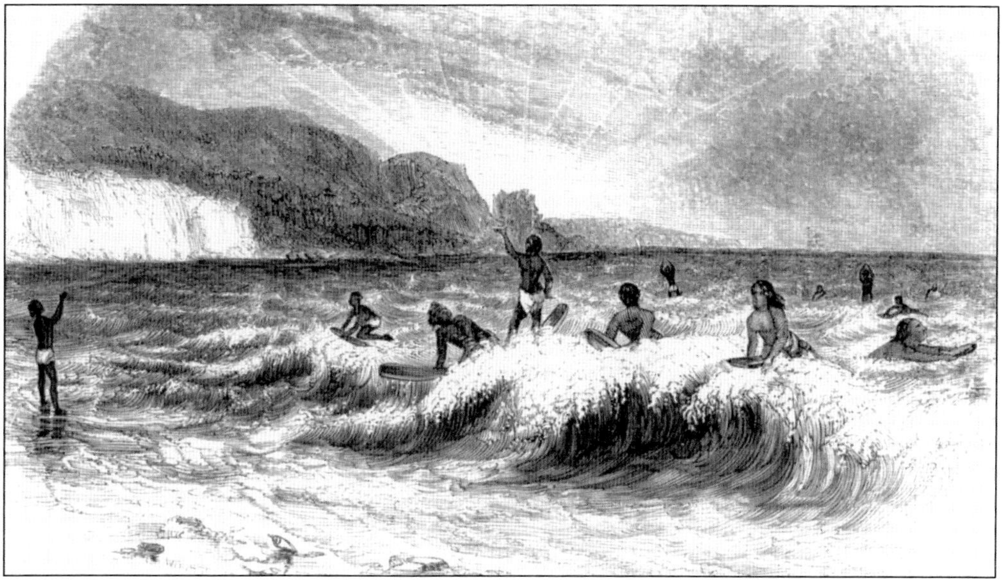

"Hawai'ian Sport of Surf Playing and Kealakekua Bay, at the Time of Capt. Cook," 1851. These sketches are from *Life in the Sandwich Islands* by missionary Henry T. Cheever. The text states, "For my part, I should like nothing better, then to get balanced on a board just before a great rushing wave, and so be hurried in half or a quarter of a mile landward with the speed of a race-horse. . . . The sport is so attractive and full of wild excitement to Hawai'ians, and withal so healthful, that I cannot but hope it will be many years before civilization shall look it out of countenance, or make it disreputable to indulge in this manly though dangerous exercise. . . . The missionaries at these islands, and foreigners generally, are greatly at fault in that they do not avail themselves more of this easy and unequalled means of retaining health, or of restoring it when enfeebled."

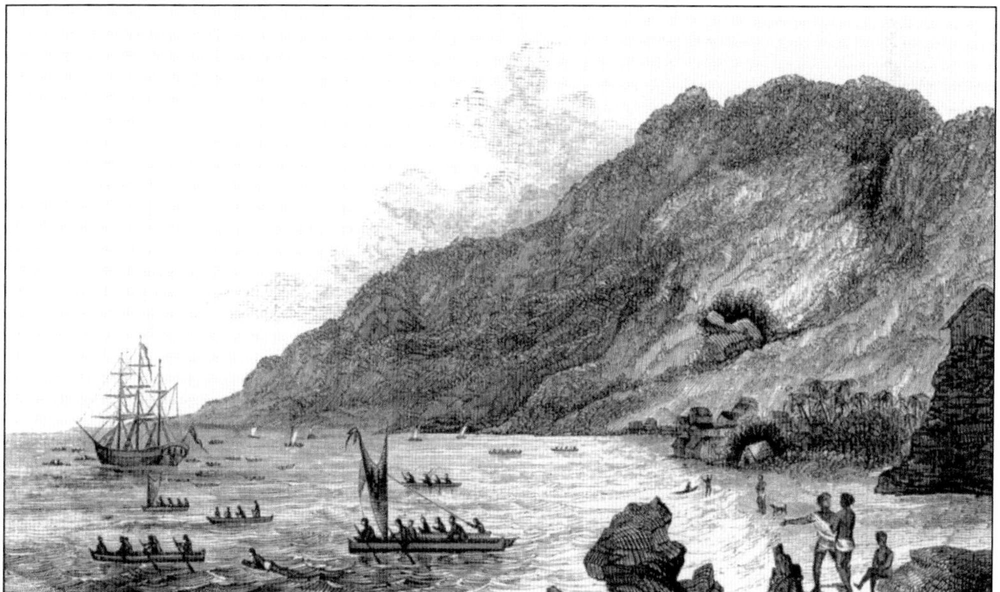

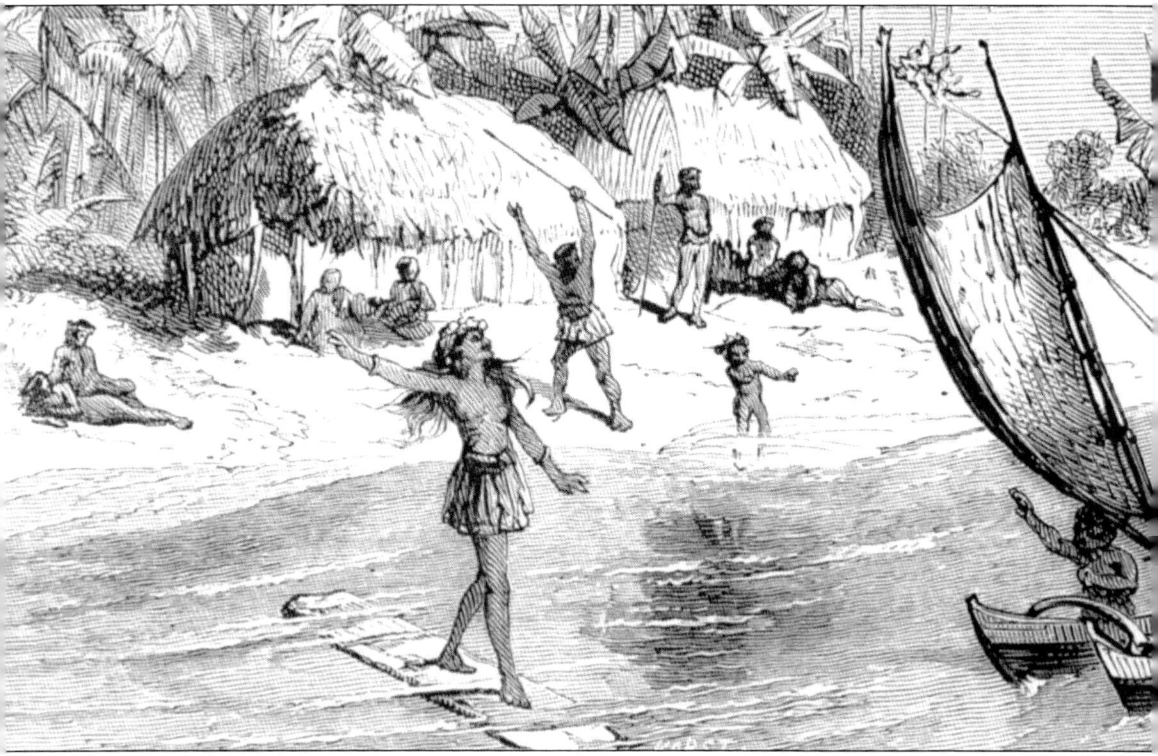

"SCENE IN POLYNESIA," 1880. All the ingredients of romantic Hawai'i are drawn into this etching that appeared in William Swinton's *Grammar-School Geography.* By the end of the 19th century, surfing was becoming a rare sight in Hawai'i for numerous reasons. Paramount was the almost complete decimation of the Hawai'ian people from alien epidemics that swept through the native population. Social changes had an impact, such as the puritan work ethic, the plantation system

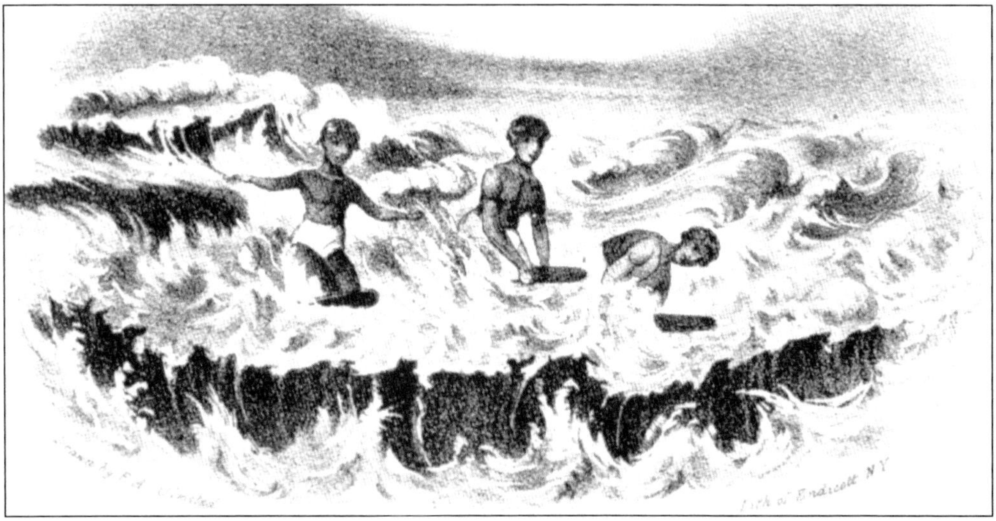

"SANDWICH ISLANDERS PLAYING IN THE SURF," 1841. Francis A. Olmsted's woodblock appeared in his *Incidents of a Whaling Voyage,* with a charming description of surf riding at Honolulu: "They amuse themselves hour after hour, in sports which have too terrific an aspect for a foreigner to attempt, but which are admirably adapted to the almost amphibious character of the natives."

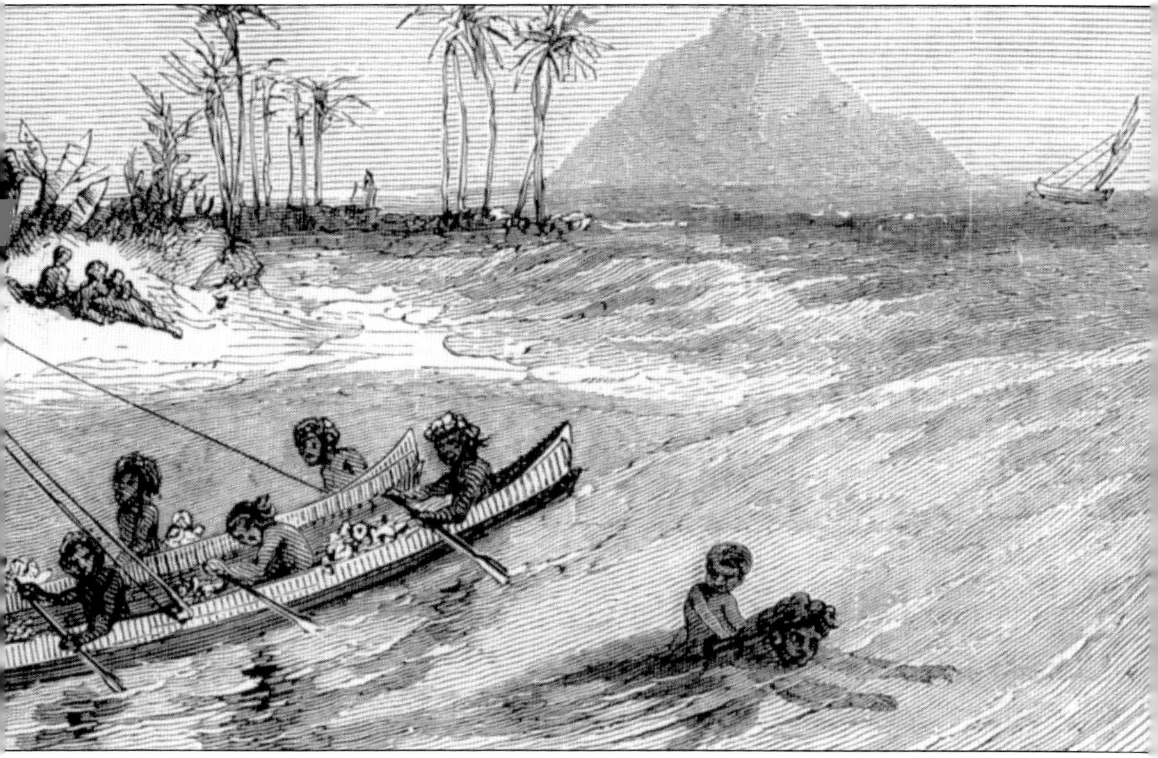

of agriculture, and the popularity of a new thrill—horses. This was noted by Hilo native Sereno Bishop, "When I returned to Honolulu in 1853, after an absence of thirteen years, I was struck by the many changes . . . it is true that as the horses became cheap and everyone had his horse, the people gave up surf-riding, as though their idea was to have rapid progress and they abandoned the older method for the newer one."

WAHINE OF THE SANDWICH ISLES, JACQUES ARAGO, C. 1819. The Western vision of Hawai'ian paradise was established early on as shown by this etching by French artist Arago. When Capt. James Cook arrived in Hawai'i and "discovered" the islands, he named them after John Montagu, the fourth Earl of Sandwich, who was his financial sponsor.

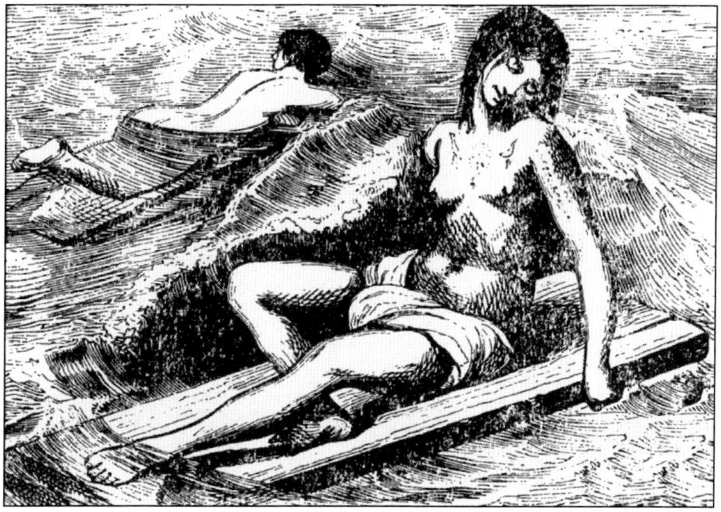

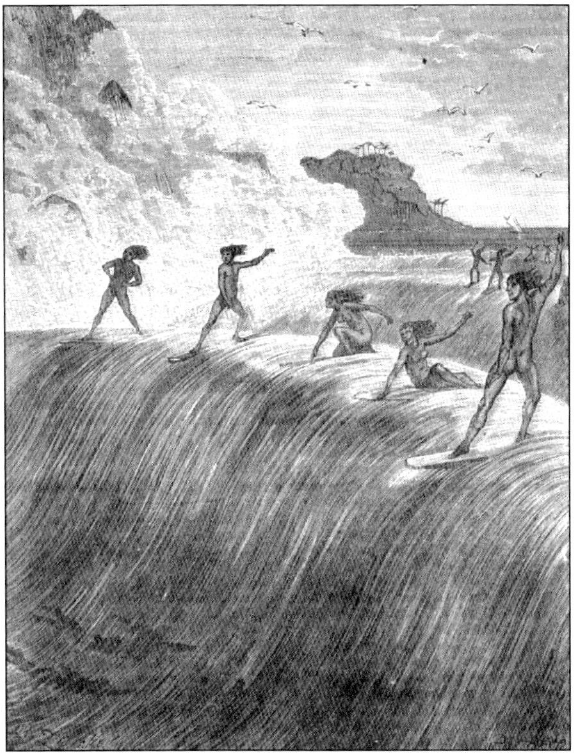

The Relationship of a Surfboard and a Breaking Wave. Few Western artists had apparently ever seen surfing. Most saw waves as waterfalls, yet there is an attempt to show the transparency of the ocean through the use of the swimmers below the surface in "Surf-Swimming" (left) from Rev. John Wood's 1868 *The Uncivilized Races of Men in all Countries of the World.* "We now come to the various games with which the Sandwich Islanders amuse themselves. Chief among them is the sport of surf-swimming. This is practiced in several of the islands of Polynesia, but in none is it carried out to such perfection as in [Hawai'i]." "Sandwich Islands' Surf Riding" (below) is from an 1883 issue of the British magazine *Boy's Own Paper.*

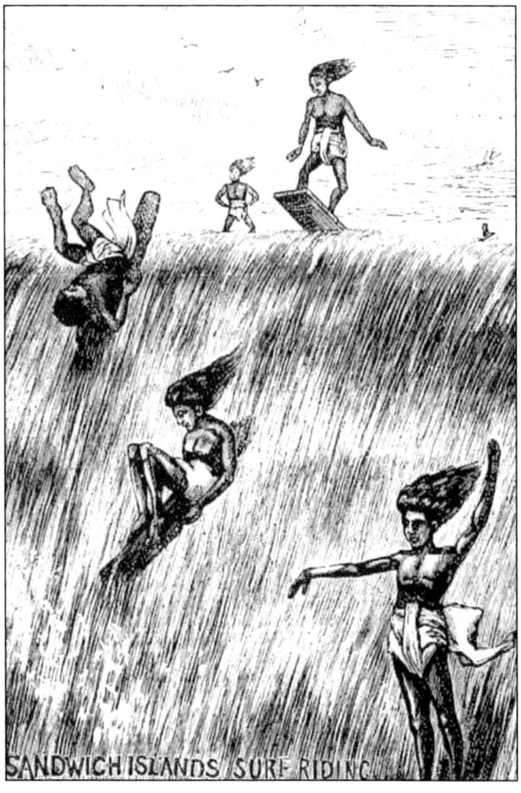

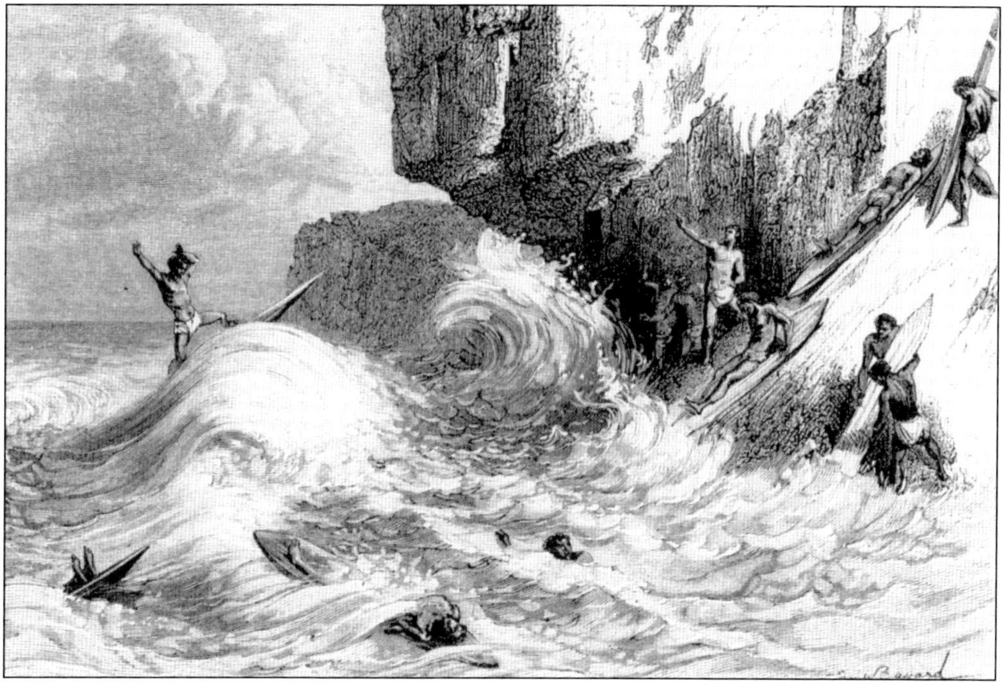

"Jeux Havaiens (Hawai'ian Games)," 1873. These French engravings, above by Bayard and below by Riou, are accompanied by text by Charles DeVargny: "One could see him then rising on the crest of the waves, descending again, and climbing anew. . . . The light board, easily maneuvered, was raised like a feather on the crest of the [wave], and [returned] to the shore with the speed of a galloping horse. . . . Almost all of the old games of the natives were of the same type. Defiant of danger, natural forces and performed in cold blood were their main attractions. The chiefs excelled at these exercises but now there are few traces of the games left. Thus they had a reason to live; today the cult of bodily strength has disappeared with it utility. It is sadly the same story with songs and legends, once easily transmitted from generation to generation and now almost forgotten."

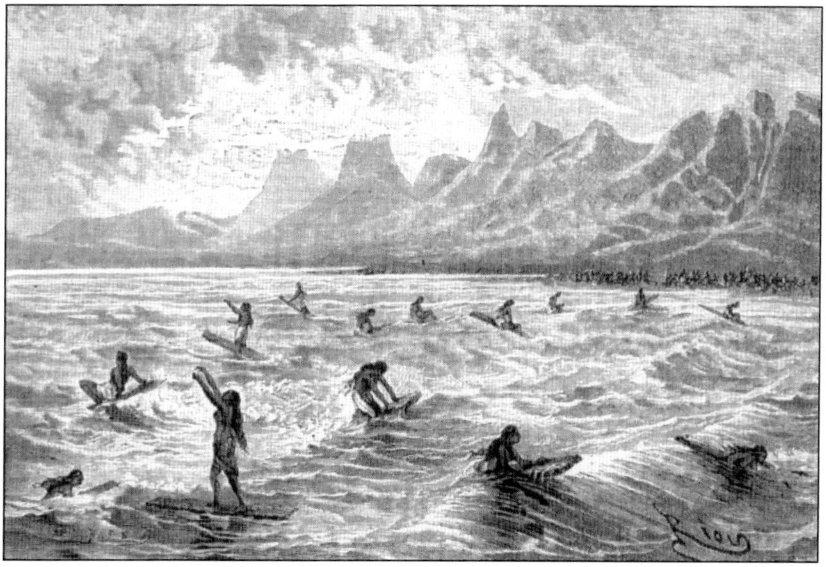

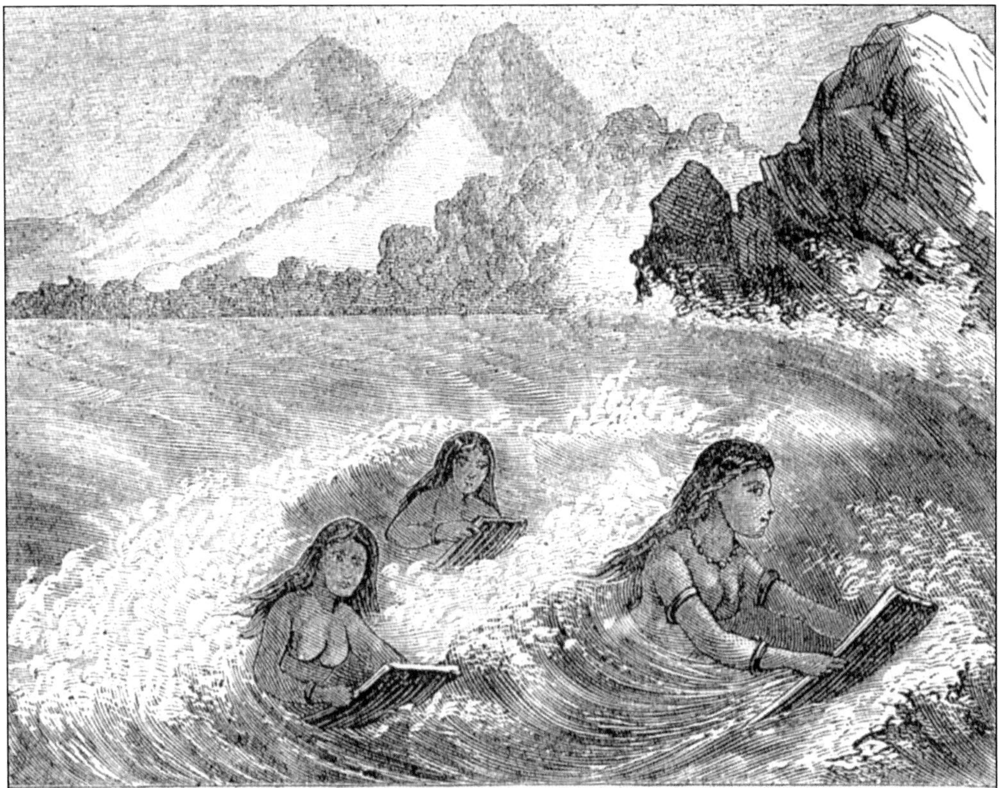

SURF-BATHING—SUCCESS.

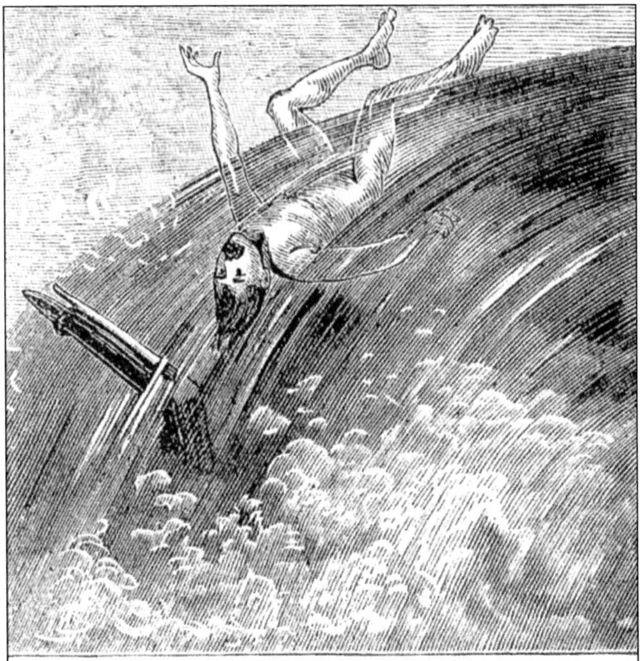

SURF-BATHING—FAILURE.

MARK TWAIN ATTEMPTS SURF RIDING, 1872. In *Roughing It,* a travel memoir, Mark Twain describes witnessing surf-bathing south of Kealakekua Bay: "In one place we came upon a large company of naked natives, of both sexes and all ages, amusing themselves with the national pastime of surf-bathing. I tried surf riding once, but made a failure of it. I placed the board right, and at the right moment, too, but missed the connection myself. The board struck the shore in three quarters of a second, without any cargo, and I struck the bottom at the same time, with a couple of barrels of water in me. None but the natives ever master the art of surf riding thoroughly." (Both courtesy Dan Pincetich.)

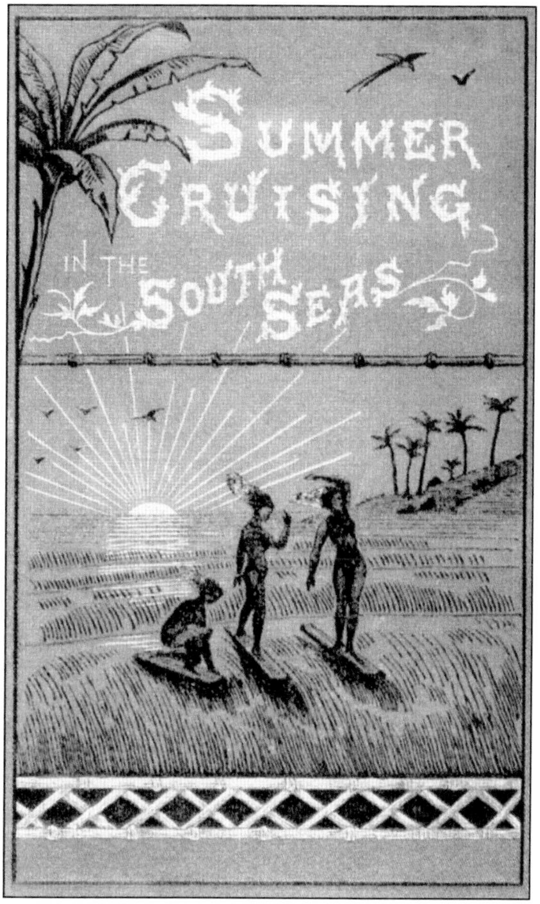

"Kahe'le and I Watched the Surf-Swimmers for Some Time, Charmed with the Spectacle," 1873. These etchings by Wallis Mackay appeared in Charles Stoddard's travel memoir *Summer Cruising in the South Seas*, the first book to depict surfing on its cover. Stoddard viewed surfing on Maui, where a whole village turns out when the surf is running "just like the old days." Kahe'le, his guide, could not resist the temptation of good surf and went out. It continues: "As it rose he climbed to the top of it, and there, in the midst of foam seething like champagne, on the crest of a rushing sea-avalanche about to crumble and dissolve beneath him, his surf-board hidden in spume, on the very top bubble of all, Kahele danced like a shadow."

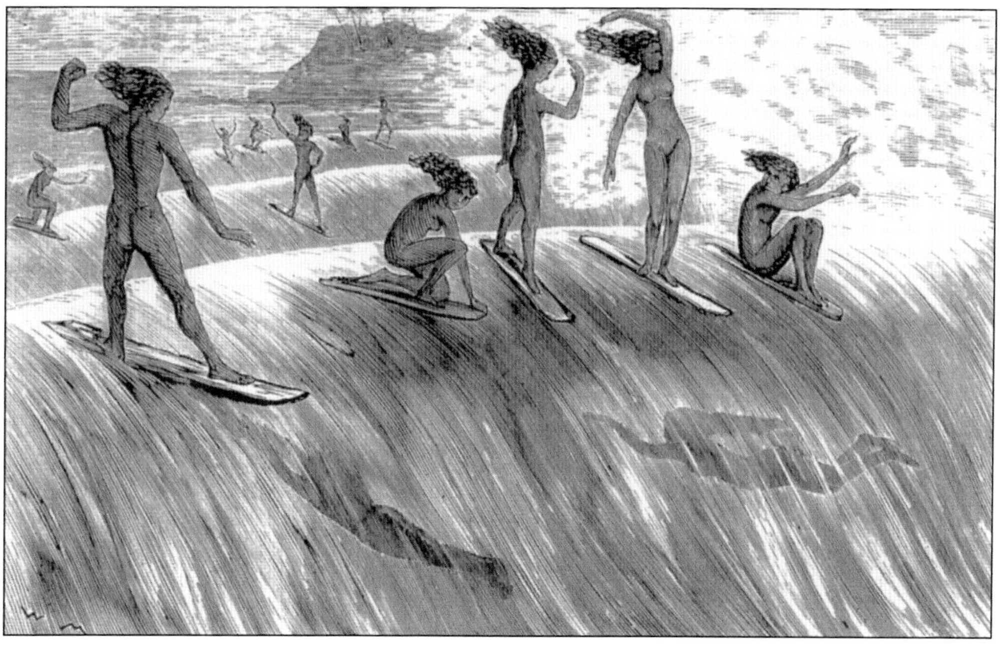

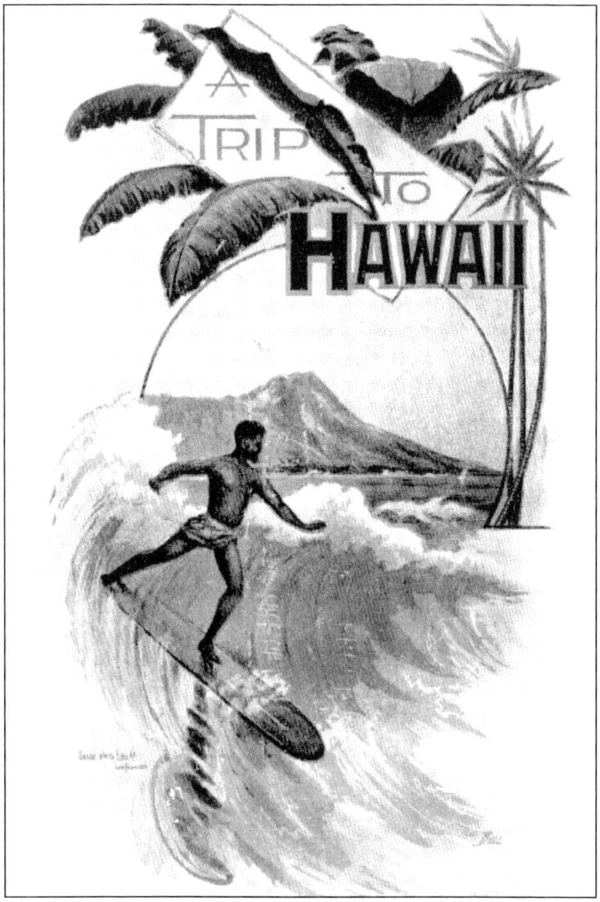

OCEANIC STEAMSHIP COMPANY OF SAN FRANCISCO BROCHURES, 1887. By the end of the 19th century, as travelers were noting that surfing was disappearing from the islands, publicists were already using it as one of the iconic images of paradise. Renowned travel writer Charles Warren Stoddard wrote this promotional piece that is mentioned in the flyer below. Rates for passage from San Francisco to Honolulu were $75 one-way, $125 round-trip, and $25 steerage; round-the-world tickets cost $650 first-class. The advertisement suggests readers "send for pamphlet 'A Trip to Hawai'i.' " (Below, courtesy Dan Pincetich.)

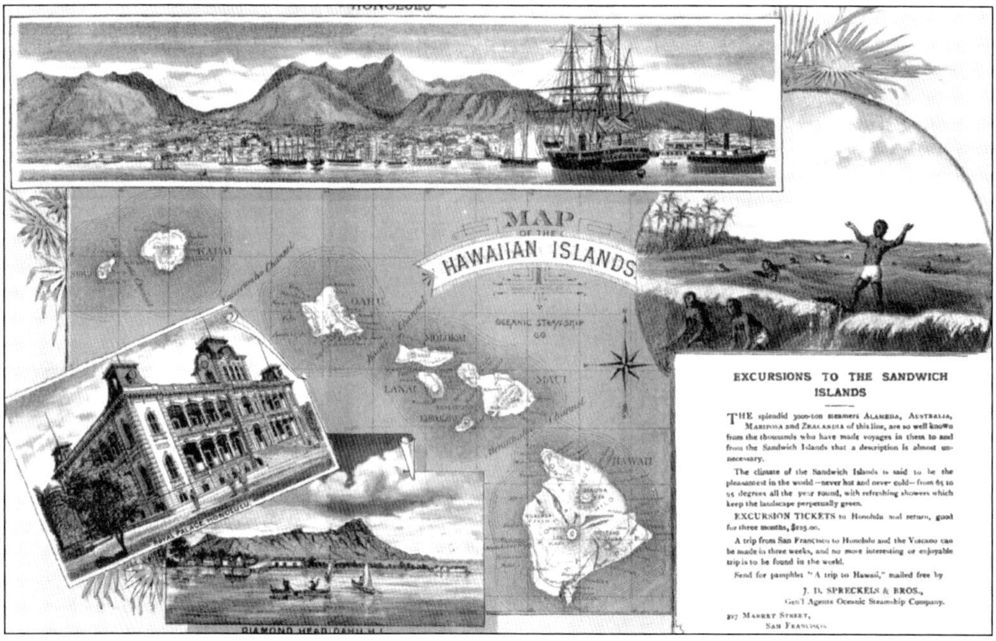

Surfing and Alligator Hunting in Hawai'i, 1893. This is the first commercial surfing image that was used throughout Europe on collectible cards. A quote from the American version of the card reads, "The religion of these people is primitive and crude. . . . Girls arrayed in all the magnificence of barbarism dance at religious festivals and add to the weirdness of the worship. . . . Alligator-hunting is very popular; seldom does a native go forth on such a quest without bringing home a huge carcass for his pains." Of course, alligators have never existed in Hawaii. (Courtesy Dan Pincetich.)

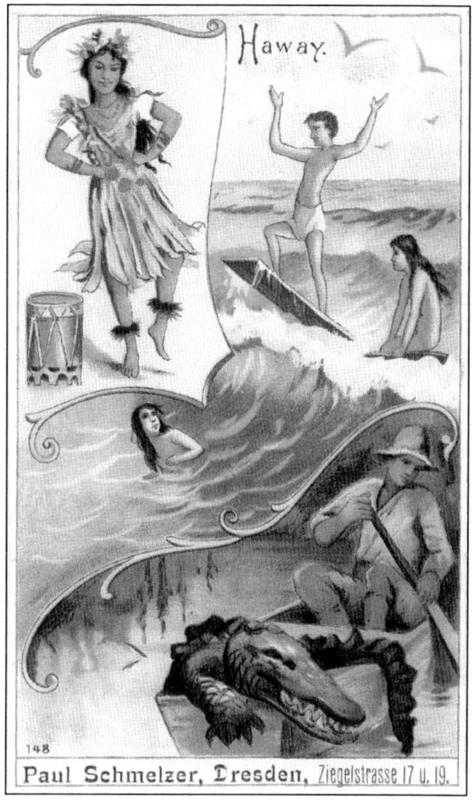

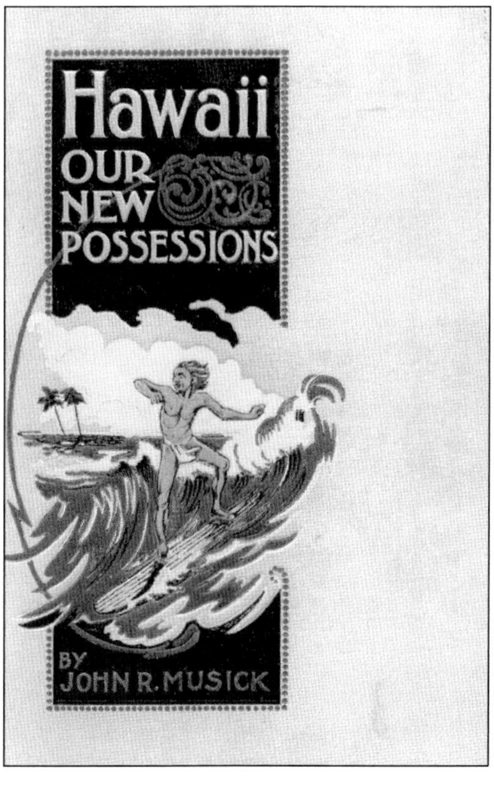

***Hawai'i, Our New Possessions,* John R. Musick, 1897.** In 1893, the Hawai'ian monarchy was illegally overthrown, and in 1898 Hawai'i was officially annexed as a US territory. Meanwhile, American publishers flooded the market with numerous books and articles on the "new U.S. possessions," which included Cuba and the Philippines—spoils of the Spanish-American War in 1898.

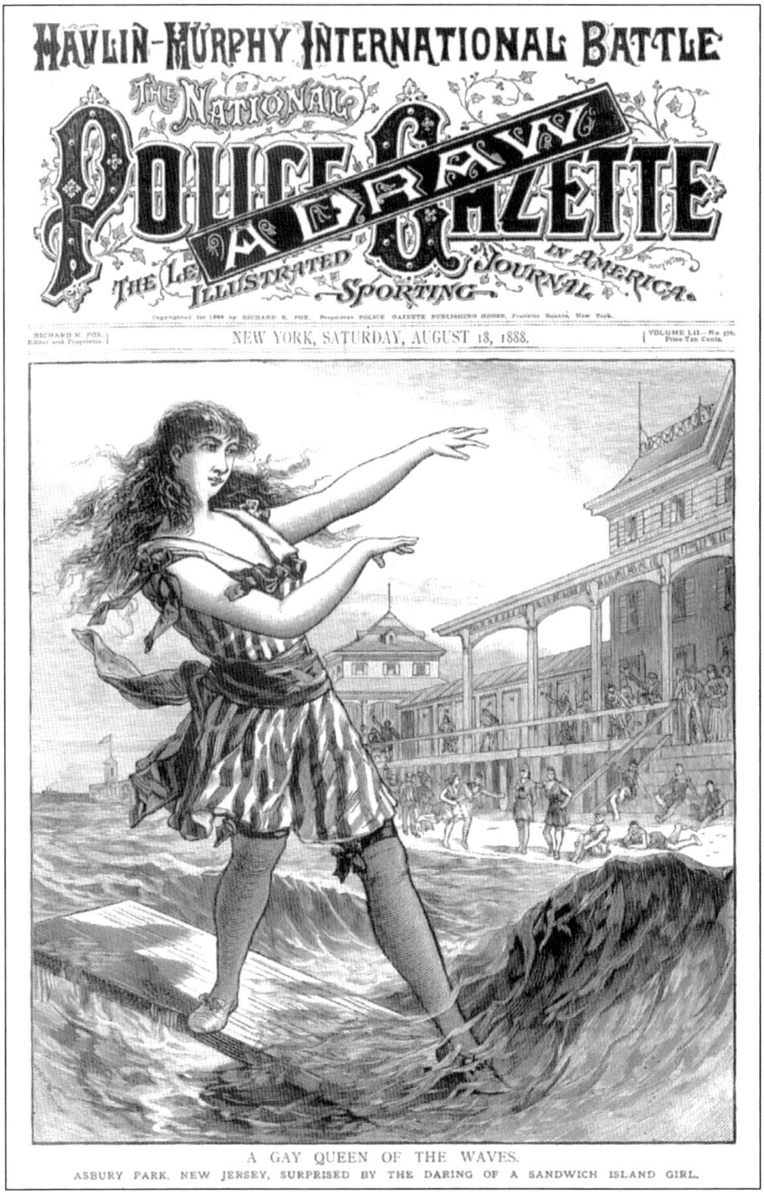

"A GAY QUEEN OF THE WAVES: ASBURY PARK, NEW JERSEY, SURPRISED BY THE DARING OF A SANDWICH ISLAND GIRL," 1888. There are numerous documented incidents of Hawai'ians surfing in distant lands before 1900, including this account from the *National Police Gazette*: "A group of summer loungers on the beach at Asbury Park, N.J. were watching the extraordinary antics of a dark eyed, bronze-faced girl in the sea a few mornings ago. The object of all this interest and solicitude was beyond the line of breakers and standing on a plank that rose and fell with the swelling waves. . . . As a wave larger than those which had gone before slowly lifted the plank upon its swelling surface, she poised herself daintily upon the support, her round arms stretched out and her body swaying to and fro in harmony with the motion of the waters. . . . So she has been amusing herself and interesting the mob for three mornings. She is as completely at ease in the sea as you or I on land, and the broad plank obeys her slightest touch." (Courtesy Al Hunt.)

Three

The Photographic Era Begins
1888–1910

by Timothy T. DeLaVega

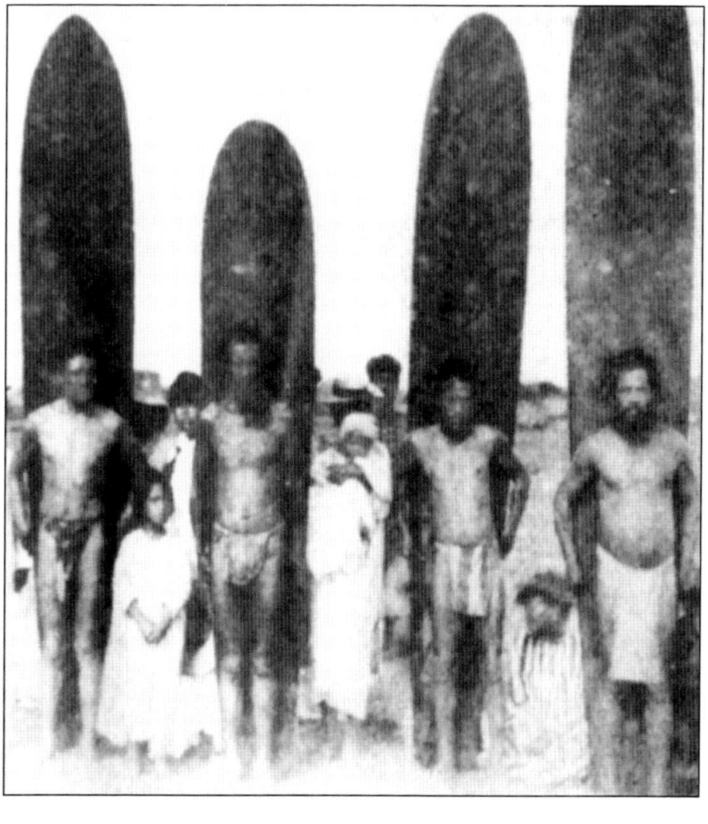

"Ni'ihau Surfers in 1890," by Dr. Henry C. Bolton. Published here for the first time, these two photographs (here and on page 28) of, from left to right, Kaika, Kawika, Keahi, and unidentified are the oldest documentable photographs of surfing. Dr. Bolton wrote, "I photographed the men of Ni'ihau before they entered the water, while surf-riding, and after they came out." This report was "illustrated with projections (glass slides) of original photographs; read at the annual Meeting of the American Folk-Lore Society, November 28, 1890." (Courtesy Chris Cook.)

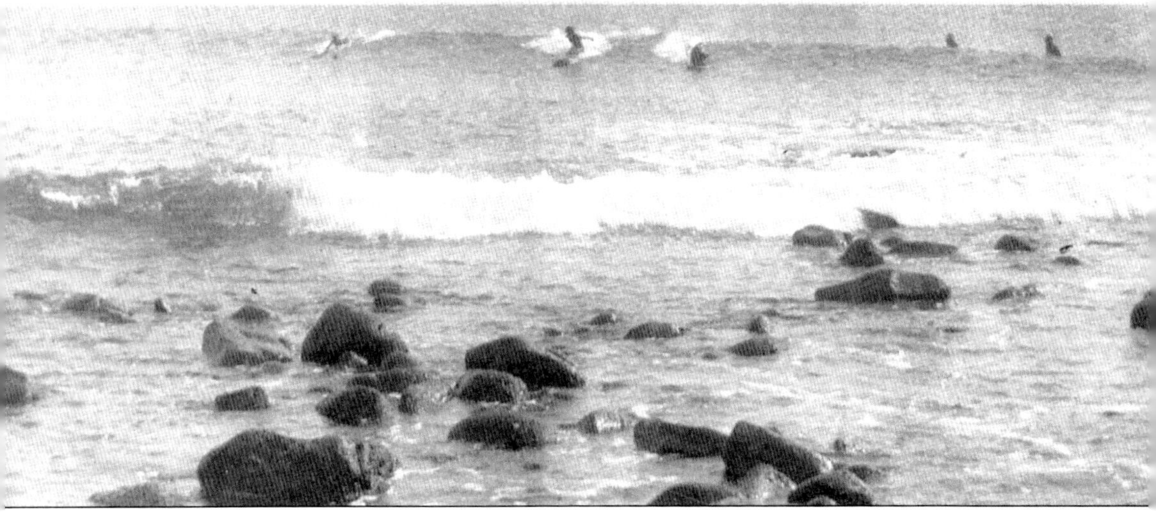

FIRST PHOTOGRAPH OF SURFING, TAKEN ON NI'IHAU BY DR. HENRY C. BOLTON, 1890. Dr. Bolton reported, "Here I witnessed, the sport of surf-riding, once so universally popular, and now but little seen. [He had traveled throughout Hawai'i.] After standing for their photograph, the men removed all their garments, retaining only the malo, or loin-cloth, and walked into the sea, dragging or pushing their surf-boards as they reached deeper water. These surf-boards . . . *Papa-he-nalu* (wave-sliding-boards), are made from the wood of the *viri-viri* (breadfruit tree) they are eight or nine feet long, fifteen to twenty inches wide, rather thin, rounded at each end, and carefully smoothed. The boards are sometimes stained black, are frequently rubbed with coconut oil, and are preserved with great solicitude, sometimes wrapped in cloths . . . watching their opportunity they lay flat upon the board (the more expert kneeled), and, just as a high billow was about to break over them, pushed landward in front of the combers." (Courtesy National Anthropological Archives, Smithsonian Institution.)

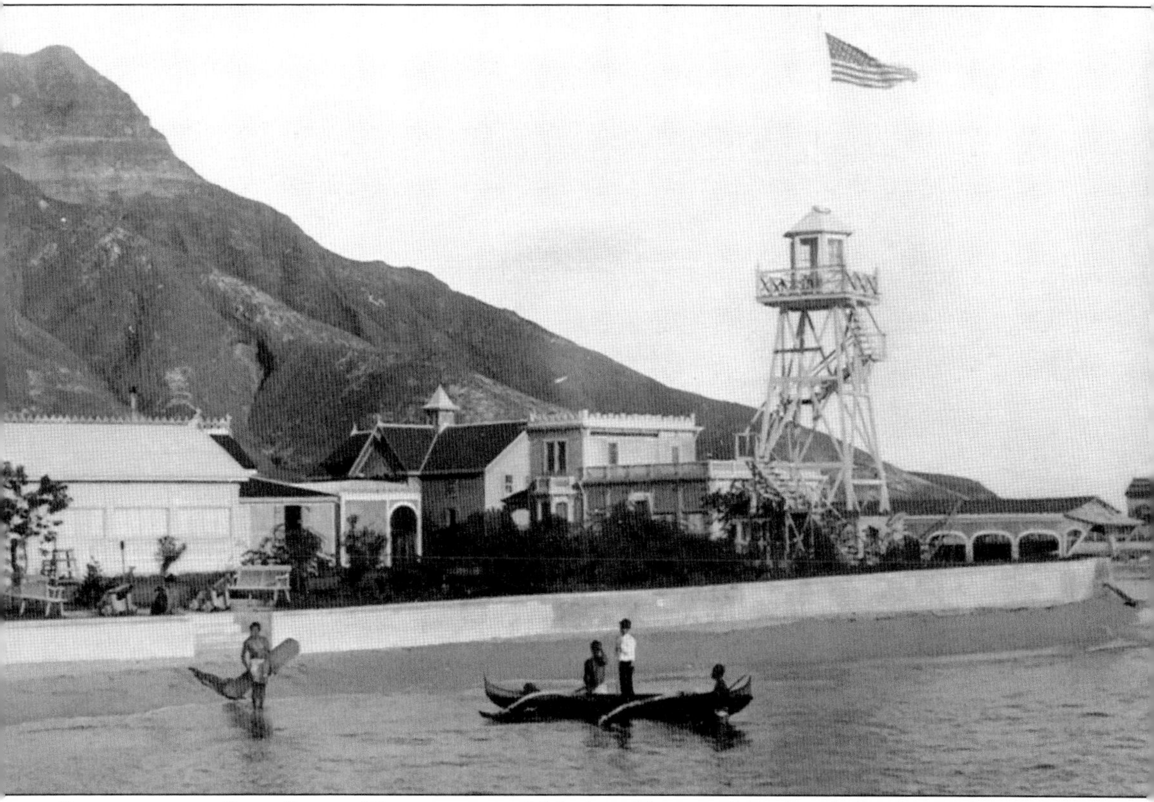

SURFER AT THE PARK BEACH HOTEL, 1888. C.N. Arnold opened the hotel, the first real one in Waikiki, in the summer of 1888 on land leased from Col. George W. Macfarlane. But it was too far from the city and was unsuccessful. In 1889, James B. Castle bought the property, demolished these buildings, and constructed a magnificent mansion Kainalu (Ocean Wave) in 1900. In the 1920s, it was sold to the Elks Club. This structure has been demolished, and new buildings at the site house the Elks and their lessee, the Outrigger Canoe Club. In 1898, *Paradise of the Pacific Magazine* noted of the same location: "Within the past two or three months a sandbar has formed off the Waikiki beach right in front of the residence of George W. Macfarlane, which gives perfect conditions. Surf-board riding has in consequence been revived, has in fact, become a fad, and a large number of both whites and natives have become expert in the art." Note how the surfer's bathing suit is cut-off pants, typical of other photographs from this period. (Courtesy Outrigger Canoe Club.)

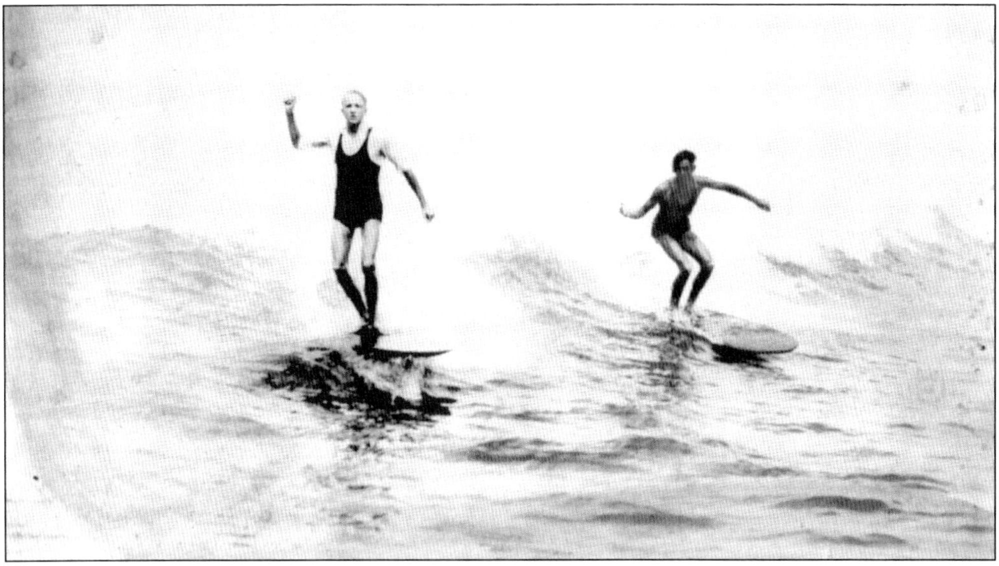

ALBUMEN PRINT OF SURF RIDING IN ACTION, C. 1899. During the 25-year span from 1860 to 1885, albumen paper was in virtually exclusive use as the general-purpose printing paper for photography. Coating paper with a layer of egg white and salt creates a smooth surface, and then adding a layer of silver nitrate forms light-sensitive silver salts. When placed in contact with a negative and exposed to the sun, a print is produced.

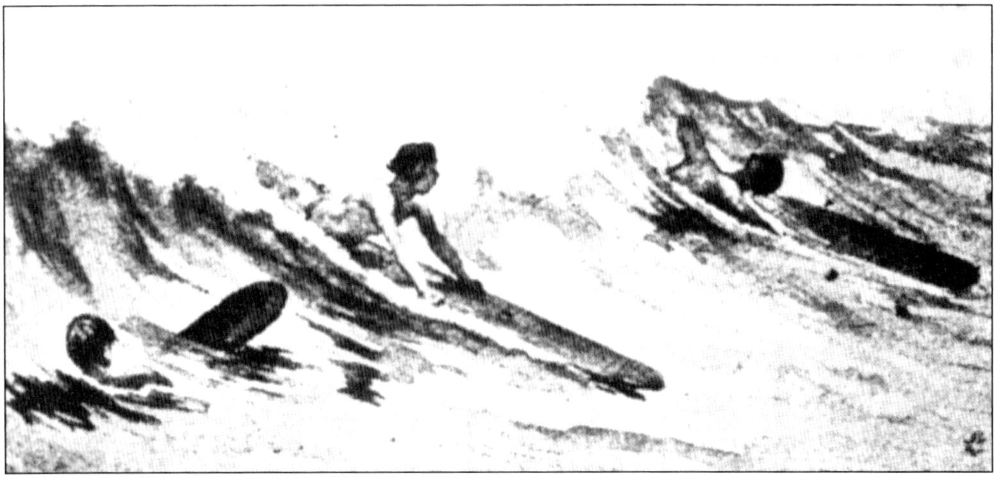

THREE *KEIKI* (CHILDREN) SURFING, FROM *HAWAI'IAN ALMANAC AND ANNUAL FOR* 1896. This drawing from a photograph appeared with a very thorough look at all the aspects of ancient Hawai'ian surfing, from preparation of the board to outer-island famous spots, mythology and chants, and even canoe surfing. The account was "prepared for THE ANNUAL by a native of the Kona district of Hawai'i, translated by Nakoina, a former surf rider." Duke Kahanamoku considered this the best of the early accounts.

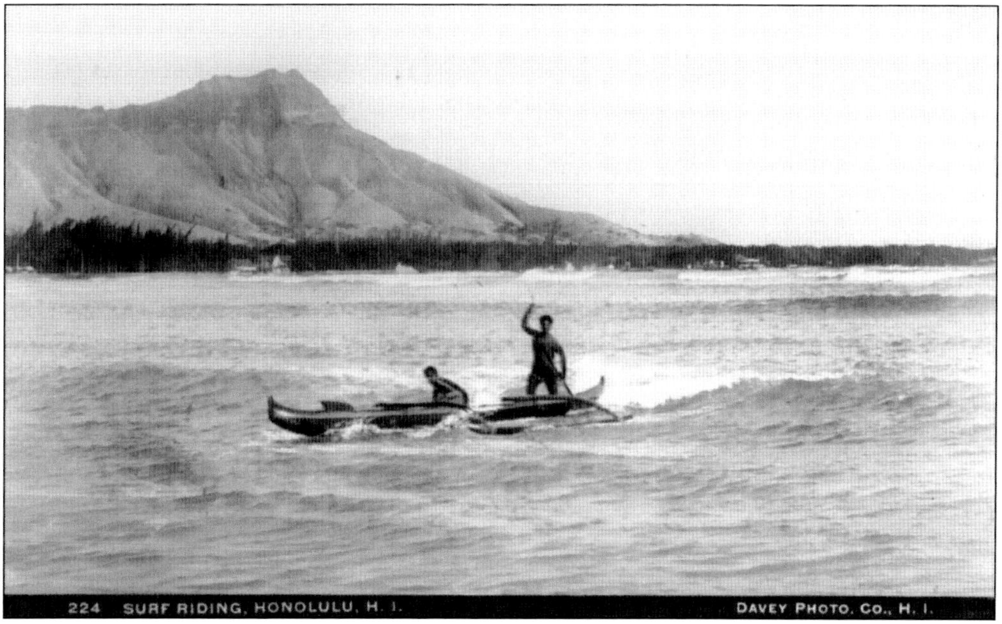

IN 1897 FOR $1 AN HOUR, A PERSON COULD ENJOY THE THRILL OF WAVE SLIDING IN AN OUTRIGGER CANOE. At the turn of the century, surf riding was generally represented by images of canoe surfing, such as these two: an 1898 image from Davey Photo Co. (above) and a c. 1906 postcard (below). In 1897, the *Dallas Morning News* noted that the beachboys started surfing canoe rides at Waikiki: "An added attraction has been created for visitors at our lovely Waikiki beach. A number of expert native canoeman have been organized into a company for the purpose of treating the visitors to the sport of wave sliding (canoe surfing) which is midway between surf riding and snow hill coasting. . . . A swift rush of a fourth mile to the beach . . . with the tossing comb of the wave overhanging the stern." (Above, courtesy Hawai'i State Archives; below, Dan Pincetich.)

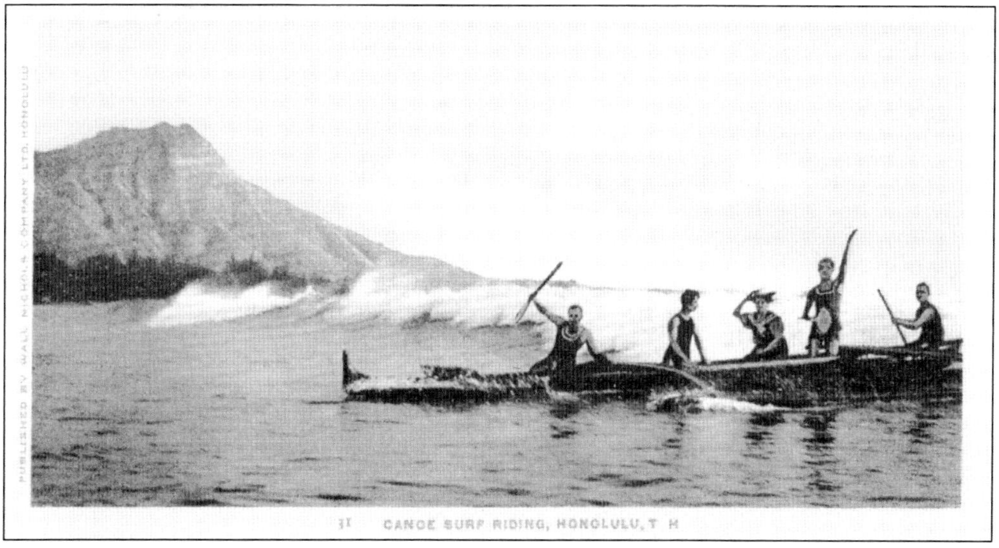

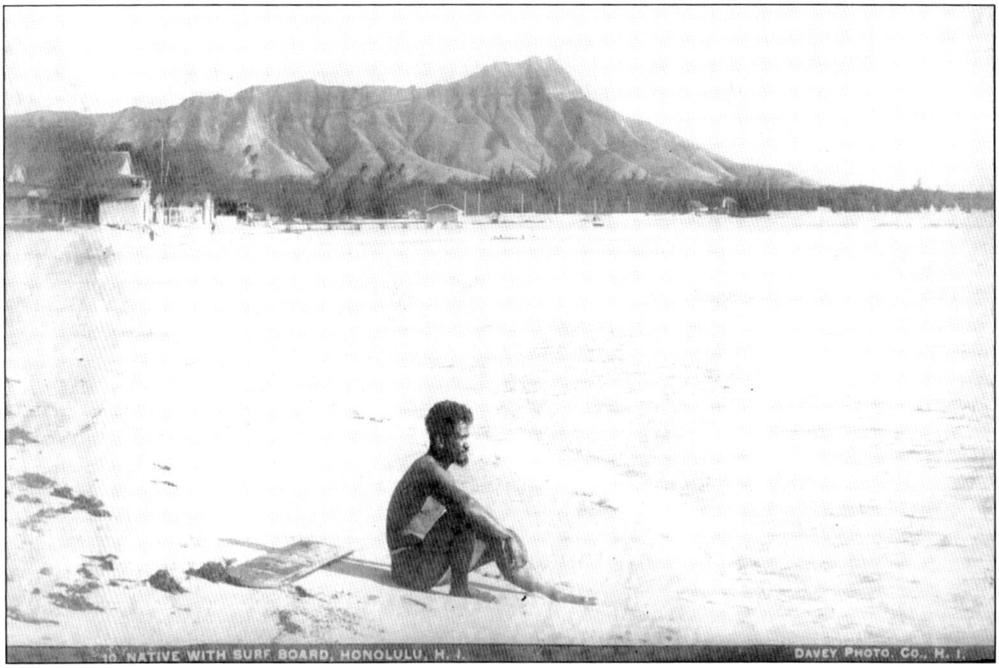

CHARLES KAUHA AND HIS ALAIA SURFBOARD, APRIL 1898. London-born Frank Davey photographed Charles Kauha in 1898 in numerous poses, but none are of Kauha surfing. Davey Photo Co. was very prolific, although Davey only documented Hawai'i from 1897 to 1901. The one similar to this book's cover is found on an Island Curio Store undivided-back postcard made between 1901 and 1907. During this time, the undivided back was for the address only, allowing no place on the card for a message. People of course started writing messages all over the postcards, which caused the government in 1907 to establish divided-back postcards so senders could write a message on the back next to the address. (Above, courtesy Hawai'i State Archives; below, Dan Pincetich.)

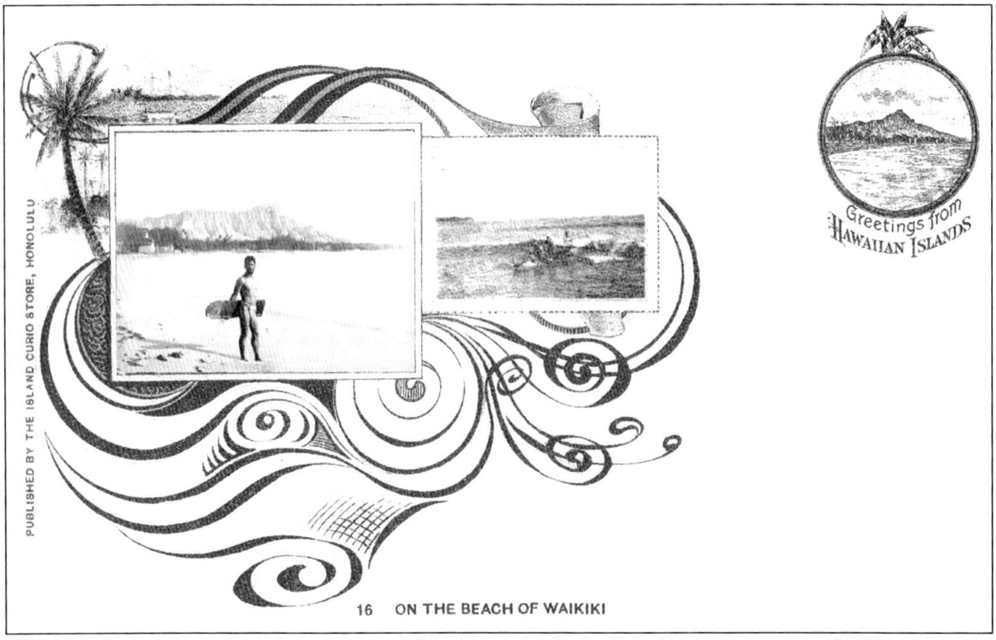

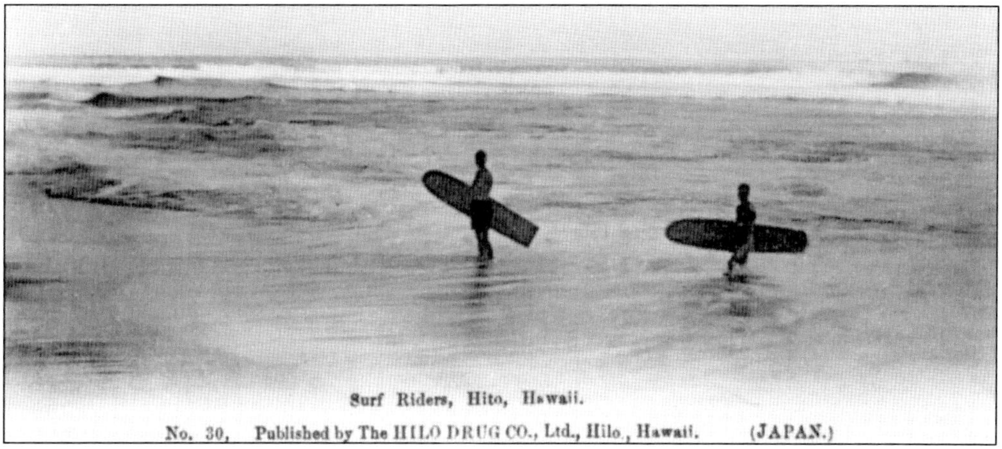

"**Surf Riders, Hilo, Hawai'i.**" This hand-tinted postcard shows Hawai'i's longest rideable surfing wave, which vanished with the completion of the Hilo Breakwater in 1926. The c. 1900 photograph is printed on a pre-1907 undivided-back postcard. Photographs of the outer islands from before 1930 are extremely rare. (Courtesy Dan Pincetich.)

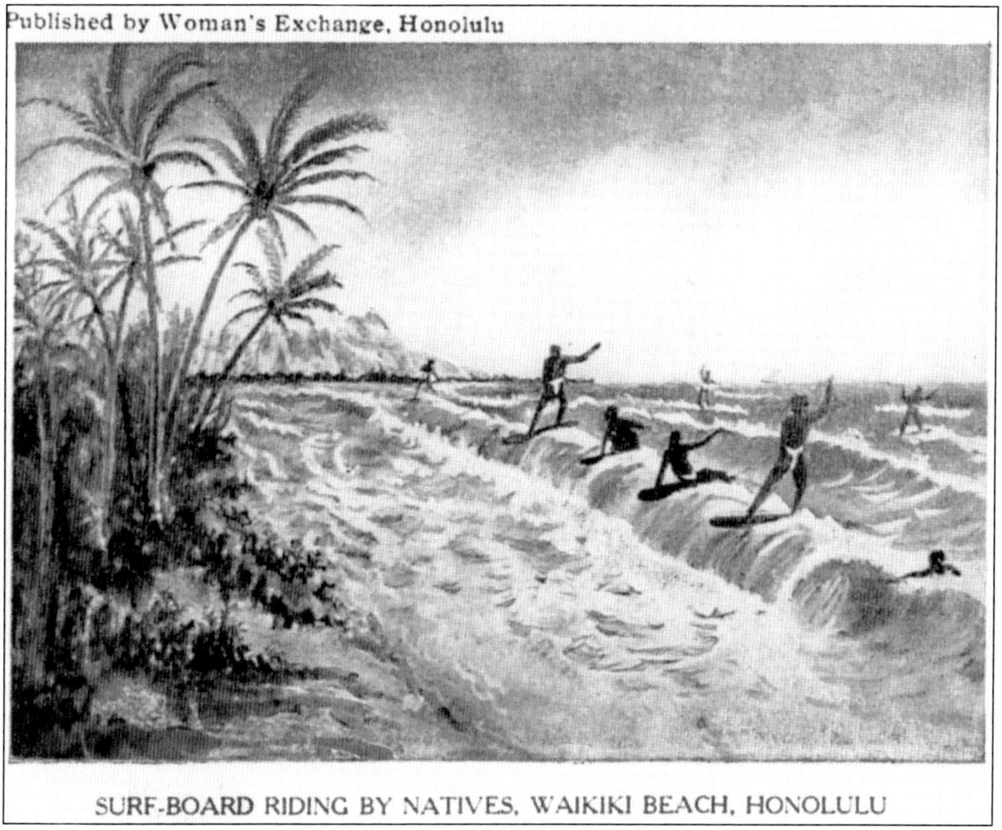

"**Surf-Board Riding by Natives, Waikiki Beach, Honolulu," c. 1904**. In 1898, the first private mailing cards were allowed by the Post Office Department. In 1901, these became known as postcards. Originally, the message was only allowed on the image side, as shown by this card with an etching of Waikiki surf riding. Collecting postcards was an early collectible craze, doubling in popularity every year. (Courtesy Dan Pincetich.)

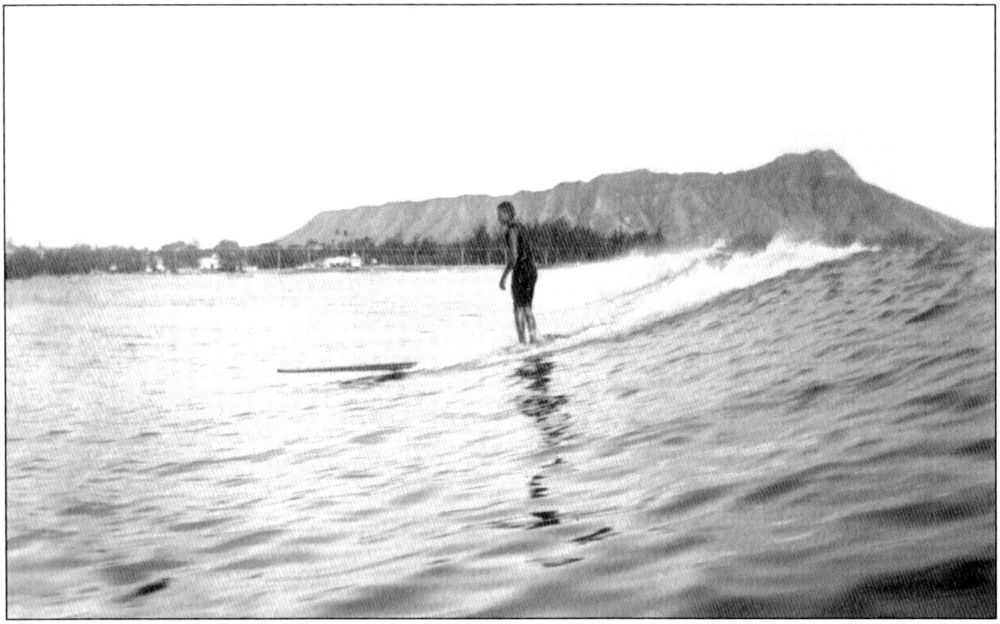

EARLIEST SURFING PHOTOGRAPHS TAKEN FROM THE WATER, C. 1905. By the angle of the photograph above, it appears the photographer was in a canoe and using a new Kodak Brownie camera. This is the only known real-photo card of a surfer standing upright and dates from the "undivided back" postcard era from 1901 to 1907. Also, with a closer look, the surfboard appears to be an olo. The postcard has notes from the night clerk of the Alexander Young Hotel, Lew E. Haehnlen: "Surfing is about the best sport I've ever tackled. I've taken some time to learn how to get a surf-board on the move."

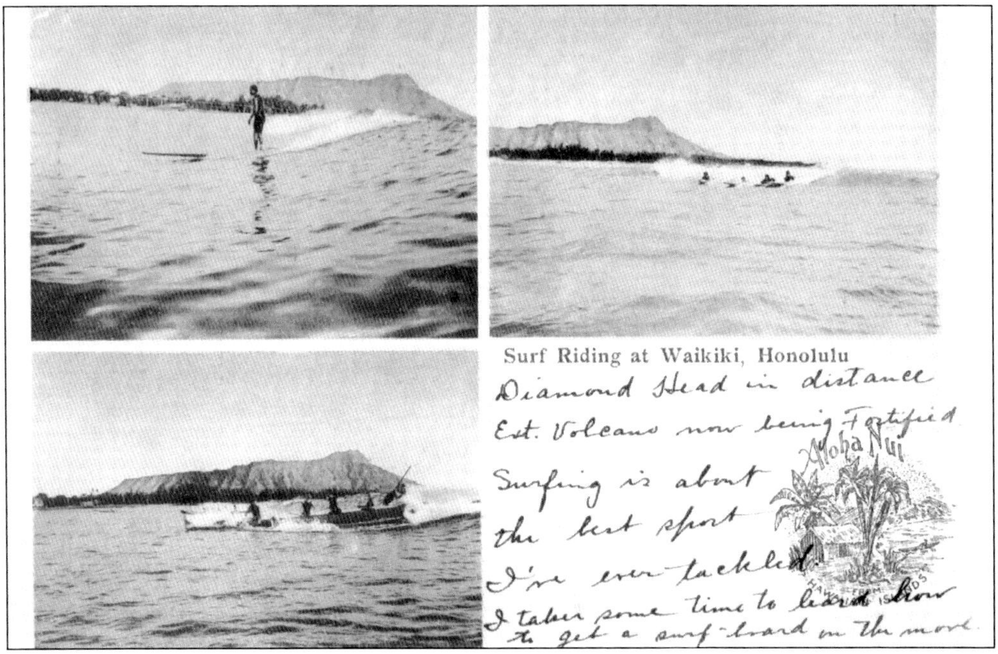

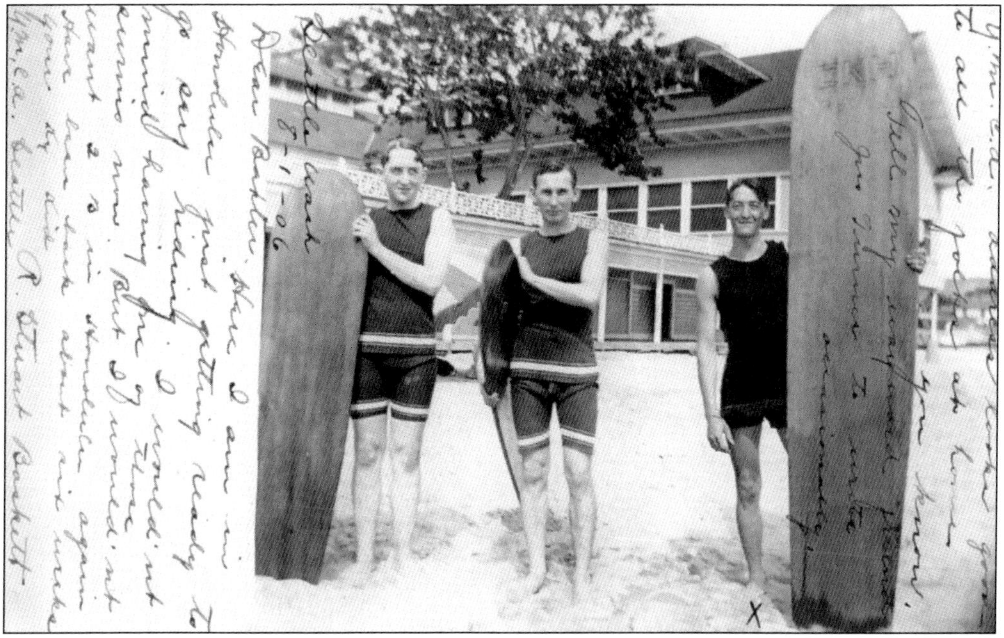

POSTCARD MUSINGS. "Here I am in Honolulu just getting ready to go surf riding. I wouldn't mind having one of those swims now," it states. This note from R. Stuart Baskett was mailed to his sister and sent from the YMCA in Seattle, Washington, in 1906. Stuart appears to be the one on the right while standing at the Moana Hotel. (Courtesy Dan Pincetich.)

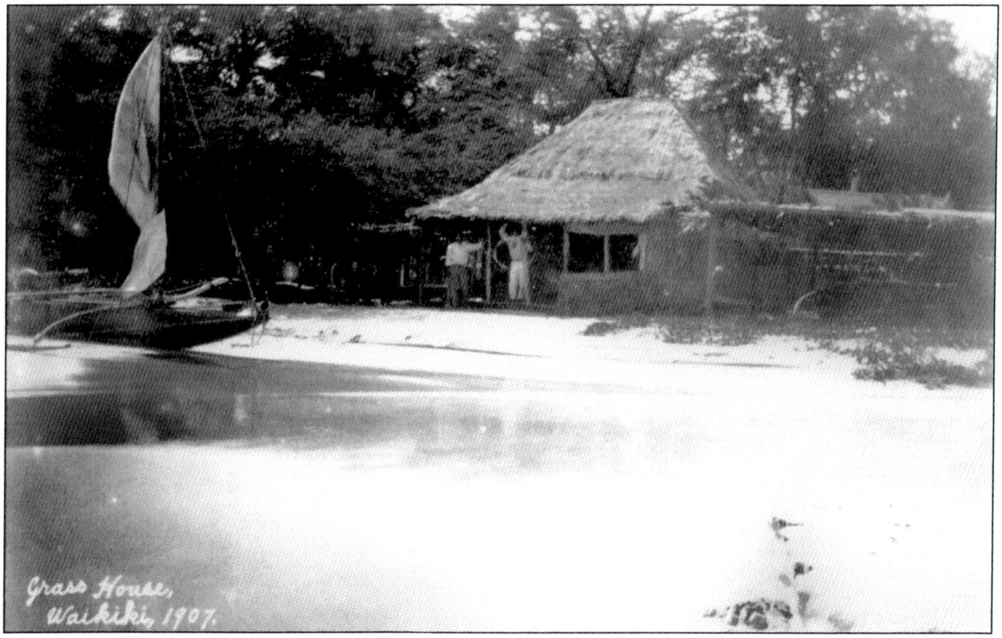

EASTMAN KODAK COMPANY'S FOLDING POCKET CAMERA. Anyone could make his or her own postcards with the folding pocket camera. Introduced in 1898, this ingenious camera made negatives the same size as postcards. It came with a metal tool that allowed a photographer to etch onto the negative, as shown on the image of the original *hale pili* (house of grass) that was brought over from Kaimuki Zoo to be used as part of the new Outrigger Canoe Club.

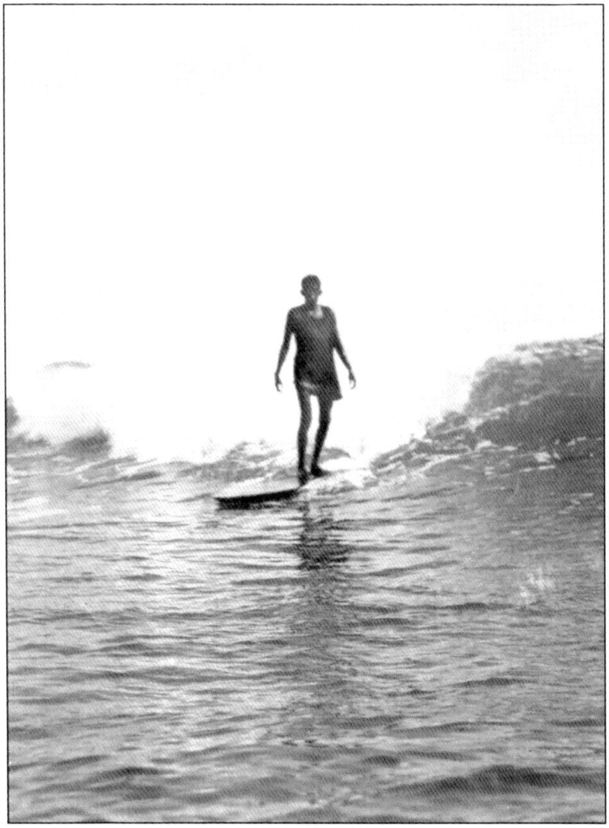

Two Action Photographs Taken from a Canoe, March 1909. At left, "First pix of a surf board rider I made, March 1909" is by R.G.L. Below, a note from an unknown photographer identifies "second from left, Kenneth Atkinson, brother of 'Jack' A.L.C. Atkinson, former Territorial Secretary." Jack was a well-known surfer. Modern photography was ushered in by the inventions of George Eastman, who in 1885 developed dry gel on paper, or film, which replaced photographic plates. In 1900, he introduced the Brownie Camera. Photography was mass marketed, with an affordable and simple process that left the complex parts to others. Ads promised, "You press the button, we do the rest." Photography was now able to capture the action of surf riding from the beach or even a canoe. (Both courtesy Hawai'i State Archives.)

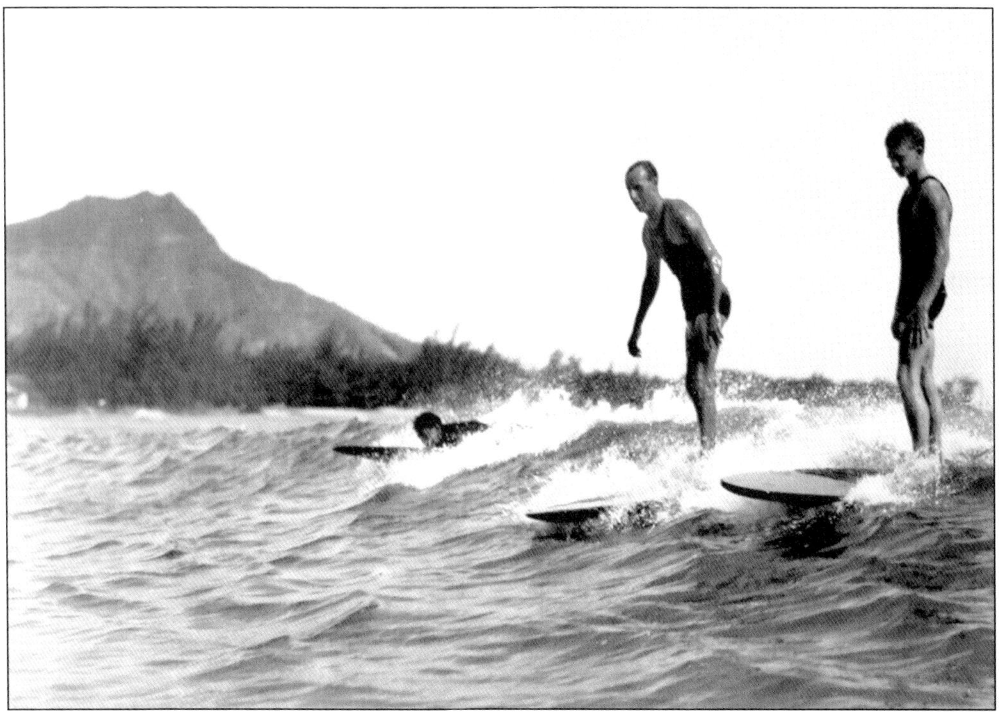

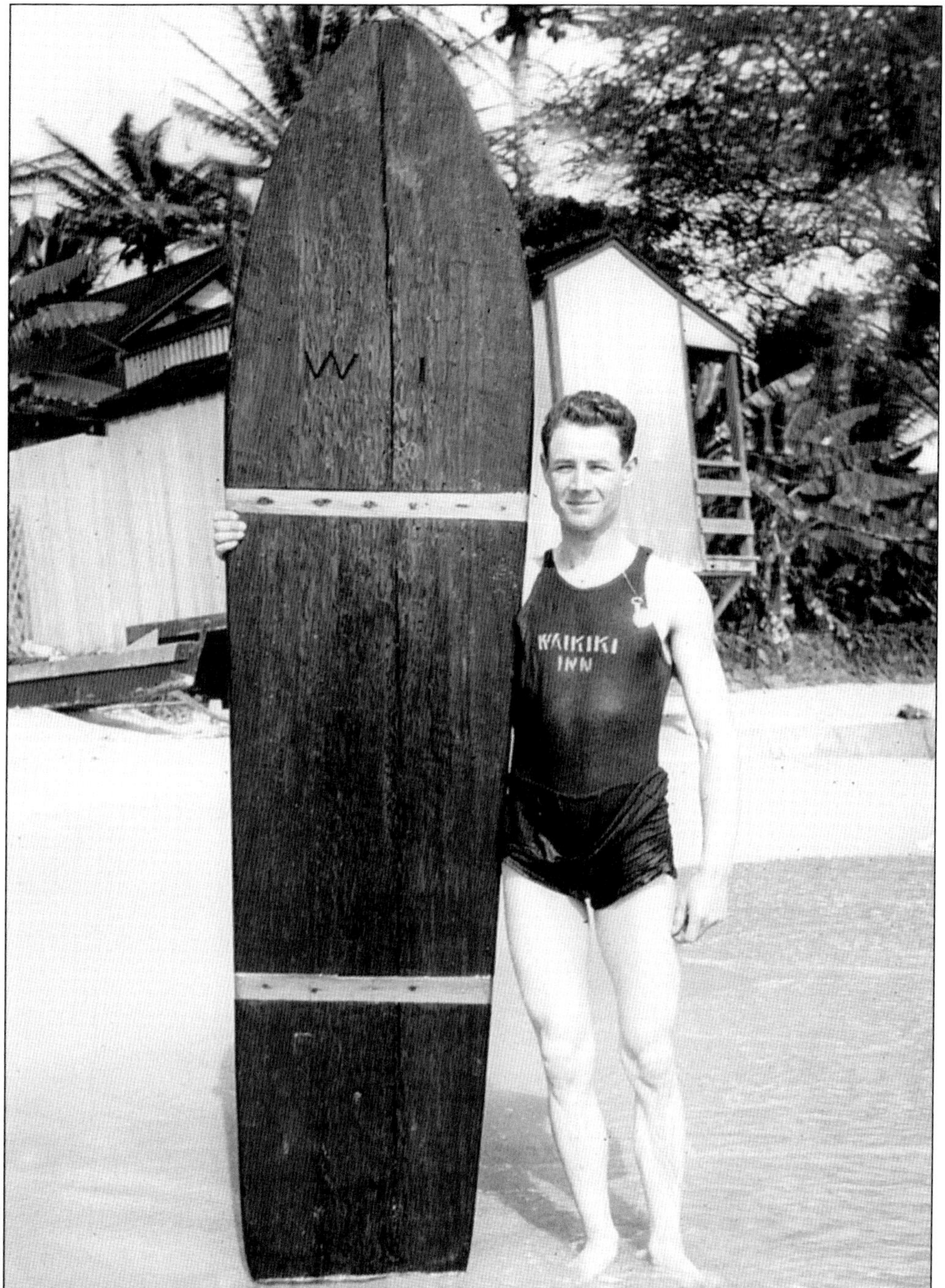

A Proud Tourist Displays the Waikiki Inn Rental Surfboard, c. 1907. With over 2,000 tourists in 1903, local establishments found enterprising ways to let visitors experience paradise. Note the way that the solid wood "plank" surfboard has been modified with straps to hold the splitting wood together. It was not until the mid-1930s that waterproof glue was available and spar varnish used to coat the wood. Without constant care, the wood would become saturated and split once it dried out.

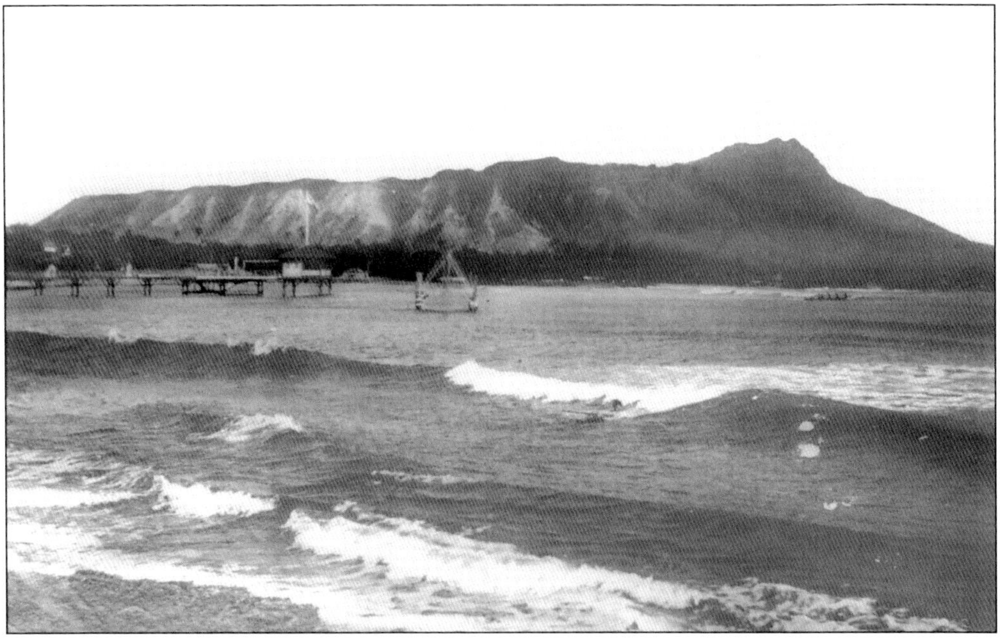

"SURF BOARD RIDING, HAWAII," A MAGIC LANTERN GLASS SLIDE. In 1902, W.C. Weedon convinced a group of Honolulu businessmen to pay him to advertise the territory of Hawai'i on the mainland through six months of lecture tours and a magic lantern show. The irresistibly named magic lantern show consisted of glass slides shown and enlarged on a screen through the use of a projector. Note the A-frame platform as seen on page 70.

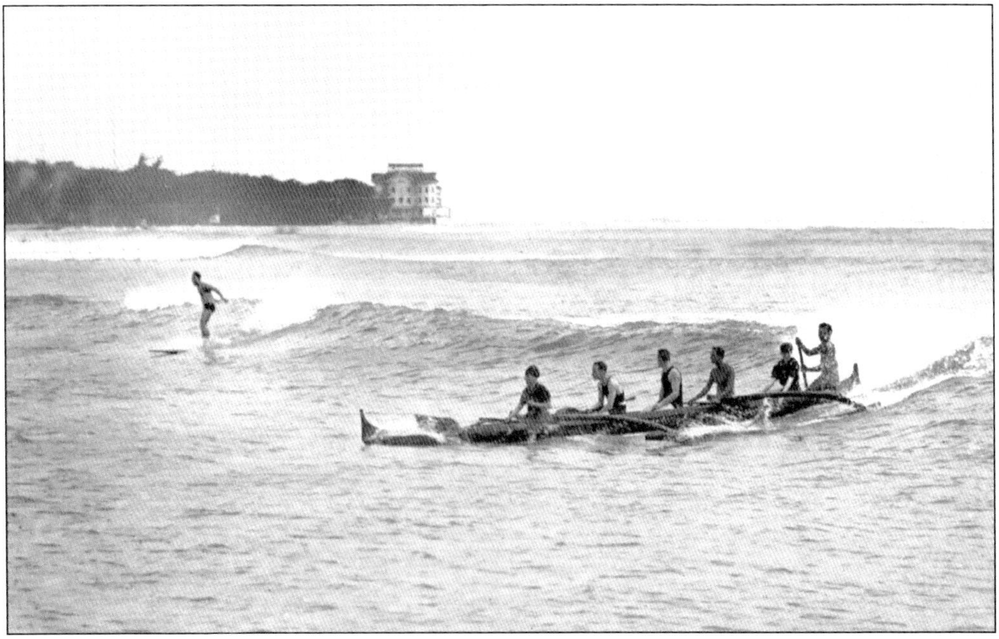

A MAGIC LANTERN SLIDE OF THE TWO WAYS OF SURF RIDING. Travelers' slide shows were a popular form of entertainment around the turn of the century and a rare chance for mainlanders to see what W.C. Weedon called "a realistic and truthful representation of those remarkable people and beautiful lands of Hawai'i."

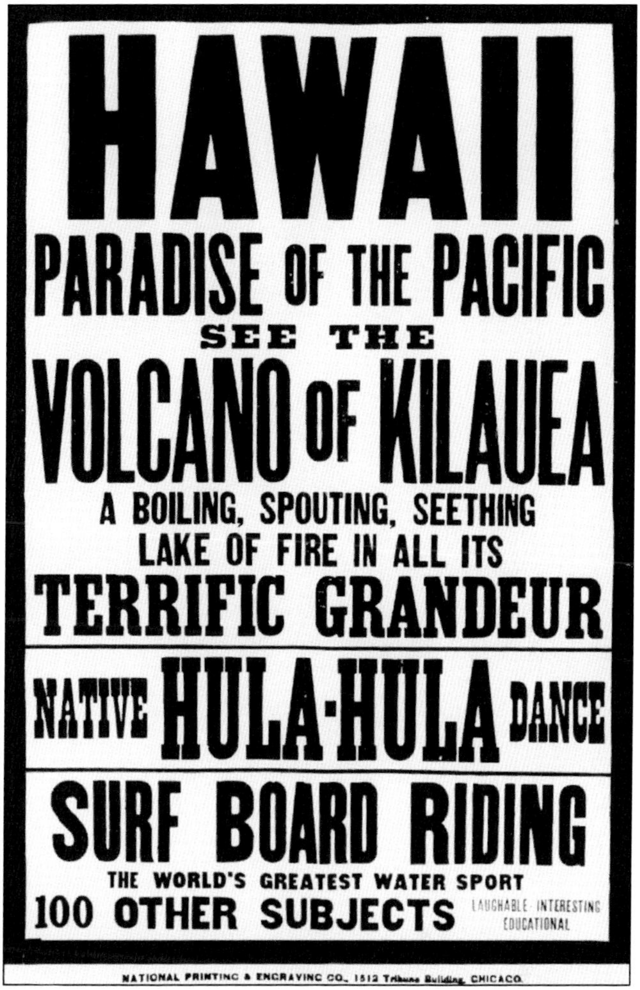

"Hawai'i, Paradise of the Pacific" and the Volcano of Kilauea. This poster was for a traveling show/presentation of Hawai'ian images. Famed photographer Ray Jerome Baker used posters similar to this for his magic lantern slides and film tours done on the mainland in summers during the 1910s and 1920s. (Courtesy Keith Eshelman.)

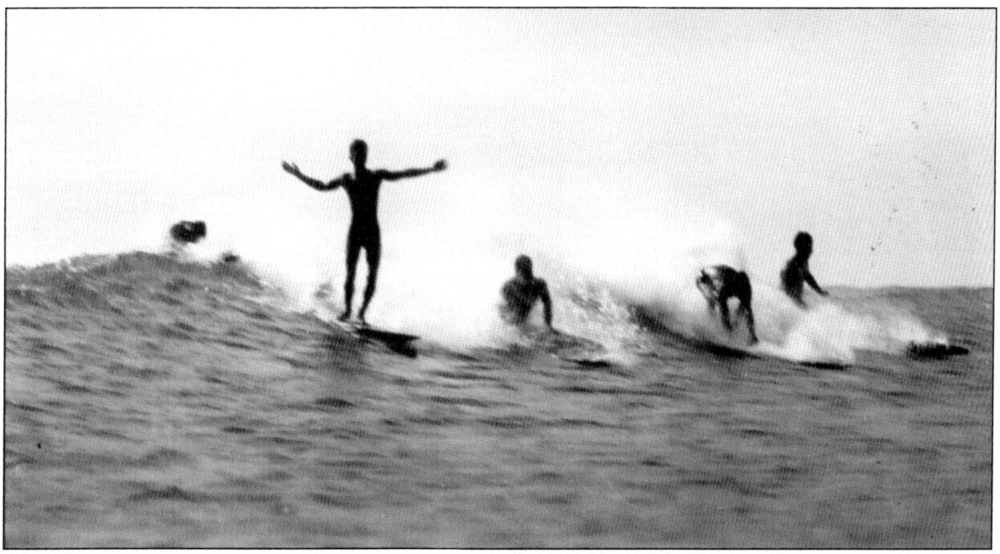

Pure Stoke. The pure joy and excitement of surfing is captured in a c. 1909 magic lantern glass slide. The exhilaration of riding a wave has always been the main reason people surf—then, now, and forever. Surfing is one of the world's oldest sports and dates back over 2,000 years.

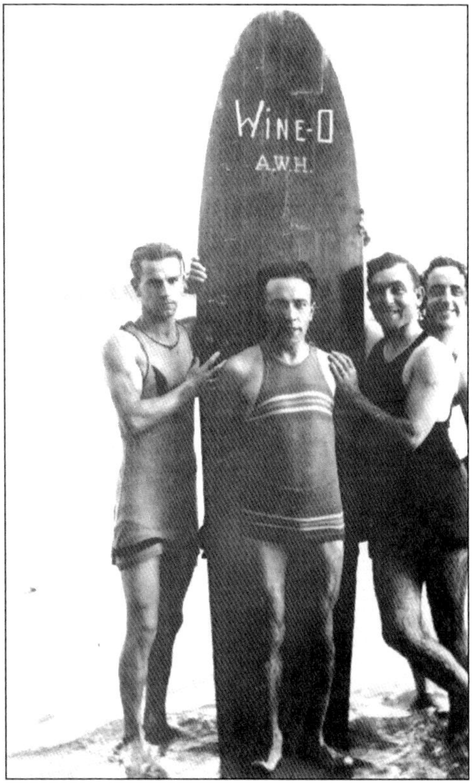

TOURISTS LEARNING TO SURF RIDE FEEL *HOPUPU* (STOKED). Unfortunately, many wonderful Hawai'ian words like hopupu are no longer used. In 1903, the Hawai'i Promotion Committee was formed by the Honolulu Chamber of Commerce and funded by the territorial legislature. Passengers on steamships and railroads were especially targeted, as they had the leisure time to read the brochures.

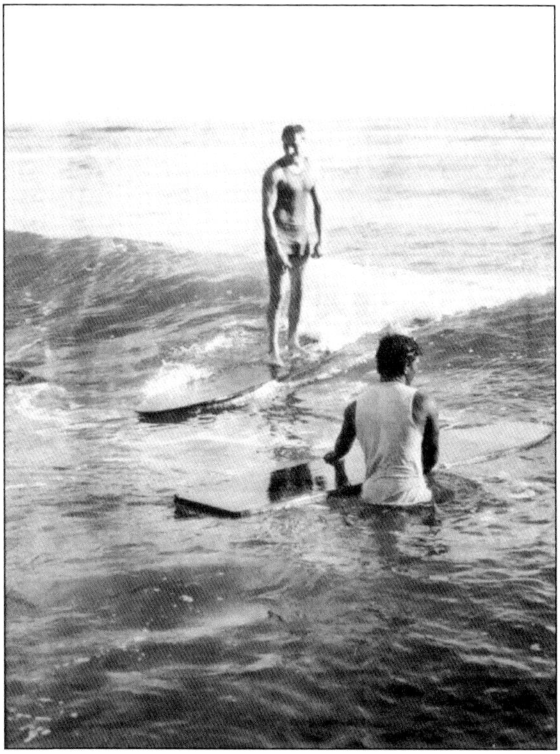

IN FRONT OF THE MOANA HOTEL, WAITING FOR THEIR WAVE TO COME IN. These surfboards are what the Hawai'ians would call an alaia and are approximately six to eight feet long, the average length for that era. According to Tom Blake in *Paradise of the Pacific Magazine* in 1931, "To Duke goes the credit of introducing a ten foot board in 1910. This board was looked upon as huge and others were slow to follow his lead." (Courtesy Cary Weiss.)

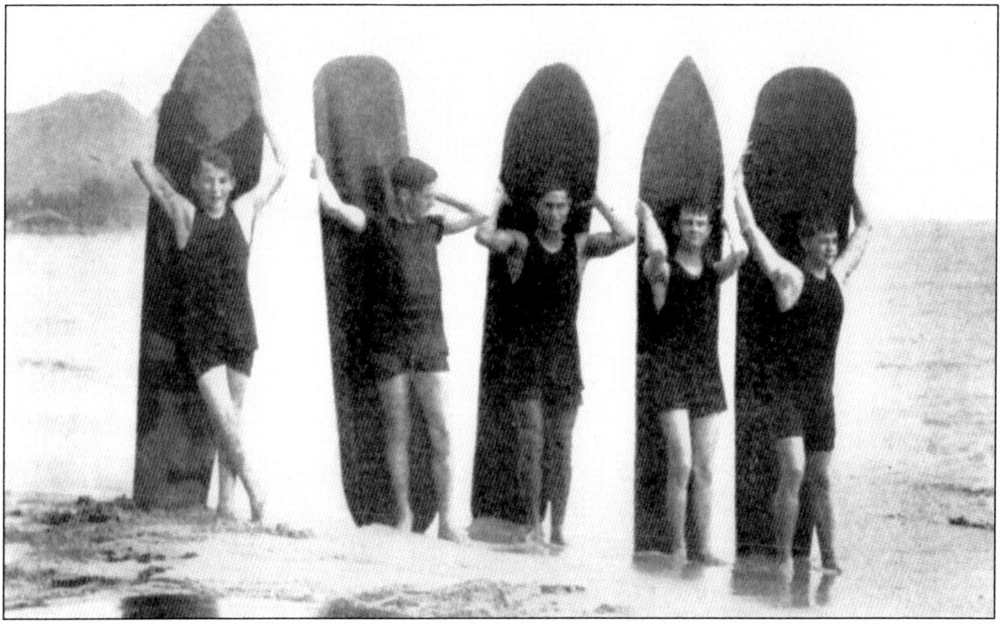

Surfboards. "Usually made of native mahogany and pointed at one end, boards will hold up the heaviest man with the force of a wave behind him, but in quiet waters they will sink with the weight of a child," wrote Alexander Hume Ford in a 1909 article in *Collier's Outdoor America*. The article also included the above photograph with a young Edward K. "Dude" Miller (pronounced "Dudie," who is seen in the center) of later renown as a leading beachboy, first Hui Nalu captain, and front man of *The Dude Miller Band*, which performed nightly at the Moana Hotel. (Both courtesy Dan Pincetich.)

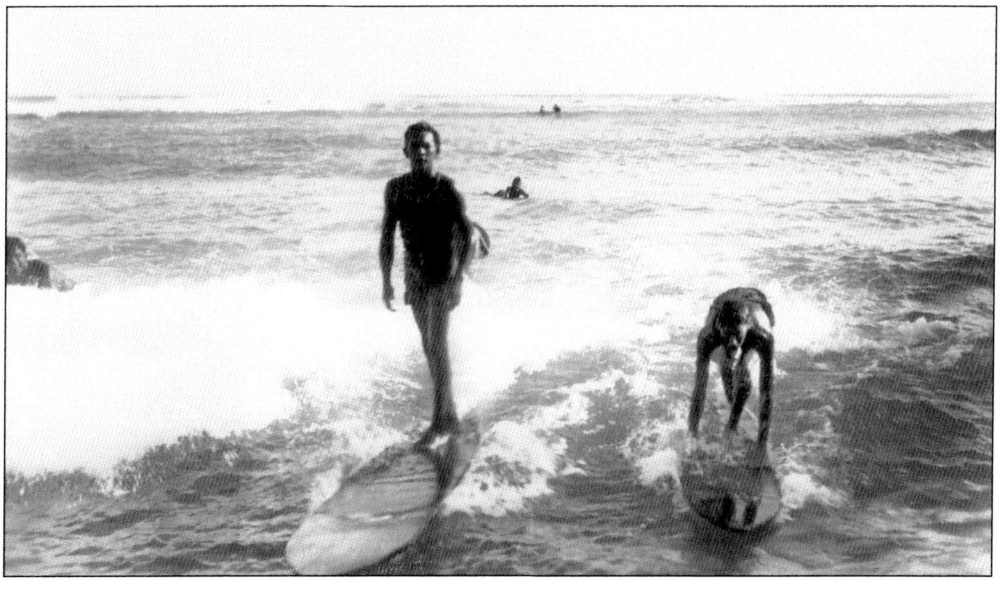

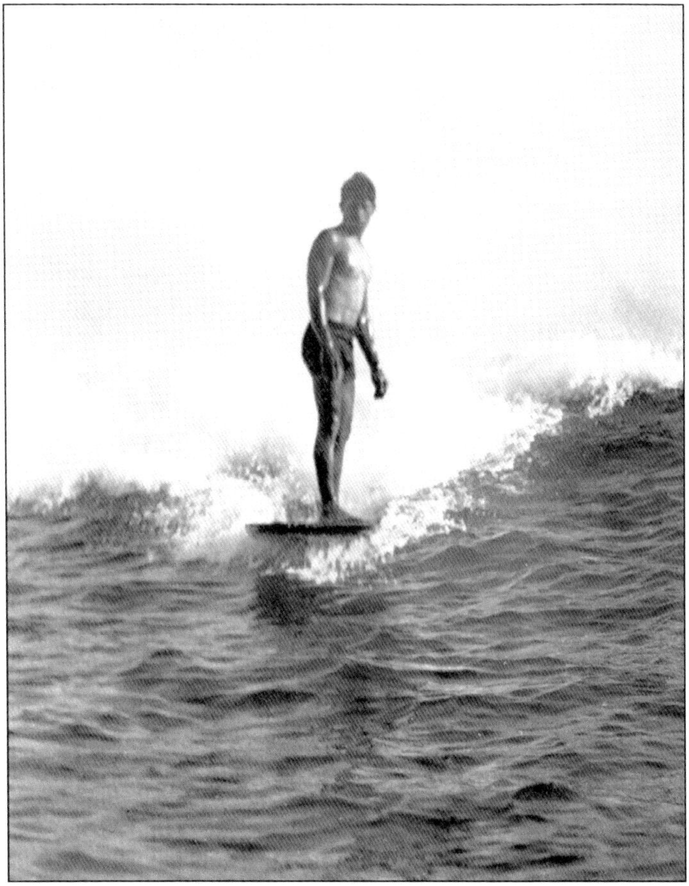

Surfing Captured while Riding in a Canoe. This popular image was used by the Island Curio Co. in one of its early divided-back, full-face postcards printed between 1907 and 1910.

A Day at the Beach, c. 1909. This photograph was taken looking down the beach in front of the Outrigger Canoe Club towards the Moana Hotel. Notice that the women are all in full dress—even those lying on the beach, and a young man is practicing his surfing moves on his surfboard up on the sand. The Moana bathhouse can be seen in the background. (Courtesy Outrigger Canoe Club.)

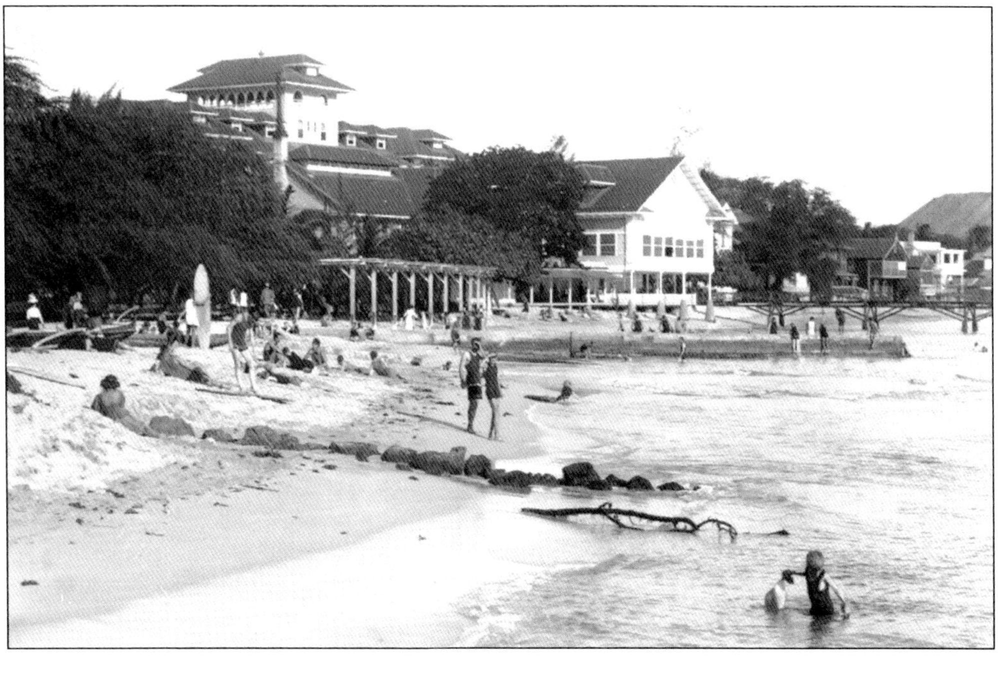

READY FOR THE BIG ROLLERS. This rather happy unidentified man with a stylish bathing suit is ready for the big rollers on the outside reefs. (Courtesy Dan Pincetich.)

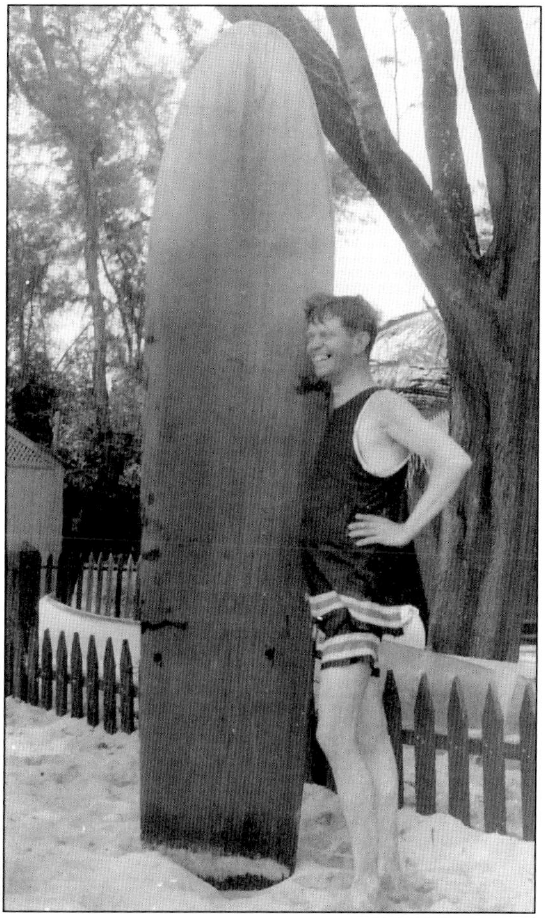

WHILE WAITING FOR WAVES, KEIKI FIND THINGS TO DO, AS ALWAYS. Then as now, keiki always seem to find the time to get out in the surf and make the best of any conditions. This was the elevated view from the Moana Pier looking east. (Courtesy Outrigger Canoe Club.)

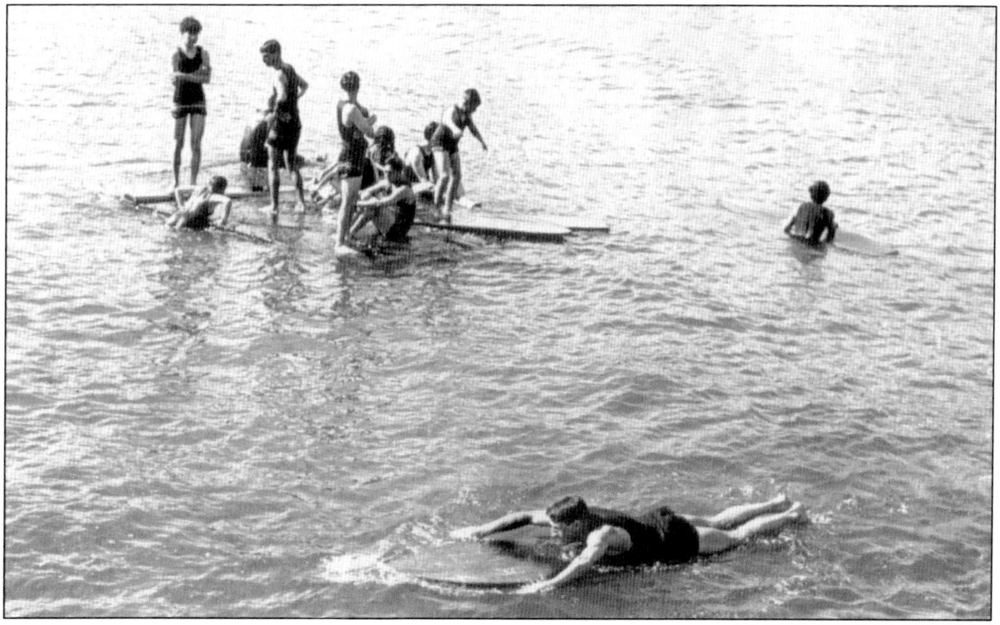

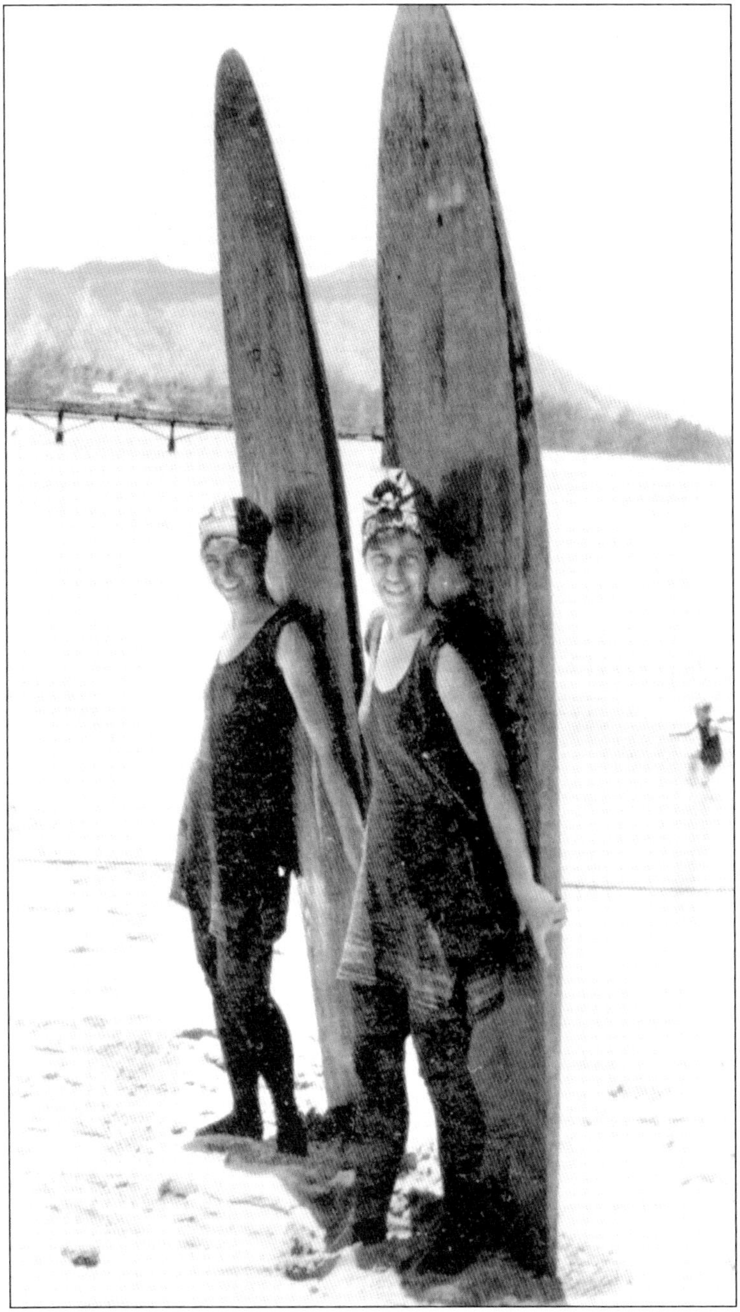

Modeling the Proper Victorian Bathing Costumes while Supporting Solid Wood Surfboards. Strict rules of modesty prevailed at the turn of the century. It was considered immoral for women to show any skin while bathing. Proper attire included leggings, long sleeves, cap, and shoes; the suit was made of wool or flannel. The "Australian Mermaid," Annette Kellerman, introduced a woman's one-piece swimsuit in Boston in 1908 and was arrested for indecency. In 1921, the territorial legislature passed the Desha Bathing Suit Law: "No person over 14-years of age shall appear on any highway within the . . . city or county of Honolulu, in a bathing suit unless covered suitably by an outer garment reaching at least to the knees. (Courtesy Cary Weiss.)

Four

The Outrigger Canoe Club 1908

by Timothy T. DeLaVega

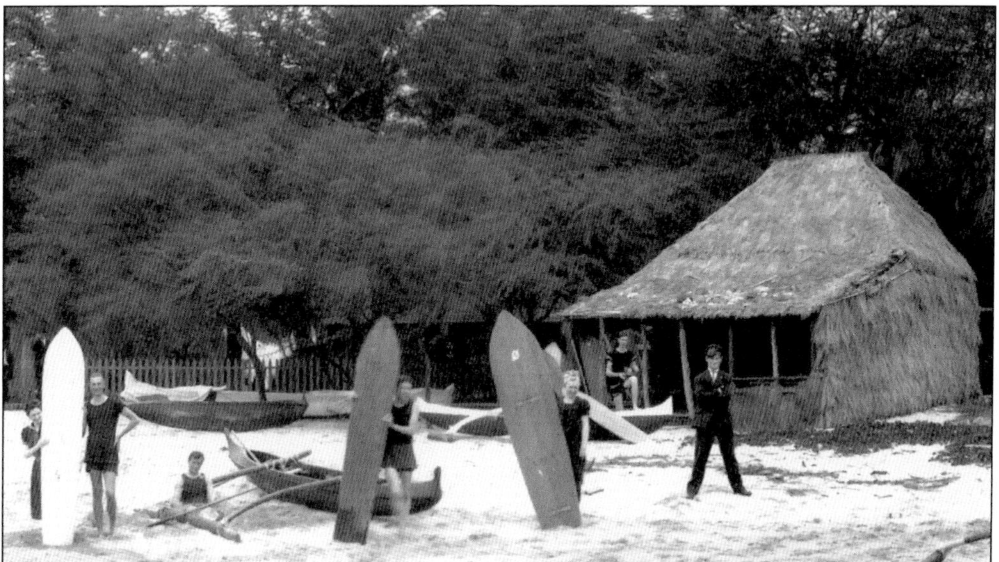

The Beginnings of the Outrigger Canoe Club (OCC). The idea of Burton Holmes and Alexander Hume Ford, the club was established May 1, 1908. Its mission was stated in a 1908 letter sent out to the community promoting the idea of "a place where surfboards may be revived and those who live away from the waterfront may keep their surfboards . . . to make Waikiki always the House of the Surfers, where men and boys ride upright upon the crests of waves."

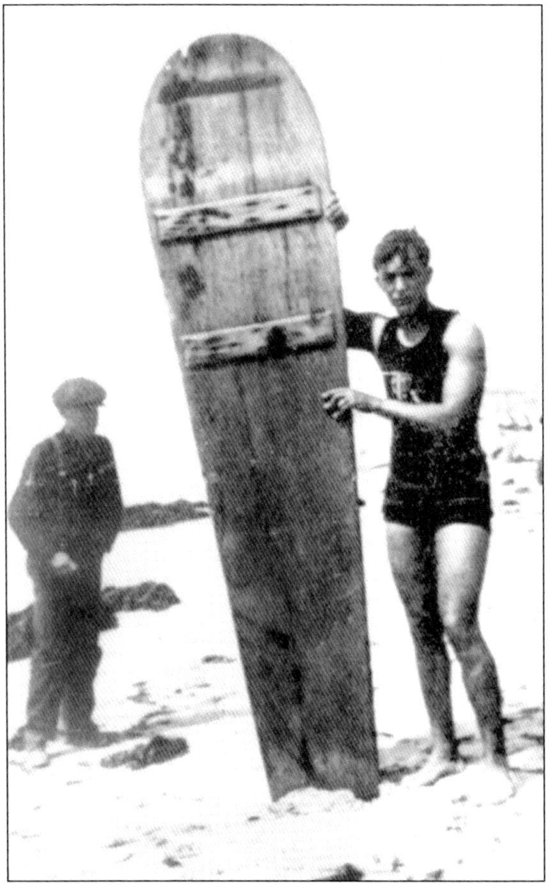

George Freeth, 1907. The 1908 *Honolulu Star* called George Freeth "the most expert surf board rider in the world." Freeth taught Jack London and A.H. Ford to surf. London wrote about Freeth: "He is Mercury—a black Mercury. His heels are winged, and in them is the swiftness of the sea." Freeth moved to California to teach surfing and swimming. He is considered one of the most influential lifeguards in US history. (Courtesy Outrigger Canoe Club.)

Jack London and His Wife, Charmian, at the Outrigger Canoe Club, 1916. Jack London was a world-renowned author when he first visited Hawai'i in 1907. At the urging of A.H. Ford, London attempted surfing and marveled at the prowess of George Freeth, whom London described as the "Black Mercury" in his internationally published short story on surfing at Waikiki, "Riding the South Seas Surf," later named "A Royal Sport." (Courtesy Outrigger Canoe Club.)

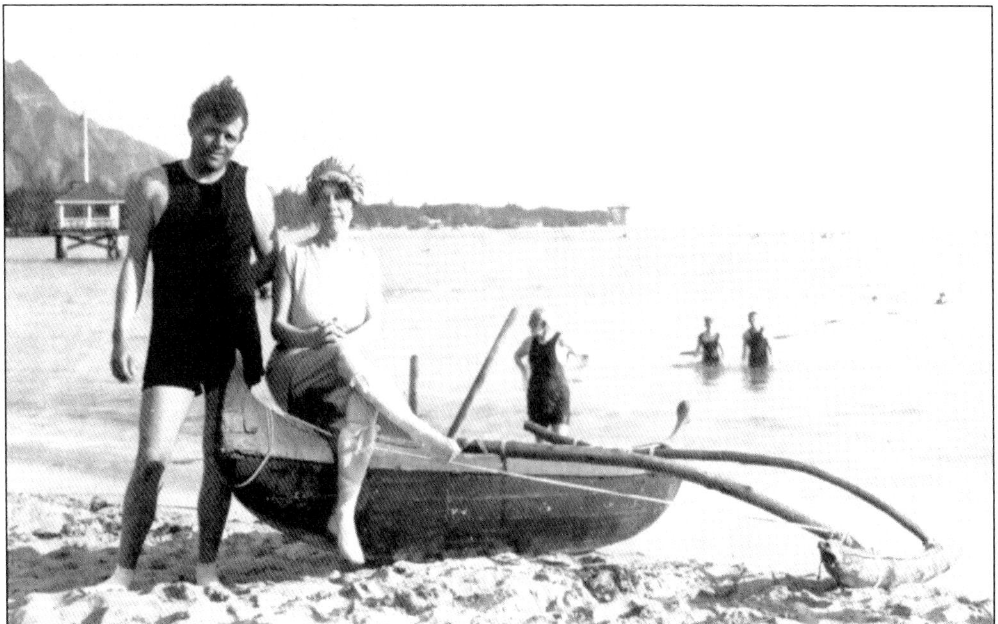

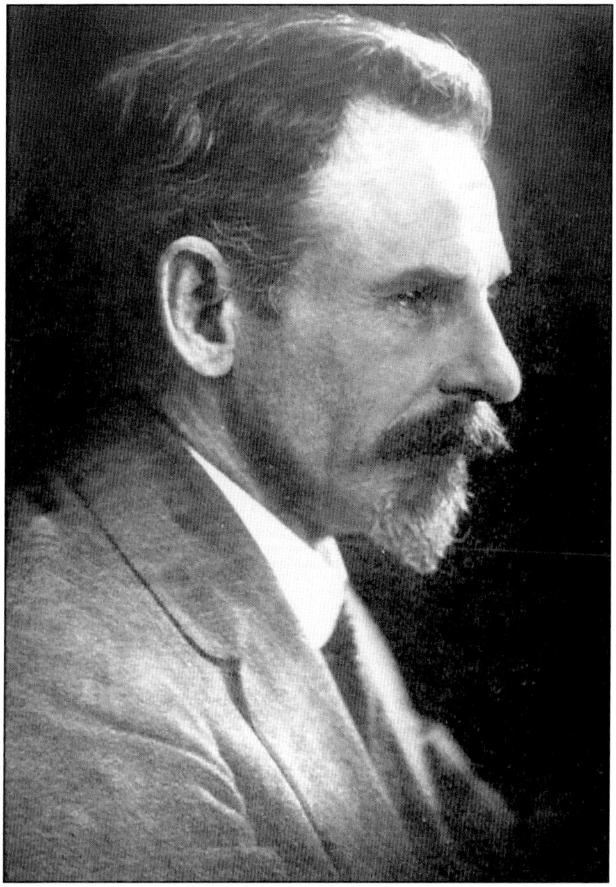

ALEXANDER HUME FORD, SURFING'S FIRST PROMOTER. The image below shows Ford overseeing the production seen on page 45. At age 39, Ford fell in love with surfing and from then on devoted his life to the promotion and revitalization of the sport. As the founder of the Outrigger Canoe Club, he guided the club's promotion of the sport through surf carnivals and magazine articles. In a 1909 *Collier's Outdoor America* article, Ford wrote, "The white man and boy are doing much in Hawai'i to develop the art of surf-riding" and "the white lad has taught the native boy to play baseball and the native has taught his fair-skinned cousin all the sports of his forefathers." Although he was to be sidelined later in life while trying to bring peace to the Pacific through his Pan-Pacific Union, Ford stayed devoted to the OCC and its mission. (At right, courtesy Outrigger Canoe Club.)

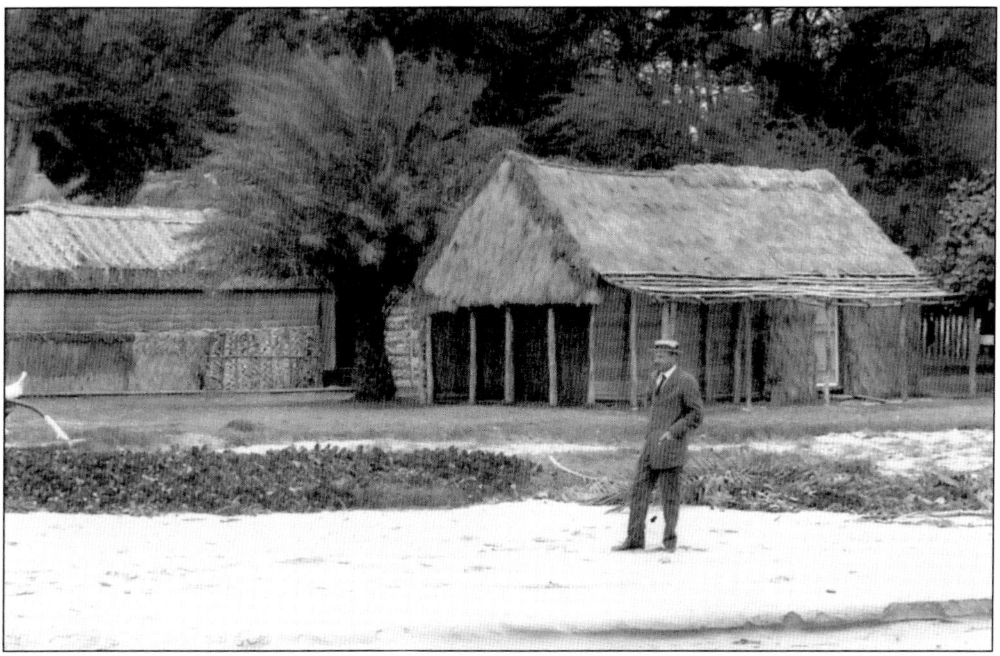

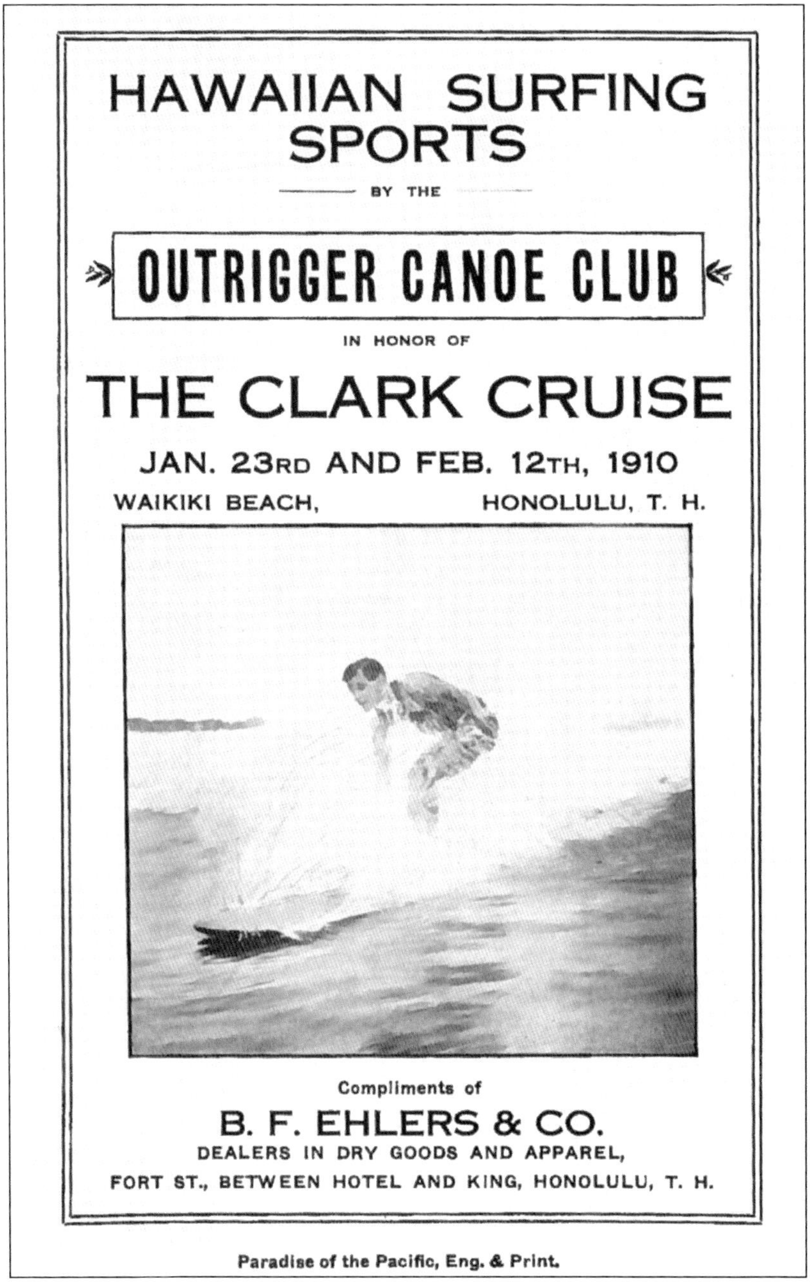

"HAWAIIAN SURFING SPORTS" PROGRAM FOR JANUARY 23 AND FEBRUARY 12, 1910. The Outrigger Canoe Club used the arrival of the cruise ships, or Regatta Day, as a promotional tool for the club. The first events were sponsored by the Clark Cruise, and cruise agent Frank C. Clark donated four silver cups, one of which can be seen at the Outrigger Canoe Club entrance lobby. In 1909, A.H. Ford described such an event in Collier's: "At the Christmas Contest. For the third time a white boy now fourteen years of age won the medal given to the most expert surfboarder; he came in a hundred yards before a monster roller standing on his head." The cover photograph was taken at Waikiki in 1908 by Edward P. Irwin, editor of the *Democrat*, a Honolulu newspaper. (Courtesy Jamie Clark.)

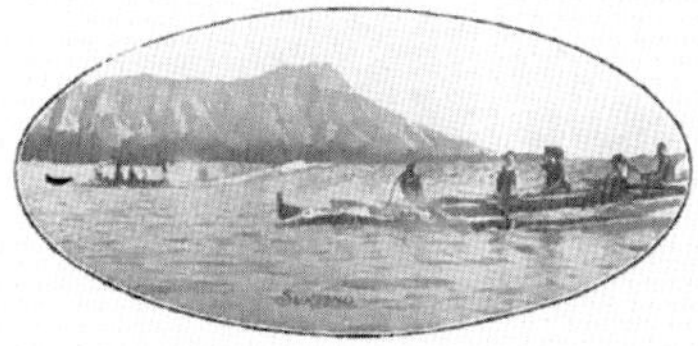

PROGRAM OF THE DAY

Sunday, January 23rd., 1910

The Promotion Committee with native singers and lei girls will meet the Cleveland in the harbor; trolley cars will be waiting to take the cruisers sight-seeing, leaving them at the Royal Hawaiian Hotel for lunch.

At 3 P. M. the Hawaiian water sports will take place in front of the Outrigger Club grounds, the Moana and the Seaside Hotels at Waikiki Beach; the Hawaiian Band will be in attendance from 3:00 to 5:30.

EVENTS:

(1) SURFBOARD RIDING, for a Clark Cup. Length of ride standing erect, ability to ride standing on head, gracefulness, etc., will be considered by judges in making award.

(2) SURFING CANOE CONTEST, for a Clark Cup. Winner to be the crew that brings its canoe closest to beach before the biggest wave.

(3) Races between surfboard-riders and outrigger canoes.

INSIDE PAGES OF THE SURFING PROGRAM FOR JANUARY 23, 1910. The "Program of the Day" (right) explains the events for Sunday, January 23: "at 3 P. M. the Hawai'ian water sports will take place in front of the Outrigger Clubs grounds." The page seen below explains the early history of the club. Of note is how rapidly the group grew in less than two years—from approximately 100 members to over 300. By 1915, there were 1,200 members. The original annual fee was $5. The eight-page program also contained the events for Saturday, February 12, a map of the area, numerous ads, and closed with the musical score to "Aloha Oe" by Her Majesty Queen Liliuokalani. (Both courtesy Jamie Clark.)

THE HAWAIIAN OUTRIGGER CANOE CLUB

Waikiki Beach, Honolulu

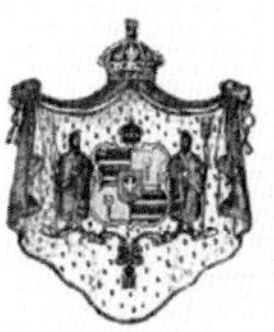

Two malihinis (new-comers, walking along the beach at Waikiki some two years ago noticed a wilderness of hau trees surrounding a stagnant lagoon; to their eyes this seemed the ideal place to secure for those who would keep alive the distinctly Hawaiian sports of riding the surf-board and manipulating the outrigger canoe.

A lease was secured on an acre and a half of land facing the sea and the Outrigger Canoe Club organized; two Hawaiian grass houses, fast disappearing relics of a former age, were purchased and removed bodily to the Club grounds, where they now face the sea at the very spot where Kamehameha, the Hawaiian Napoleon, landed to conquer the island; the property was owned by the late Queen Emma. The grass houses on the Outrigger grounds and the one in the Bishop Museum are among the few ancient relics of this kind to be seen on Oahu island.

There are now about 300 members of the Outrigger Club, and the art of riding the surf-board has reached a degree of development by many of these that was attained in the old days only by the Chiefs of the highest rank.

The Hawaiian Outrigger Canoe Club is, as was intended from the beginning, a place where malihini (new-comer) and kamaaina (old resident) can meet to strive for perfection in Hawaiian surfing sports, the fame of which has long been world-wide.

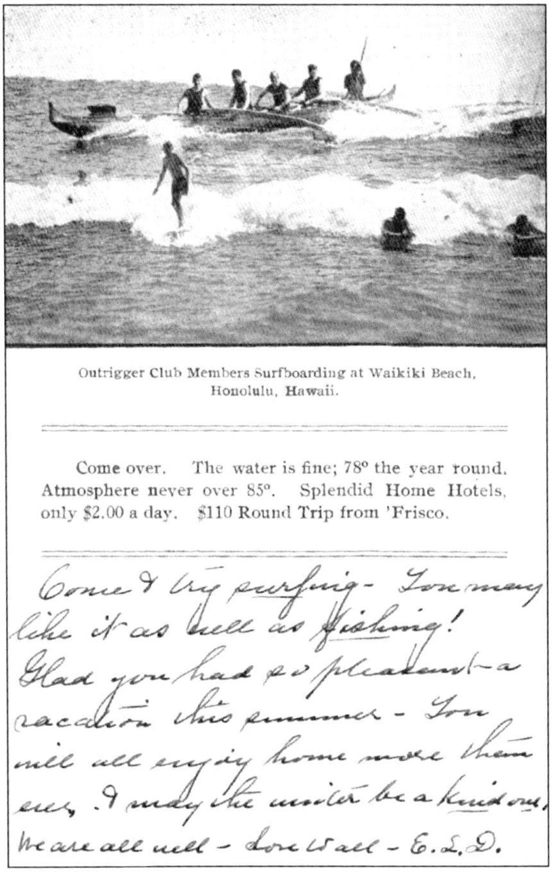

OUTRIGGER CANOE CLUB POSTCARD, 1909. The note on the postcard reads, "Come and try surfing—you may like it as well as fishing!" (Courtesy Dan Pincetich.)

IN 1909, THE CLUB BUILT A THATCHED-ROOFED DANCE HALL. The *Pacific Commercial Advertiser* in 1908 noted, "These are busy days at the Outrigger Club; school has closed and the boys are hard at work cutting out surfboards. Sometimes there are a dozen of them under the lanais of the grass houses cutting planks." And a carpenter was kept busy making surfboards for $2 each. (Courtesy Outrigger Canoe Club.)

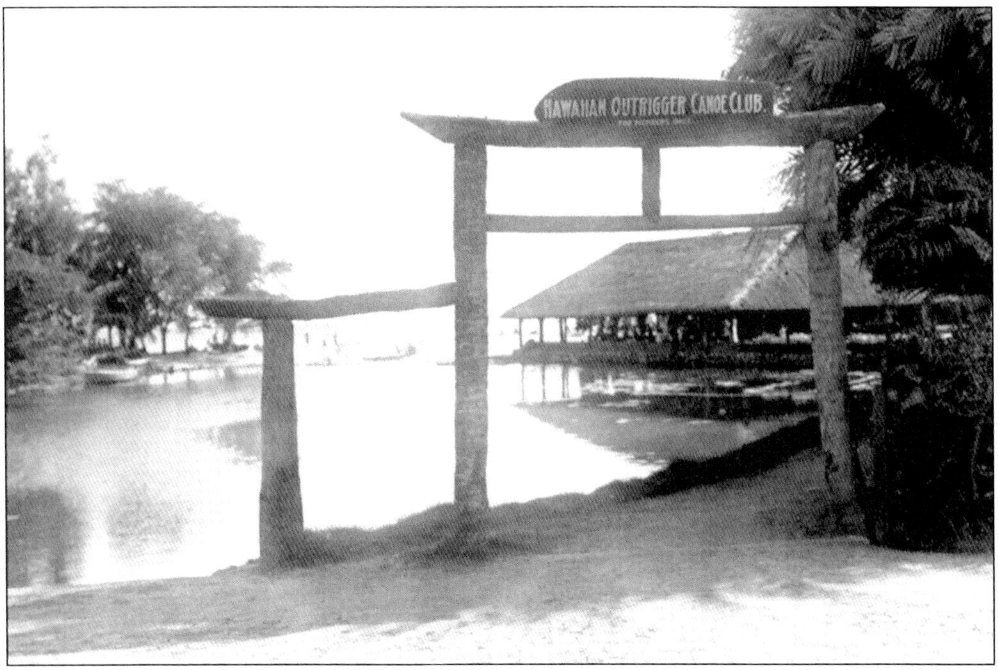

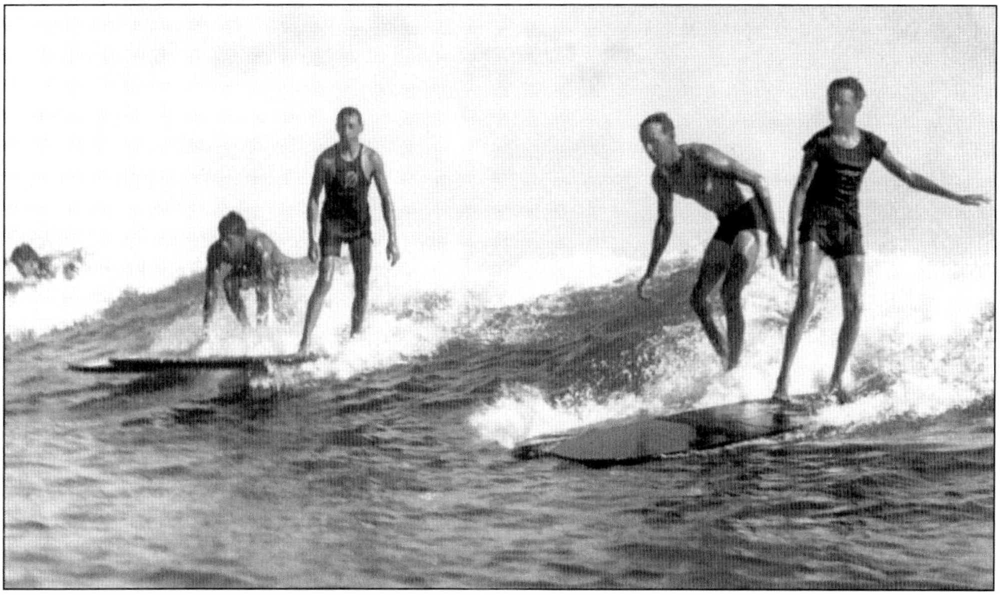

The Outrigger Logo on a Magic Lantern Slide by R.K. Bonine, July 18, 1912. The college student third from left and wearing the Outrigger Canoe Club shirt is Harry Steiner, whose father established the Island Curio Co. The original Outrigger Club logo has stood the test of time and is still used by the club. By 1915, members of the club included the territorial governor and several judges of the territorial supreme court.

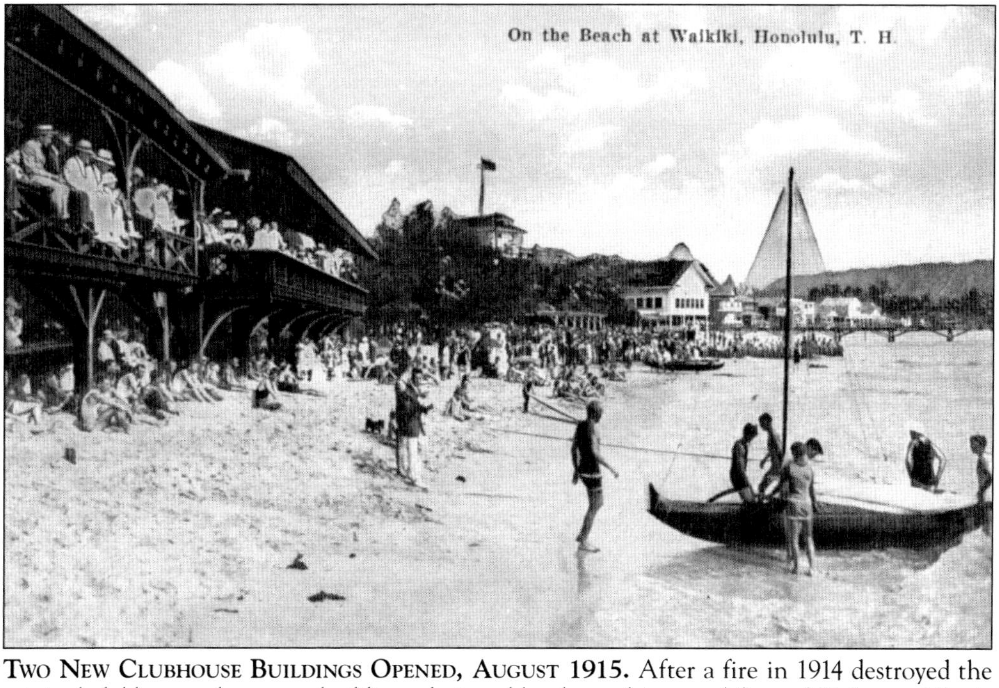

Two New Clubhouse Buildings Opened, August 1915. After a fire in 1914 destroyed the original clubhouse, these new buildings designed by the architectural firm of Ripley and Davis were opened. The buildings had the dance floor on the second floor and storage for canoes and surfboards below, with the clubhouse to the west (left). This postcard depicts the excitement of a Regatta Day with the new buildings.

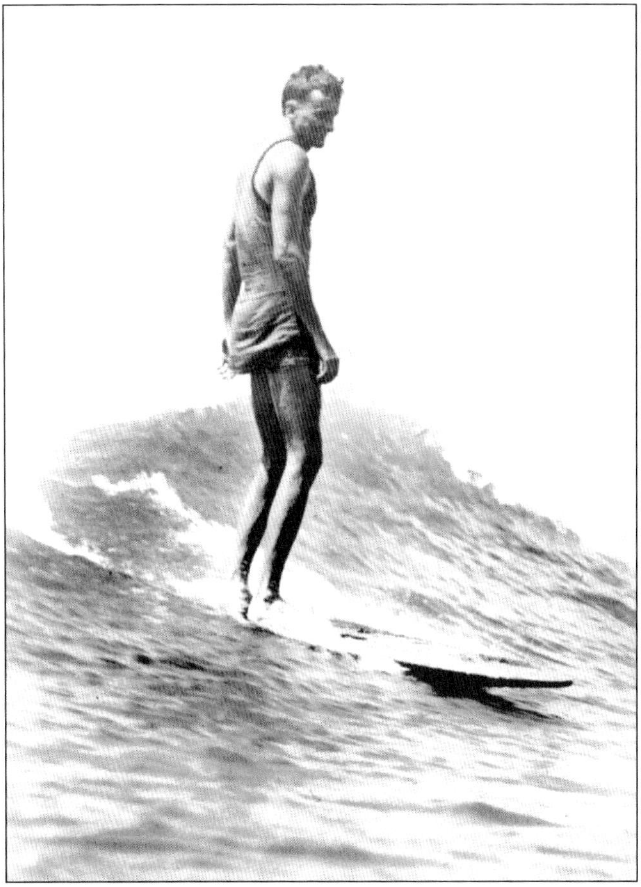

George David "Dad" Center. Center was the Outrigger Canoe Club captain, a renowned canoe-racing coach, a swimming coach at the 1920 and 1924 Olympics, and, according to A.H. Ford and Tom Blake, one of the finest surfers of the era. Dad is also credited with starting the first beach volleyball game on a rather poor day for surfing in 1918. (Photograph by Ray Jerome Baker.)

Keiki and Their Papa Li'ili'i Surfboard, Outrigger Club Beach in Background. In 1944, Alexander Hume Ford wrote, "I got a 20 year lease on what is now the Outrigger Canoe Club grounds for $5 a year, provided the dues for boys and under 16 would not be over $5 a year . . . Such dues made it possible for every kid with guts to live at least half the day fighting the surf."

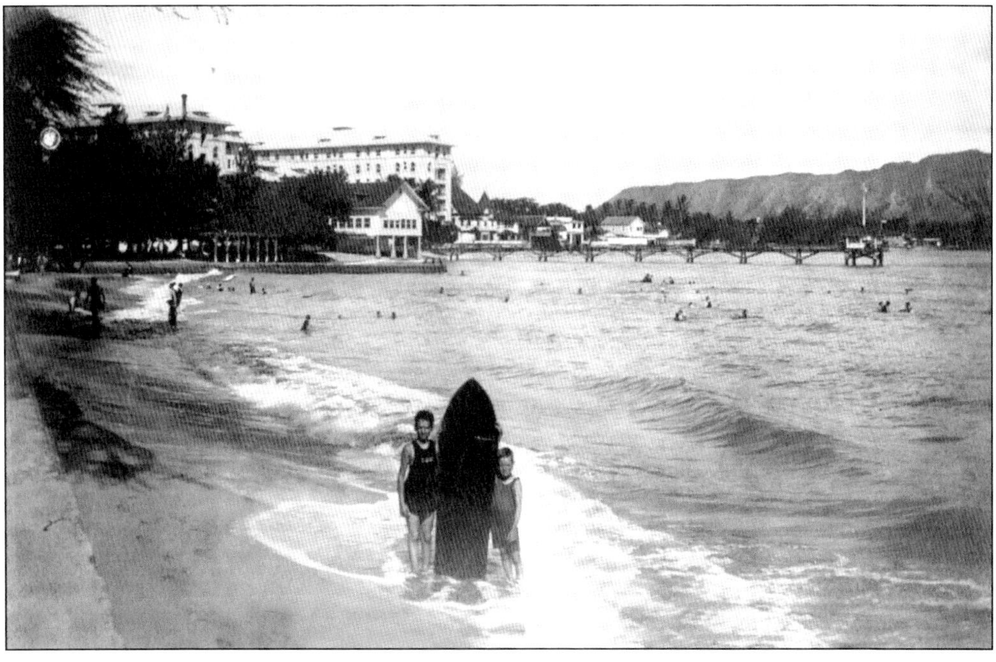

Five

HUI NALU (CLUB OF THE WAVES) 1908

BY TIMOTHY T. DELAVEGA

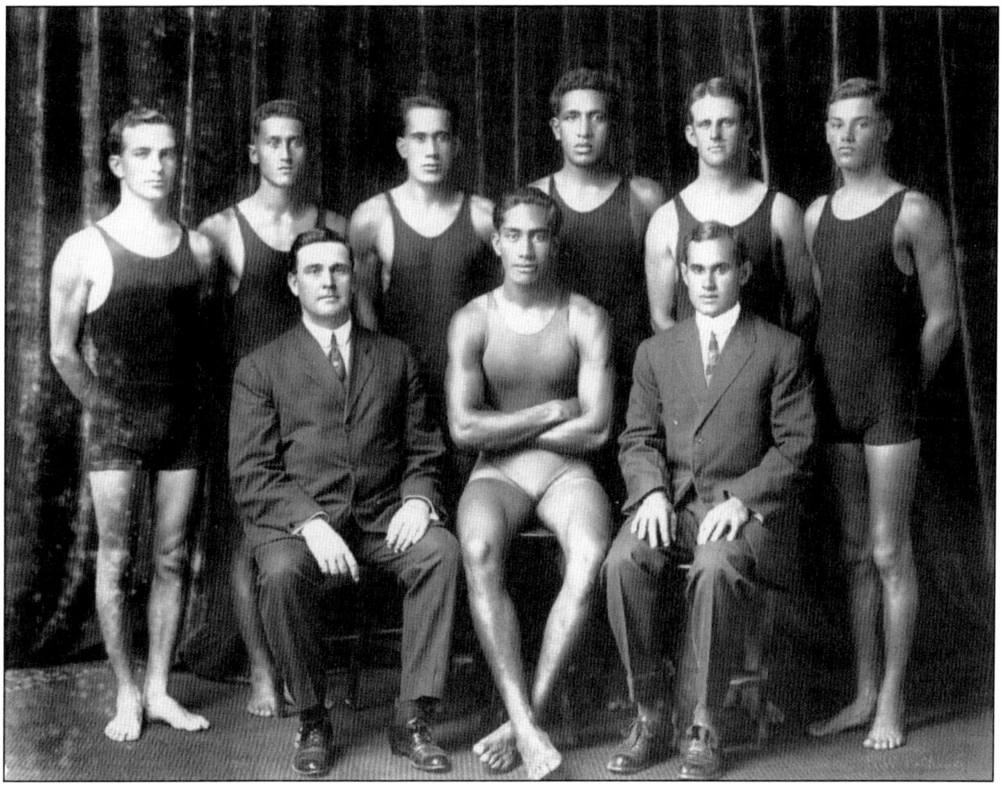

HUI NALU SWIM TEAM CHAMPIONS, 1913. They are, from left to right, (first row) W.T. Rawlings (manager), Duke P. Kahanamoku, and E.K. Miller (captain); (second row) W.H.D. King, Lukela Kaupiko, Dan Keaweamahi, Hiram Kahele, Curtis Hustace, and Fred Wilhelm. The Hui Nalu was established in 1908 by Ken Winter, Duke Kahanamoku, and William A. "Knute" Cottrell. Until the mid-1920s, the "Club of the Waves" was one of America's most successful swimming clubs. (Photograph by Roscoe W. Perkins, courtesy Outrigger Canoe Club.)

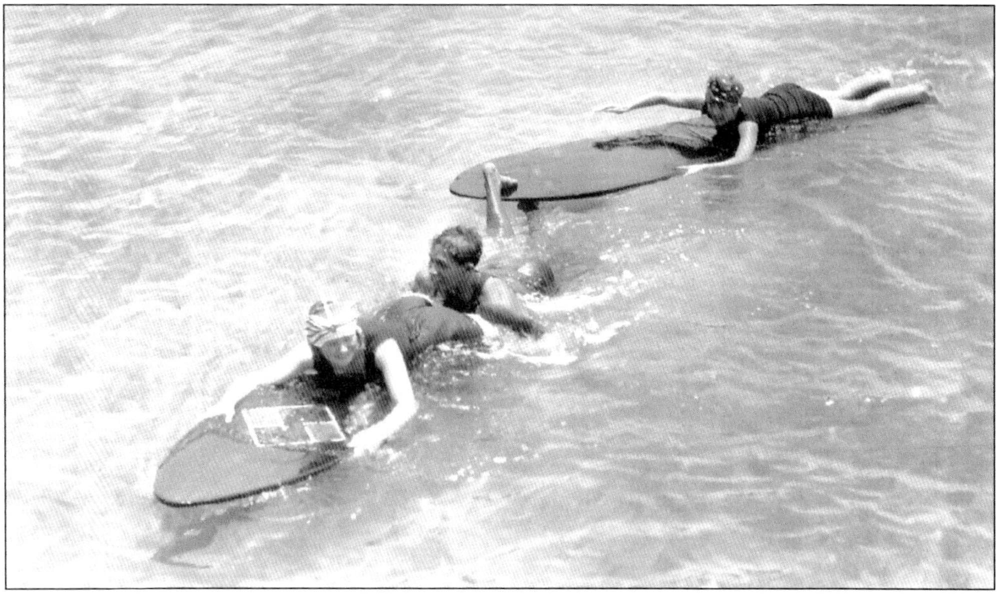

TEACHING TWO AT A TIME. The Hui Nalu was composed of nearly all Hawai'ians or part-Hawai'ians and, as such, most of the early beachboys. They met under a large hau tree in front of the Moana Hotel, and membership fees were $1 a year. Hui Nalu member Dude Miller arranged the first beach concession with the Moana Hotel around 1915. (Courtesy Dan Pincetich.)

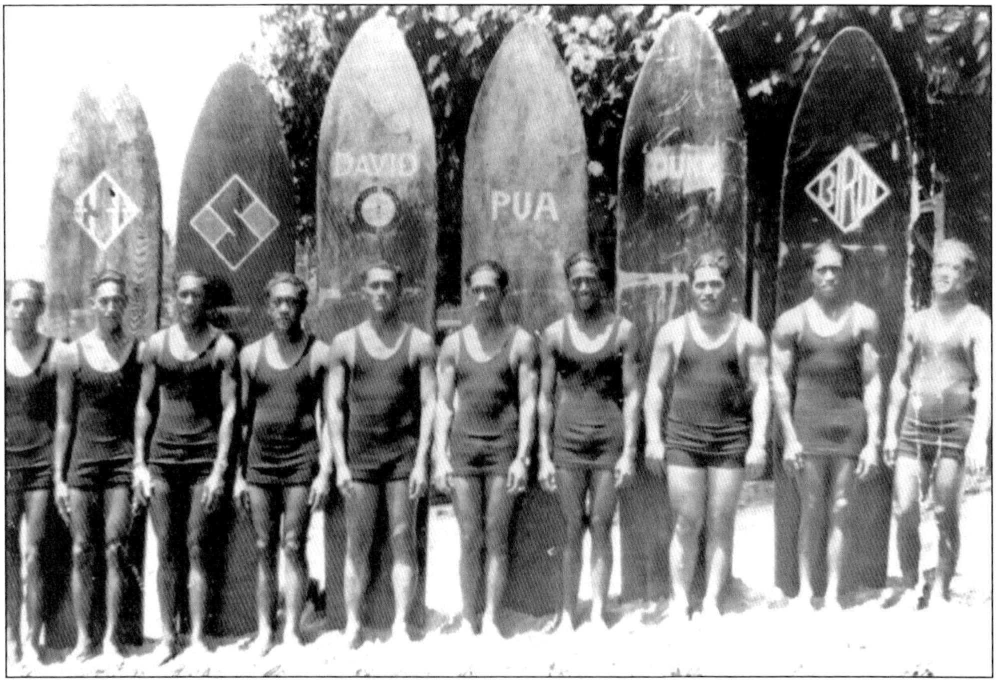

BEACHBOYS IN FRONT OF THE MOANA HOTEL HAU TREE. The Hui Nalu included all six Kahanamoku brothers and Johnny Noble, the renowned musician. According to Grady Timmons, they were also known as the "Moana Bathhouse Gang." Besides canoe and surfing lessons, their biggest role was keeping the beach clean and safe for tourists. The second surfboard on the left is the same one shown in the photograph above.

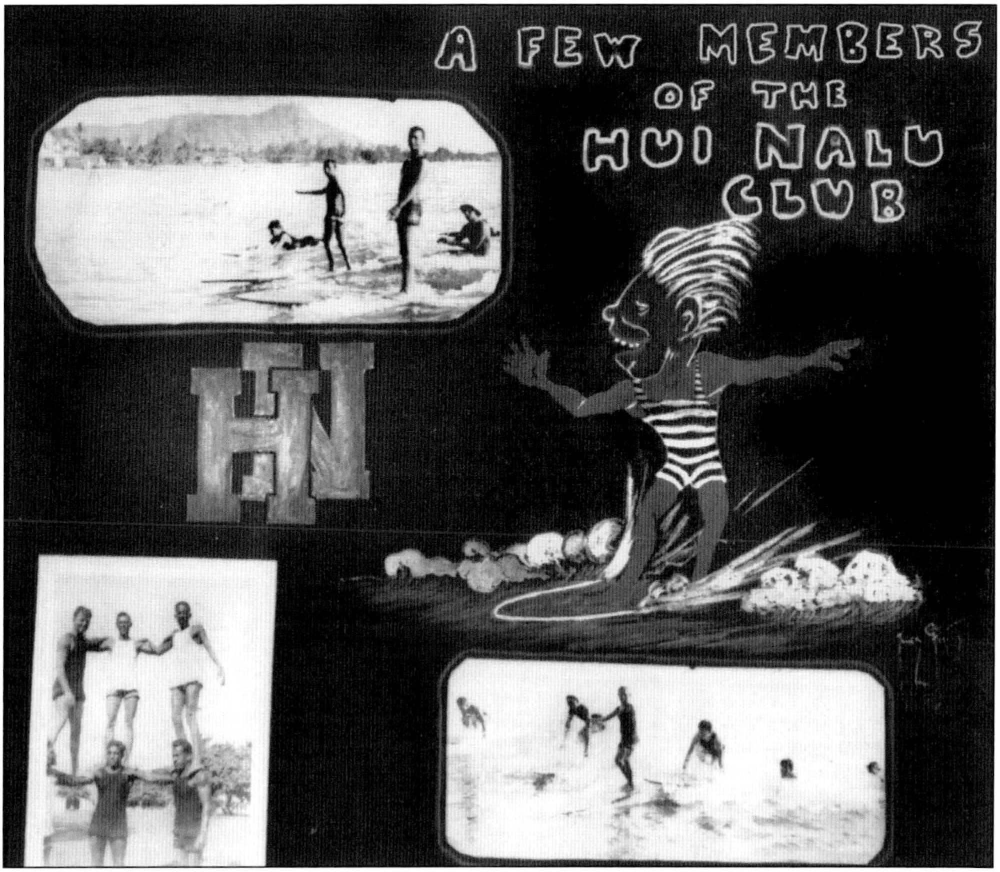

A Few Members of the Hui Nalu Club, 1912. Above, Kaniau Evans's scrapbook shows the pride and joy Hui Nalu members had in the good old days. They had a glee club, their own song, pennants, and a logo. The image below shows, from left to right, Curtis Hustace, Dan Keauwamahi, David Kahanamoku, Lew Henderson, and Kaniau Evans with a canoe loaded down with surfboards that is landing next to the Apuakehau stream breakwater. (Courtesy Hawai'i State Archives.)

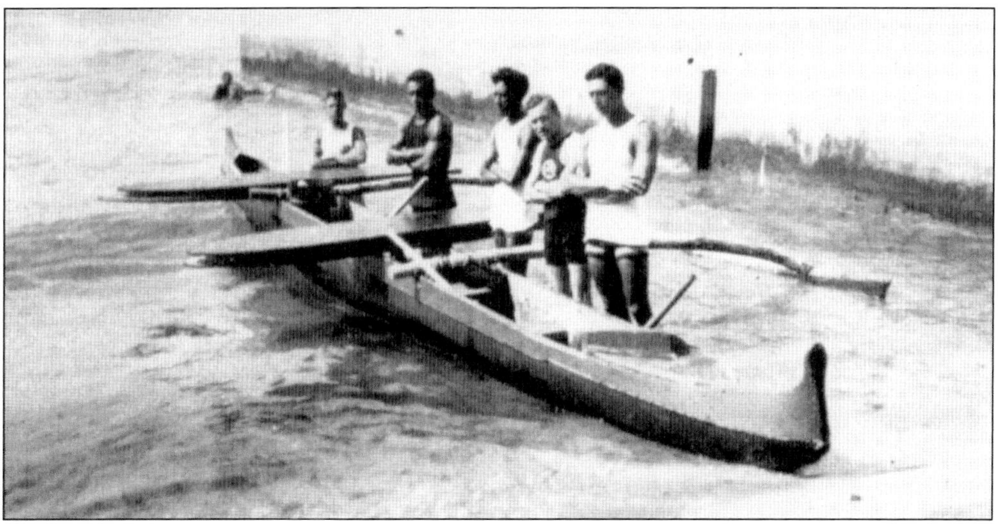

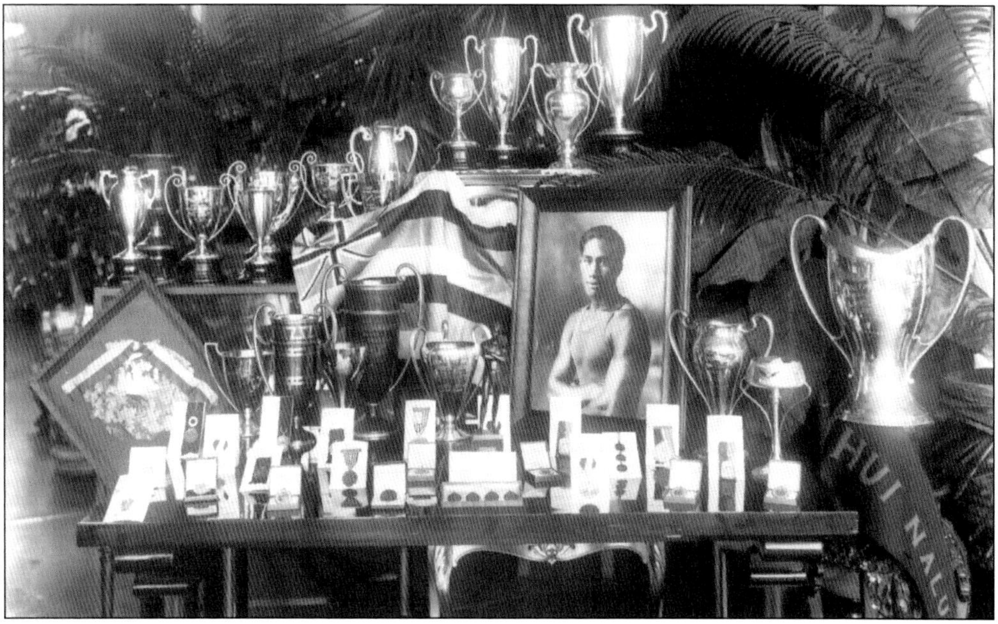

DUKE'S TROPHIES INSIDE THE MOANA HOTEL. Duke's Olympic success was mirrored by a 15-man Hui Nalu team, which competed at the 1915 Panama-Pacific International Exposition (PPIE) in San Francisco. As Kaniau Evans told his family, "We wiped out everybody!" The Hui also dominated the 1920 Olympic swimming events in Antwerp, Belgium. (Photograph by L.E. Edgeworth, courtesy Outrigger Canoe Club.)

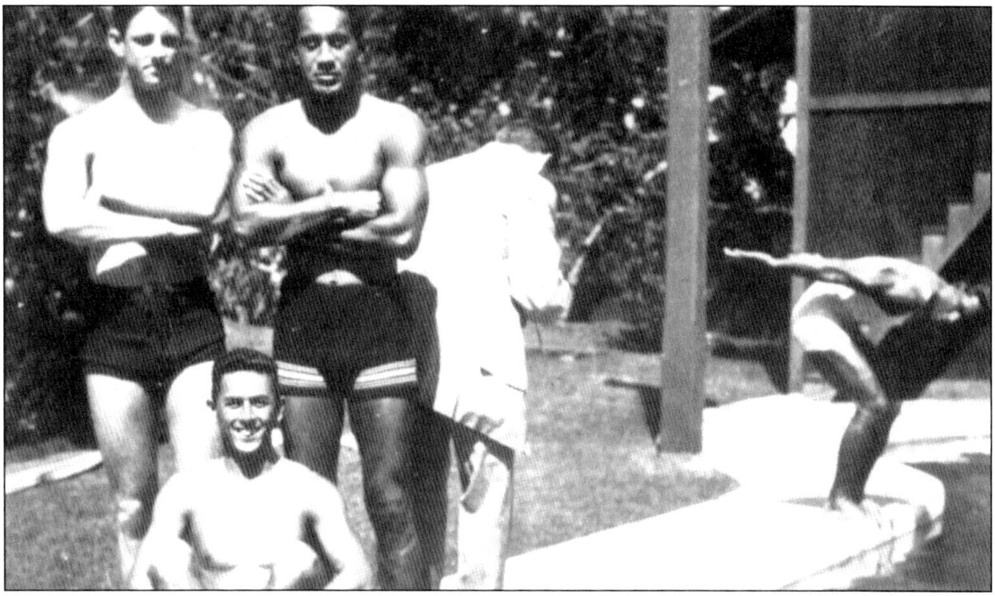

FROM LEFT TO RIGHT, KANIAU EVANS, CURTIS HUSTACE, AND DAN KEAUWAMAHI POSE WHILE A SAN FRANCISCO SPORTSWRITER SNAPS DUKE DIVING IN. Duke commented to the *Red Wing Republican* on the team's one loss at the PPIE: "The man who mopes when he's beaten shows something in his make-up which will usually prevent him from winning high honors. He's not a sportsman. A man's got to keep cheerful to be a victor. . . . Keep smiling and trying. A smile develops energy." (Courtesy Hawai'i State Archives.)

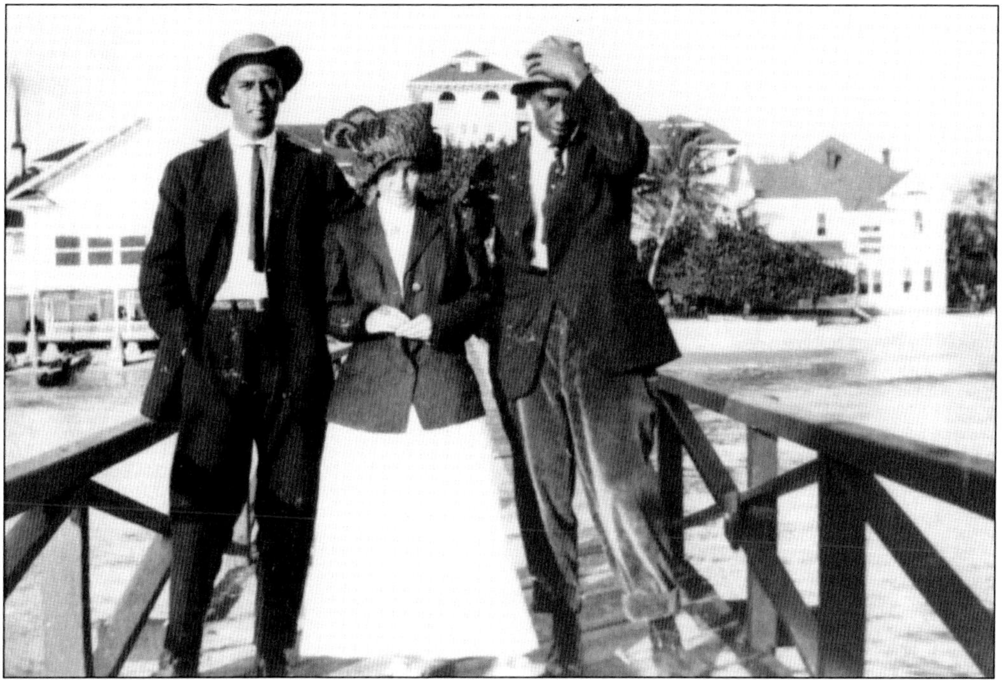

Kaniau Evans (Left), Hazel ? , and Duke at the End of the Moana Hotel Pier, 1912. The end of the Moana Pier was where the beachboys gathered: during the day to watch the surfing and act as lifeguards and at dusk and into the velvety night to sing and play *hapa-haole* music on their ukuleles and guitars for an appreciative crowd. (Courtesy Hawai'i State Archives.)

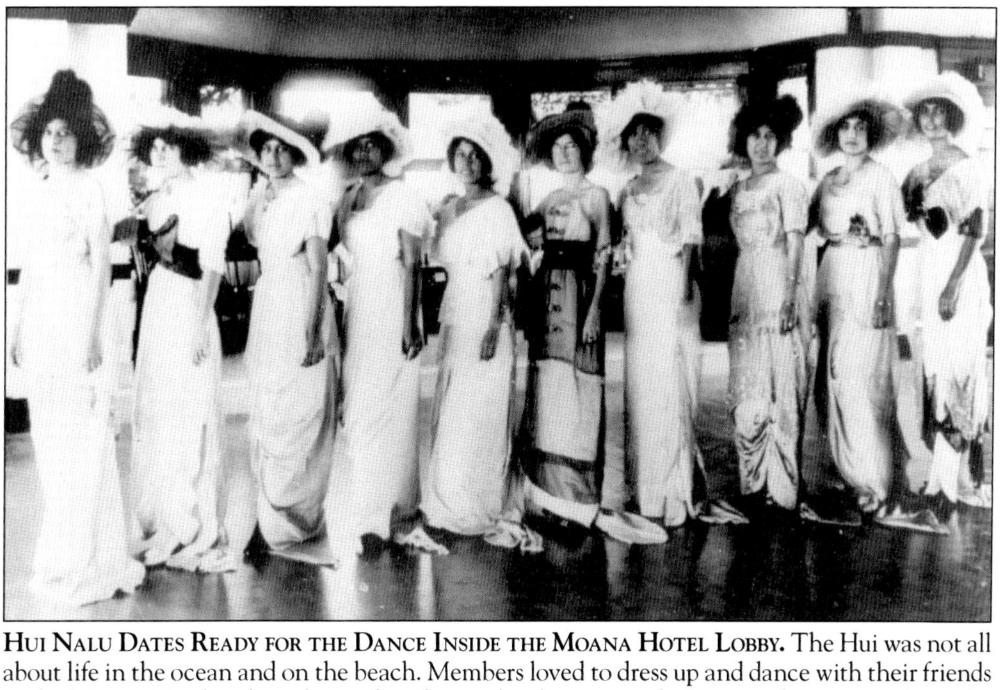

Hui Nalu Dates Ready for the Dance Inside the Moana Hotel Lobby. The Hui was not all about life in the ocean and on the beach. Members loved to dress up and dance with their friends at the Moana Hotel and on the roof garden under the stars at downtown's luxurious Alexander Young Hotel. (Courtesy Hawai'i State Archives.)

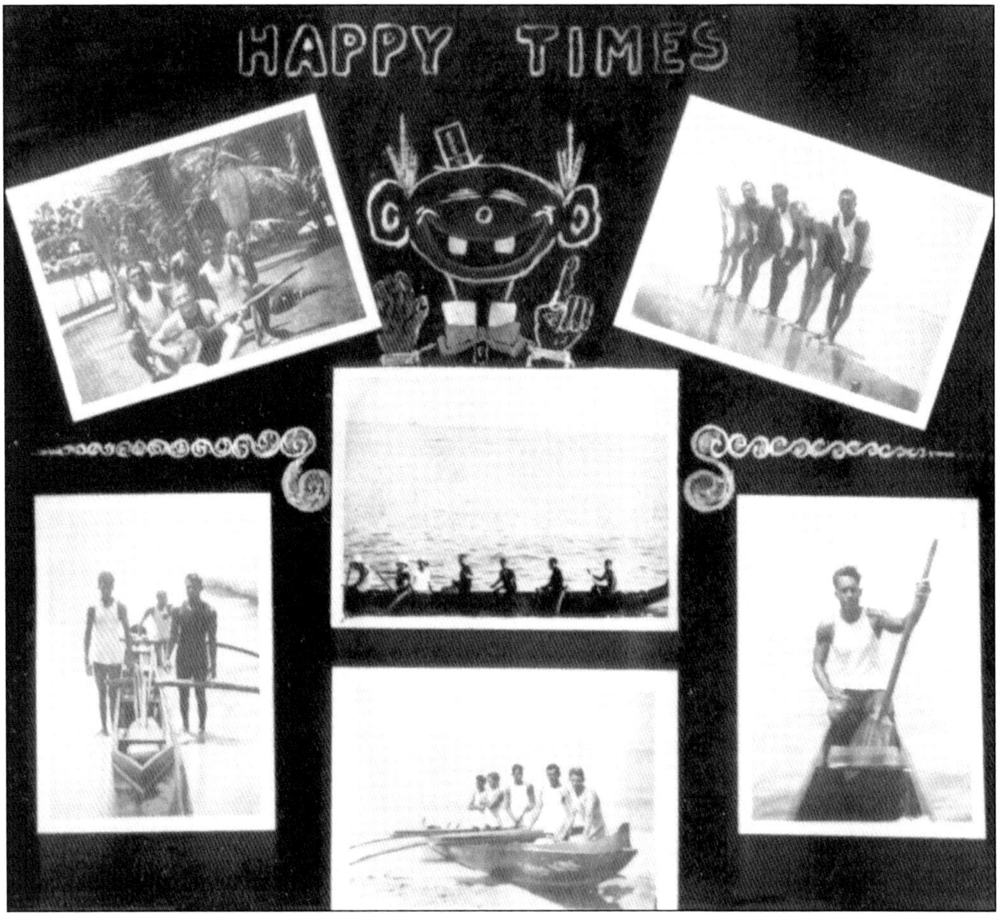

"HAPPY TIMES" HUI NALU SCRAPBOOK, BY KANIAU EVANS (ABOVE), 1912. Fiercely competitive, the Hui competed against the Outrigger Canoe Club and against other clubs in canoe racing. It became a major sport throughout the islands, as it was in days of old. A white tank top was the color of choice for members. (Above, courtesy Hawai'i State Archives; below, Dan Pincetich.)

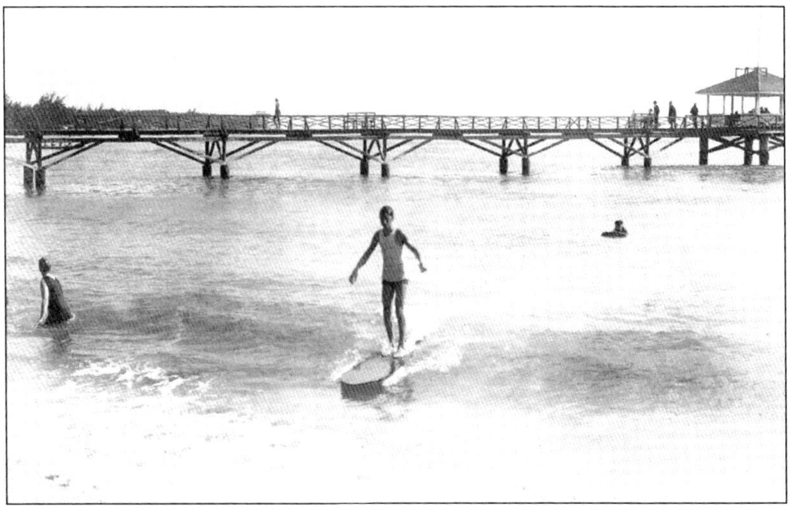

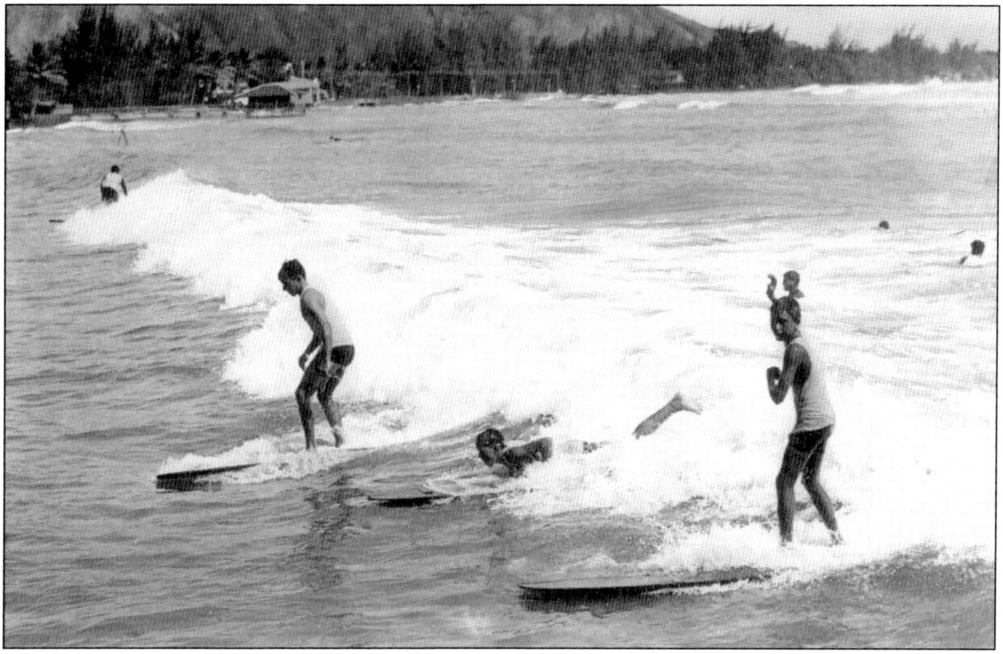

Soon Everyone Wanted to Wear Hui Nalu White Tank Tops. In this photograph taken off the popular Moana Pier, notice that the middle surfboard has a wooden brace to hold the surfboard together (similar to the one shown on page 37). (Courtesy Hawai'i State Archives.)

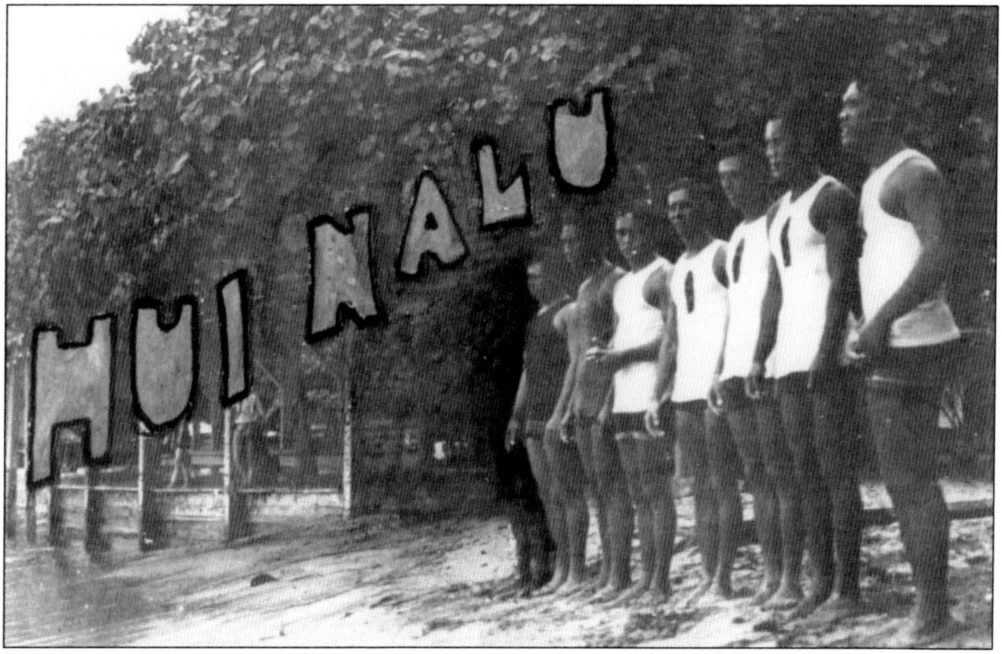

Hui Nalu and the Crew, 1912. Things to note about this photograph include the mystery identity of the crossed-out surfer on the left and the surfboard design used on the front of the shirts. It appears that the Hui worked on a few designs until it settled on the logo shown on page 60. (Courtesy Hawai'i State Archives.)

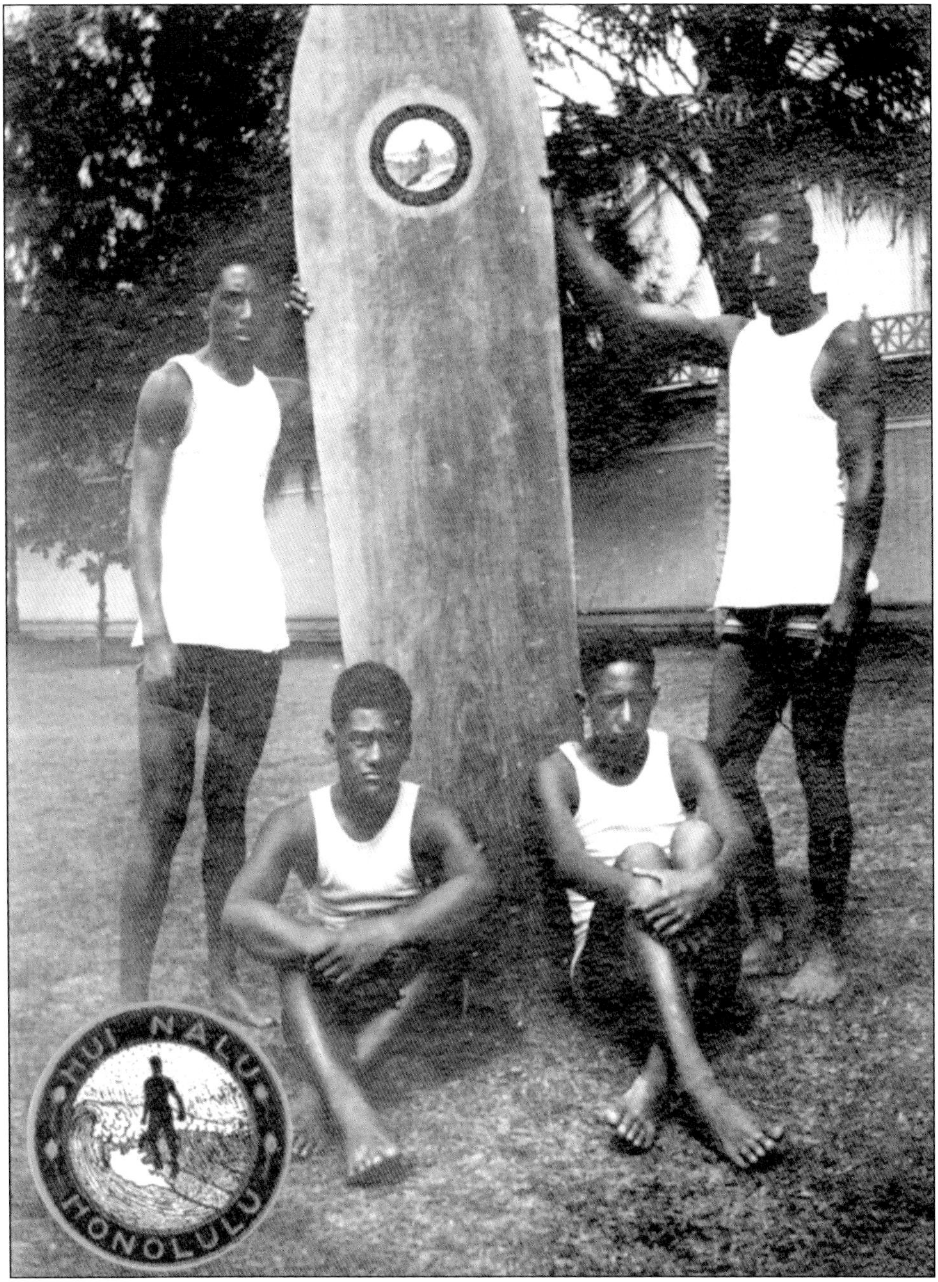

CLOCKWISE FROM TOP LEFT, DAVID KAHANAMOKU, "STEAMBOAT" BILL KEAWEAMAHI, WILLIAM KAHANAMOKU, AND HIRAM ANAHU SHOW OFF THE NEW HUI NALU LOGO, C. 1916. The logo appears to have gone through numerous changes in its early years, with the men eventually settling on this design of a surfer on a wave with the words "Hui Nalu, Honolulu" as shown by the inset. Grady Timmon, in *Waikiki Beachboy*, notes that when Dude Miller became Hui Nalu captain, "he made the beachboys wear uniforms. He made sure they were clean cut and clean-shaven, and when he was on duty there was no drinking, no gambling, and no letting your hands stray over a female tourist." (Anahu was a noted musician and can be seen on page 113.)

Six

SURFING'S FIRST BOOM

1910–1920

BY TIMOTHY T. DELAVEGA

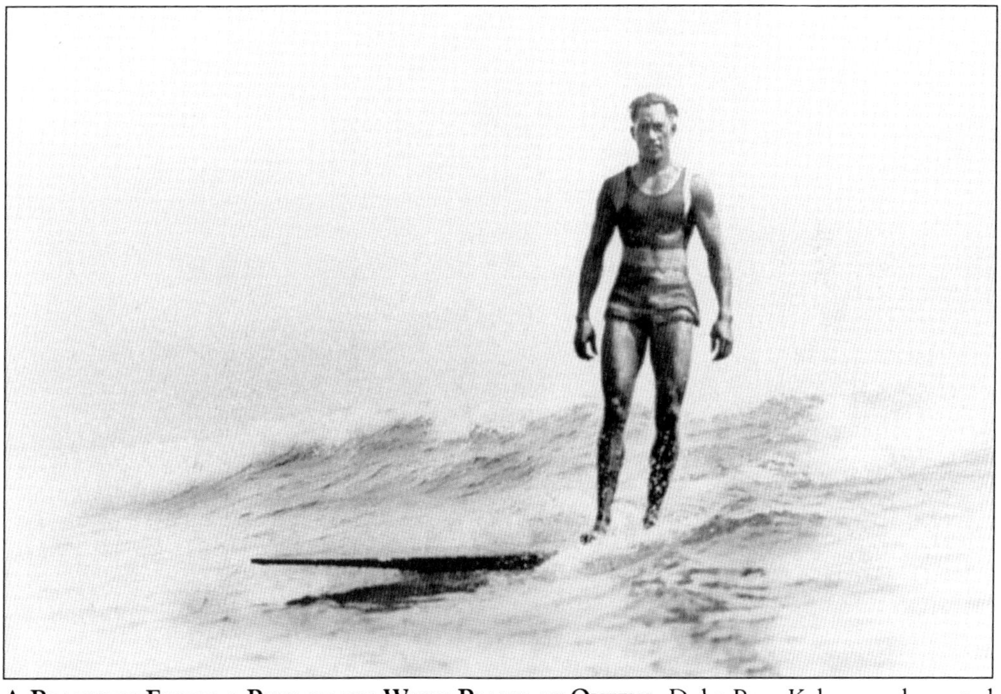

A BEACHBOY ENJOYS A RIDE ON HIS WOOD PLANK AT QUEENS. Duke Paoa Kahanamoku noted in a 1911 *Mid-Pacific Magazine* article, "Perhaps the ideal surfing stretch in all the world is at Waikiki beach, near Honolulu, Hawai'i. Here centuries ago was born the sport of running foot races upon the crests of the billows, and here bronze skinned men and women vie today with the white man for honors in aquatic sports once exclusively Hawai'ian."

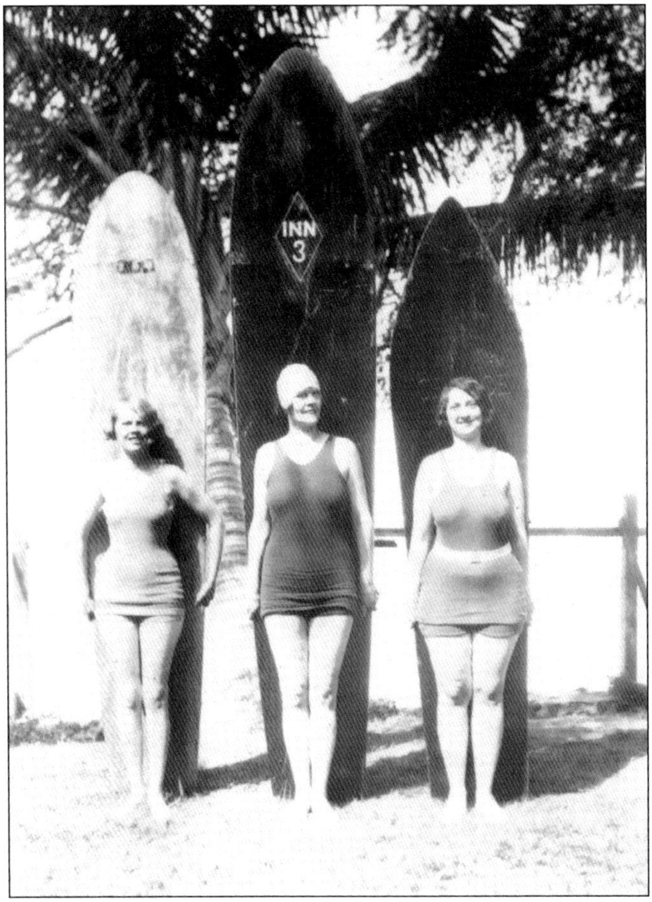

THREE WAHINE MODEL THE LATEST STYLE OF SWIMWEAR AND SURFBOARDS. Surfboards were longer after 1910. The surfboard on the right has the typical outline and length for the pre-1910 type; they were smaller and had a sharper nose outline. The Waikiki Inn rental board in the center is an example of the longer surfboard introduced around 1910, which had a much fuller nose.

SURFING IN WAIKIKI, C. 1910. This real-photo card is unusual in that it shows surfers angling along the wave instead of the usual images from this era where they are generally shown going straight ahead of the breaking wave. Note that the surfboards appear to be the smaller pre-1910 versions. (Courtesy Dan Pincetich.)

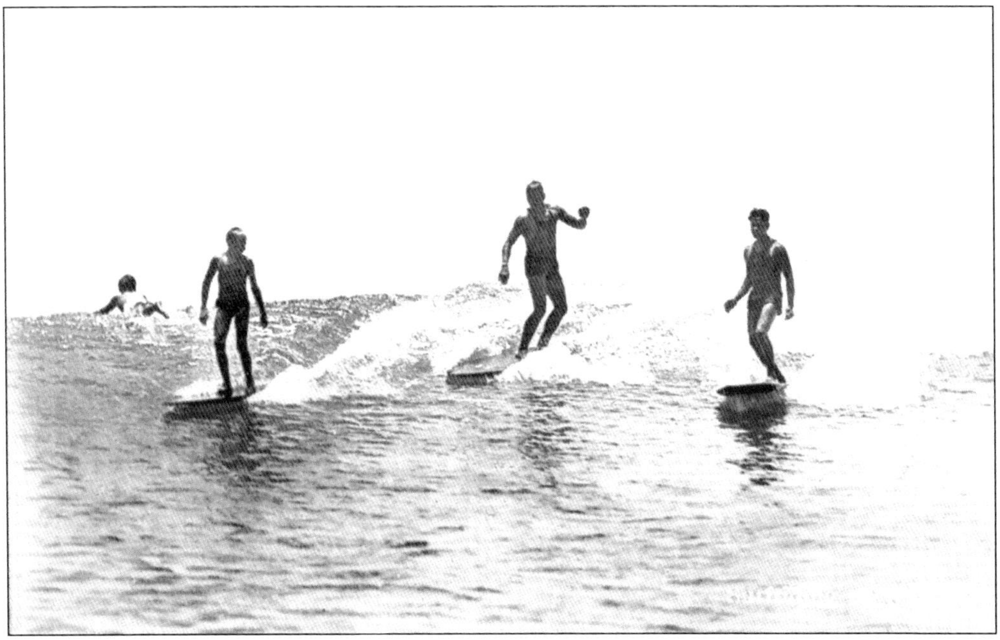

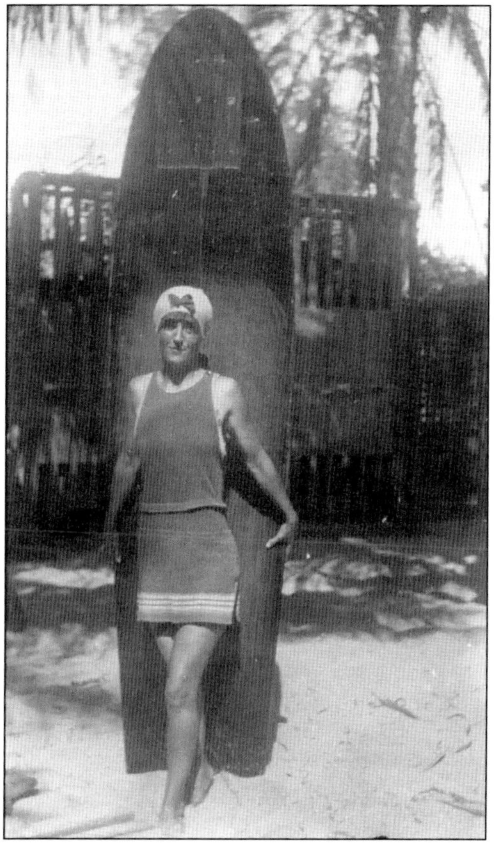

A Stylish Wahine Models for the Camera. *Seven Weeks In Hawai'i*, written by Leola Crawford in 1913, describes how she went on "a surf-board party. . . . Superintended by Duke Kahanamoku. . . . Paddling far out we would wait for a wave and as it fell we were caught in its milky surf and washed with lightning speed to the beach. This is surely a reckless sport but, O, the wild joy of it!"

Surfing at the Moana Pier. In 1908, A.H. Ford wrote in *Outing Magazine*, "First get a plank six or seven feet long by about a foot or even sixteen inches wide. Point one end and smooth the edges all round and you have a surfboard. Next . . . lie flat on the board on the water, learn to balance yourself, then send your arms flying around like a pair of windmills." (Courtesy Cary Weiss.)

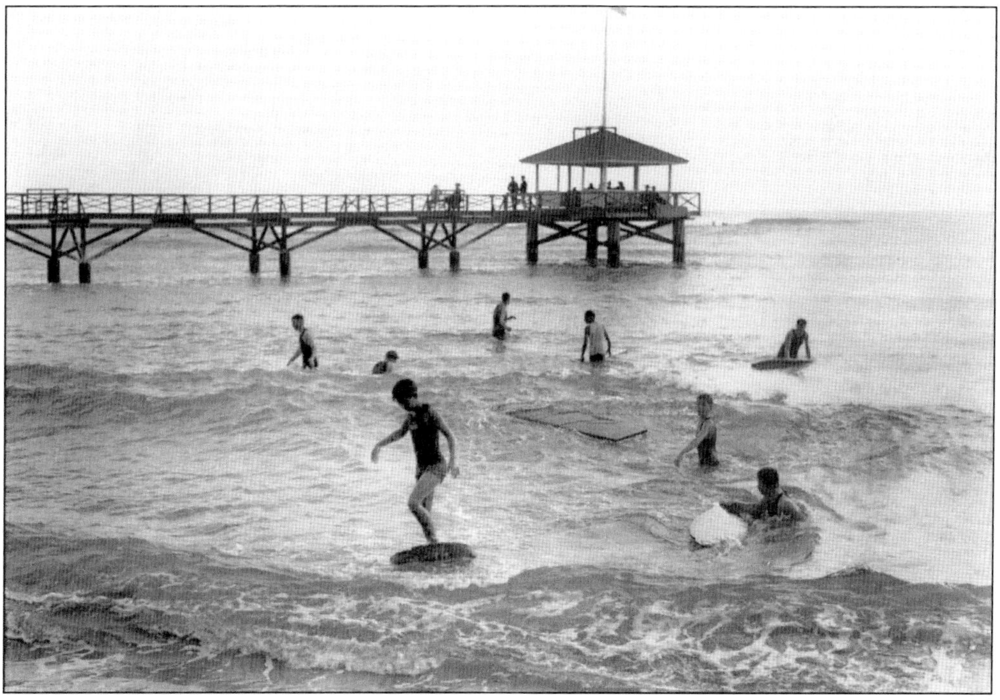

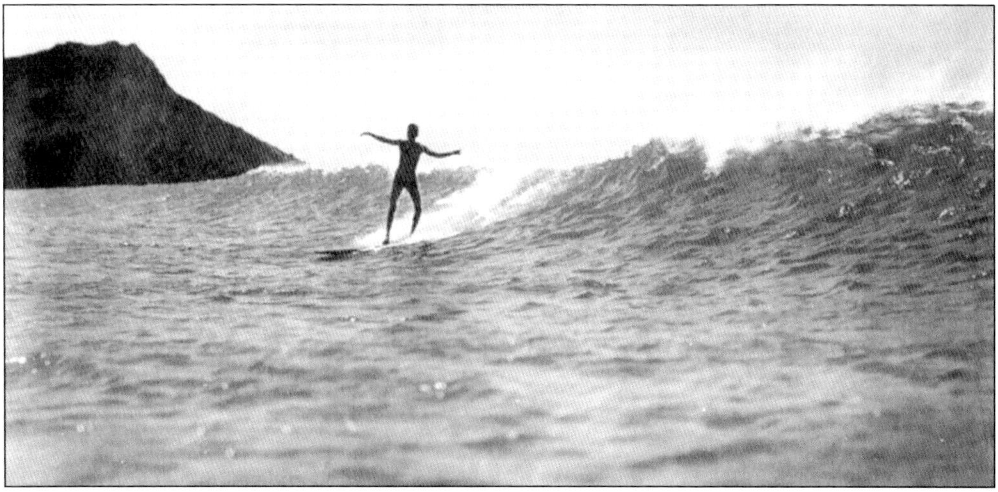

PHOTOGRAPHS FROM *THE SURF RIDERS OF HAWAI'I* BY ALFRED R. GURREY JR., C. 1911–1914. Gurrey is considered *the* pioneer surfing photographer and published the first book dedicated to surfing. It contains eight hand-printed surfing photographs. The book is exclusively about Waikiki surfing, with a short text and a stanza from Lord Byron's poem *Childe Harold's Pilgrimage*. The text describes surf riding, "On comes the surf, it strikes—arches, curves and falls; and as it plunges forward like a frightened seahorse, this fearless surf rider is at its mane. With board pointed shoreward he rides this untamed fury. He stands erect with arms outstretched, triumphant; with glittering inclined plane before him. On; on he sweeps, tobogganing in an opalescent sea, plowing up showers of liquid jewels into sunlight." It ends with a photograph of fellow Hui Nalu member Duke. (Courtesy Allen Kukel.)

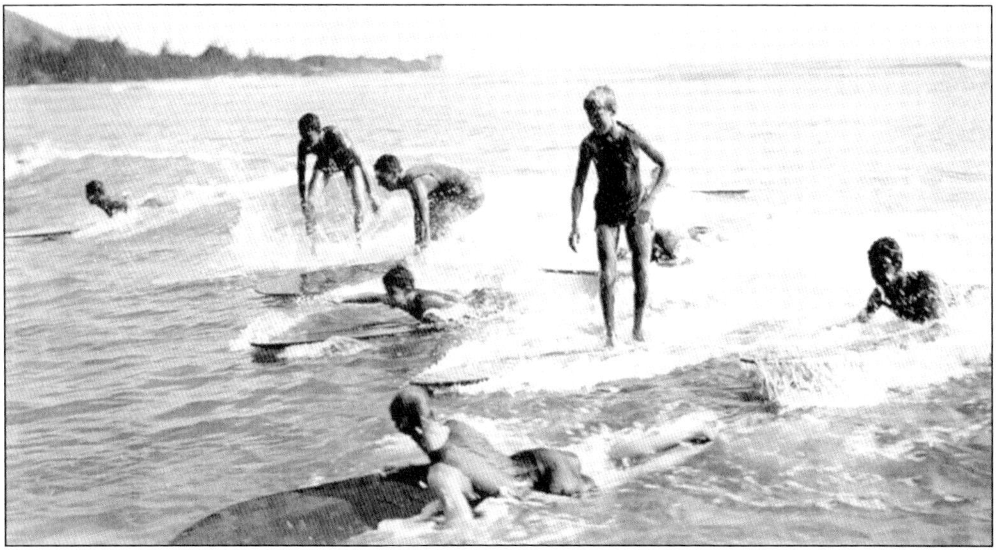

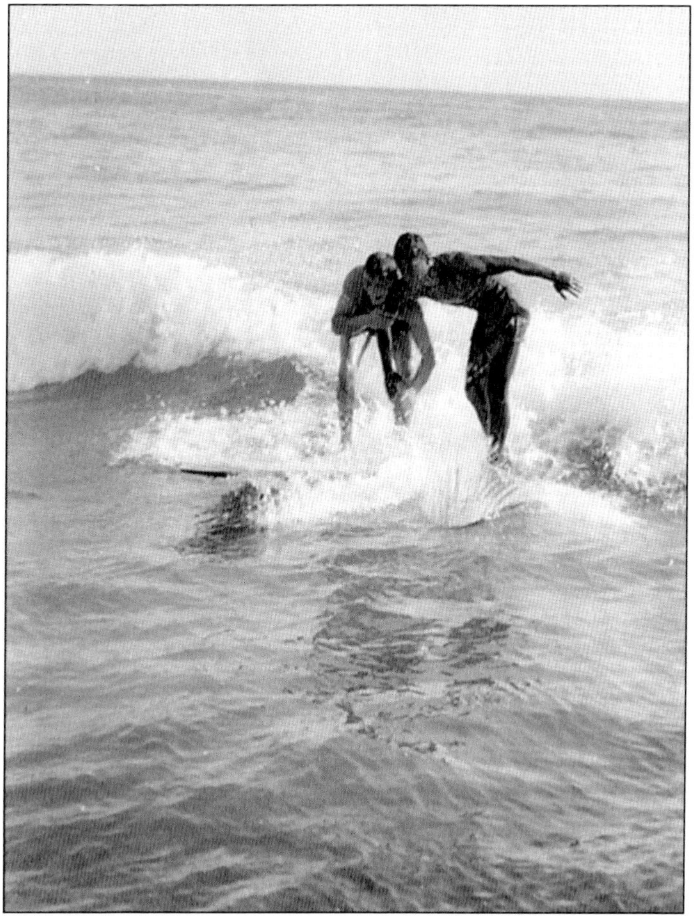

"Riding the Surf at Honolulu, Hawai'i." This 1919 article by A.R. Gurrey Jr. in *National Geographic Magazine* describes the sport: "Walking a tight rope stretched on top a speeding express train might afford some of the exhilaration of Hawai'i's distinctive sport. Here, again, geography molded the national pastime; for the conformation of the ocean bed along the island coast creates the swells that make this sport popular. The picture illustrates only one position of the native rider, who lies prone, sits and even stands on his head on his super-canoe." (Both photographs by A.R. Gurrey Jr., courtesy Joel T. Smith and Cary Weiss.)

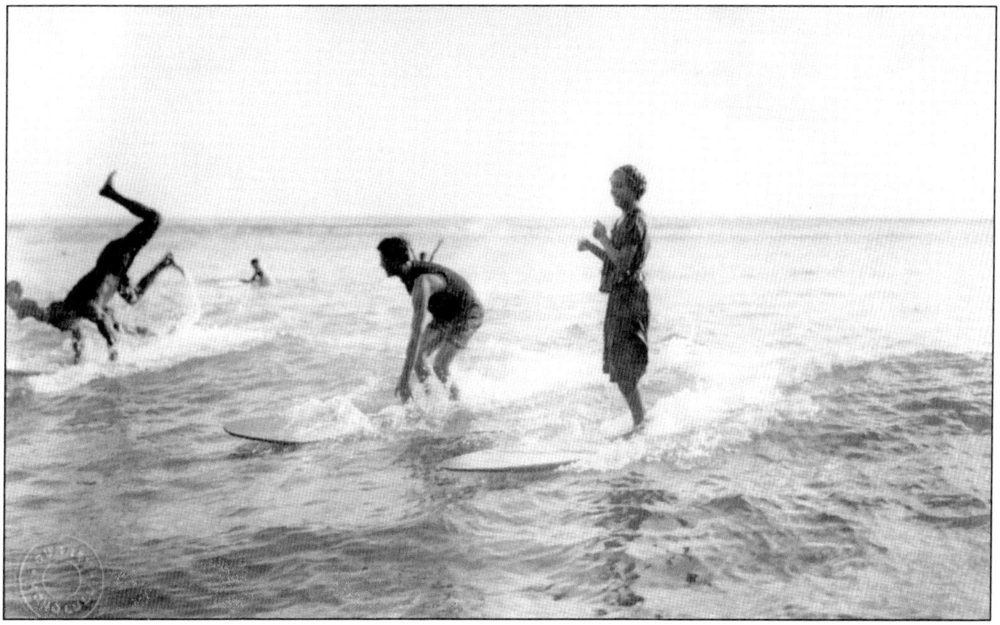

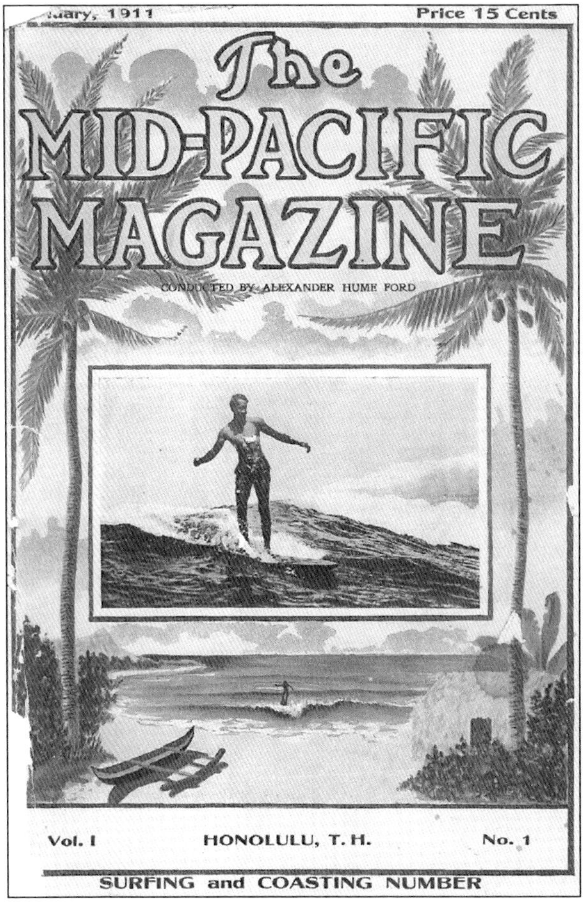

MID-PACIFIC MAGAZINE, NO. 1, JANUARY 1911. Alexander Hume Ford's magazine devoted its first issue to "Surfing and Coasting," including an article by Duke with photographs by A.R. Gurrey Jr. "I have never seen snow and do not know what winter means . . . but every day of the year, where the water is 76, day and night, and the waves roll high, I take my sled, without runners, and coast down the face of the big waves that roll in at Waikiki. . . . How would you like to stand like a god before the crest of a monster billow, always rushing to the bottom of a hill and never reaching its base, and to come rushing in for half a mile at express speed, in graceful attitude, of course, until you reach the beach and step easily from the wave to the strand?" (Both courtesy Joel T. Smith.)

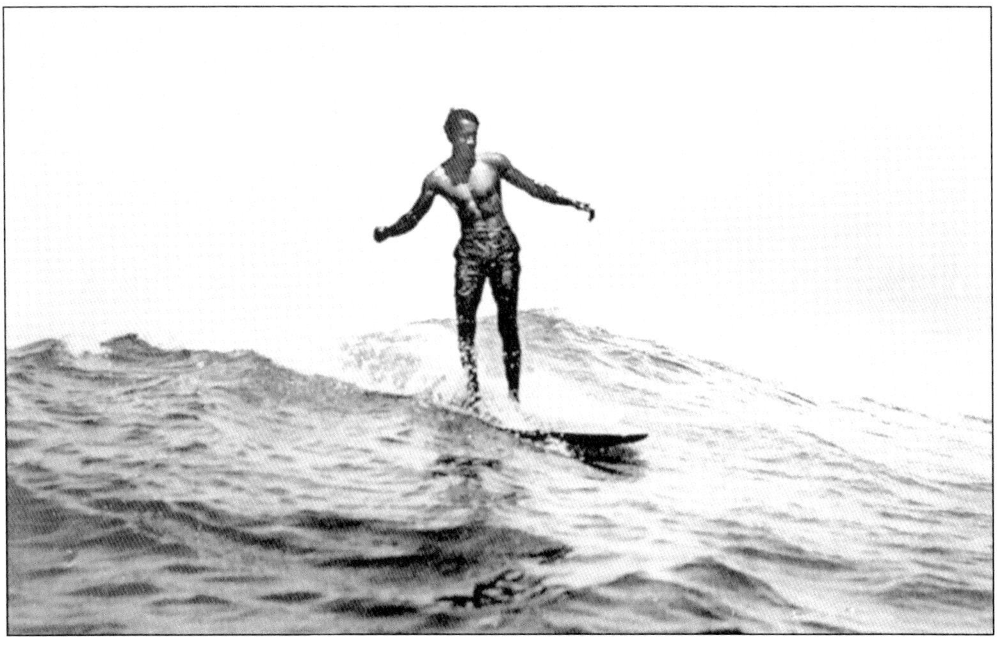

Watching the Duke Surf. In a 1914 *Outing Magazine*, George Marvin's article "Riding the Surf at Waikiki" was accompanied by photographs by A.R. Gurrey Jr. Martin sees Duke far outside when "ai-i-i-i-e-e-e-e! yells the Duke, as he goes streaming by. Light as the spray smoking after him, the last yell swallowed by the half-drowned work I make of that breaker because of watching him too long."

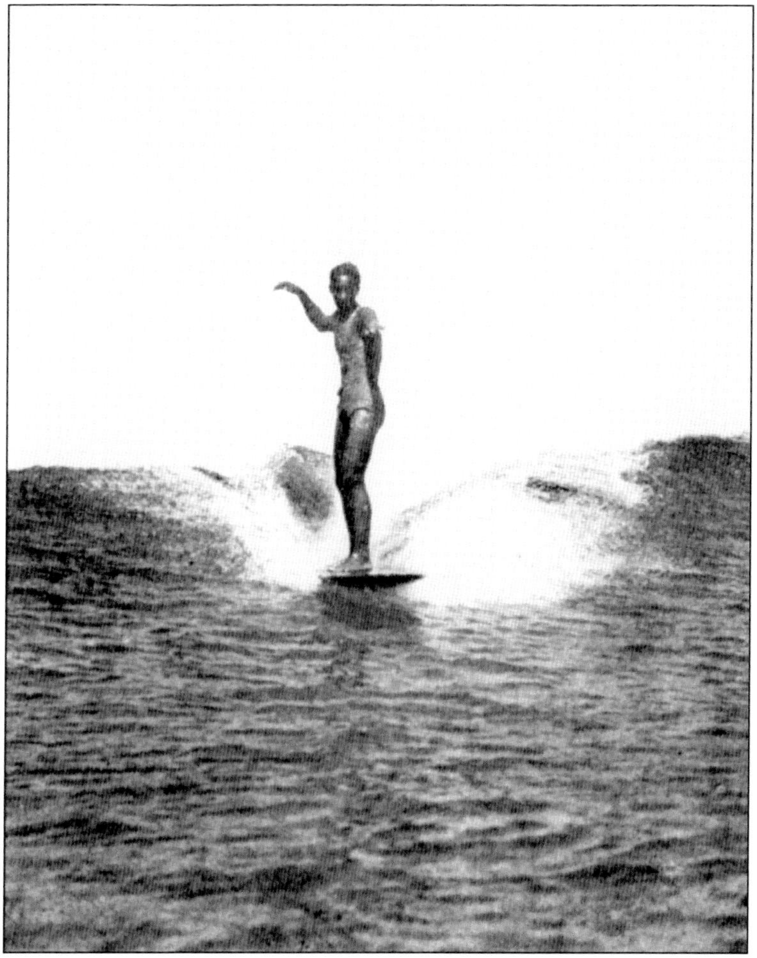

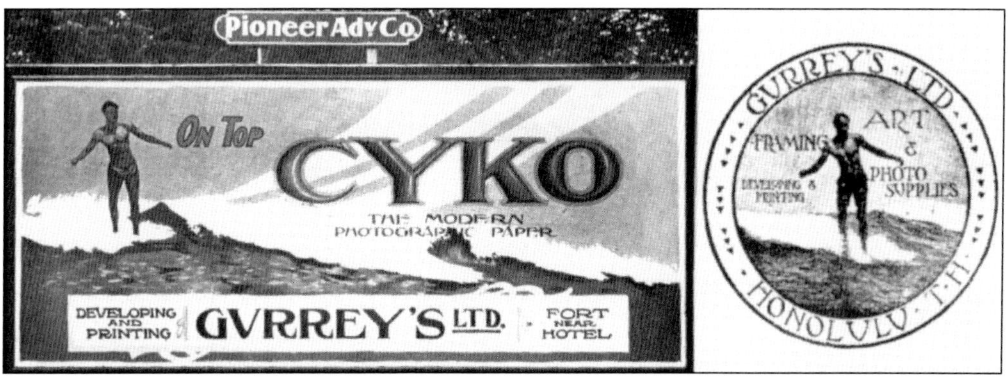

Gurrey's Ltd. Billboard and Logo, 1912. Kansas-born A.R. Gurrey Jr. moved to Hawai'i in 1903, the same year he married renowned photographer Caroline Haskins. A surfer, he joined the Hui Nalu in 1913, and his work was featured in *Mid-Pacific Magazine* throughout the decade. (Courtesy Dan Pincetich.)

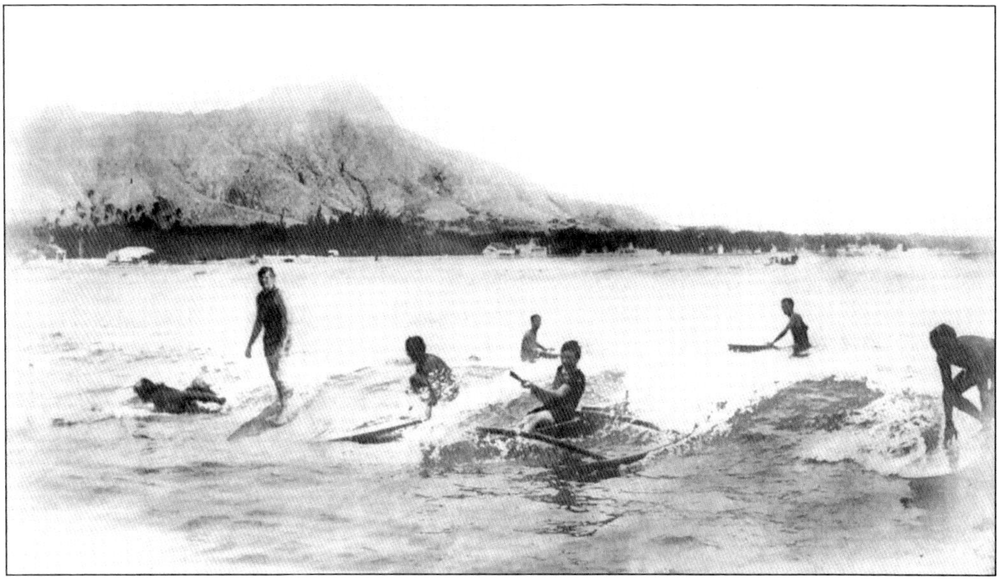

J.J. WILLIAMS' MANIPULATED PHOTOGRAPHS, 1911. Williams Photo Studio was one of the best known for early Hawai'ian photographs. The studio still flourishes under great-grandson Matt Williams. These are examples of J.J.'s early photographic manipulation, done by the use of a masking process during development that allowed objects to be added or removed. In the image above, the standing surfer to left has been added from the original photograph shown below. The surfer has been noted as Jack London, but this is doubtful. London's own writing in 1907 states he "did not learn to stand." The manipulated image copyright is later, in 1911. But the seven known manipulations J.J. did with this image imply that it was someone of importance.

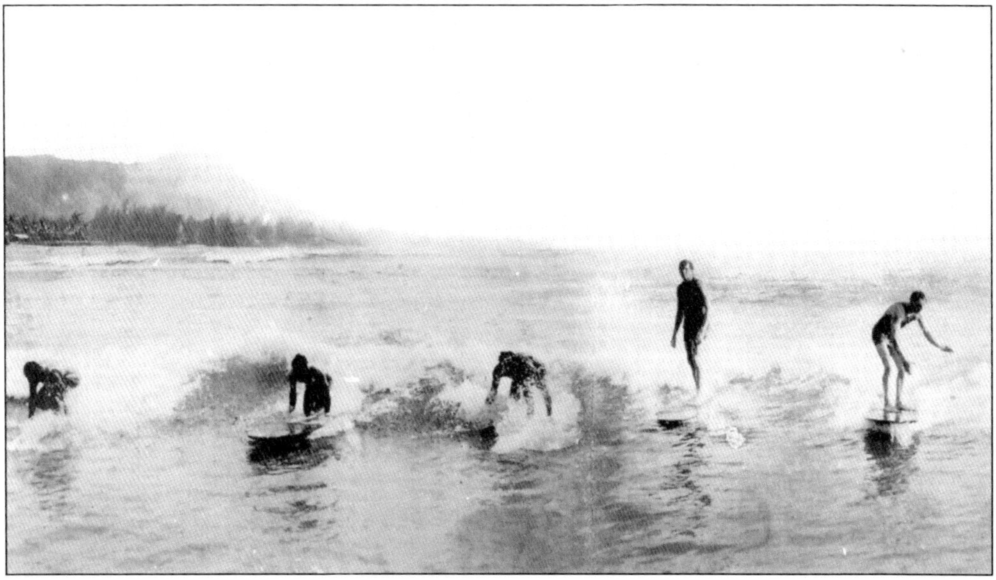

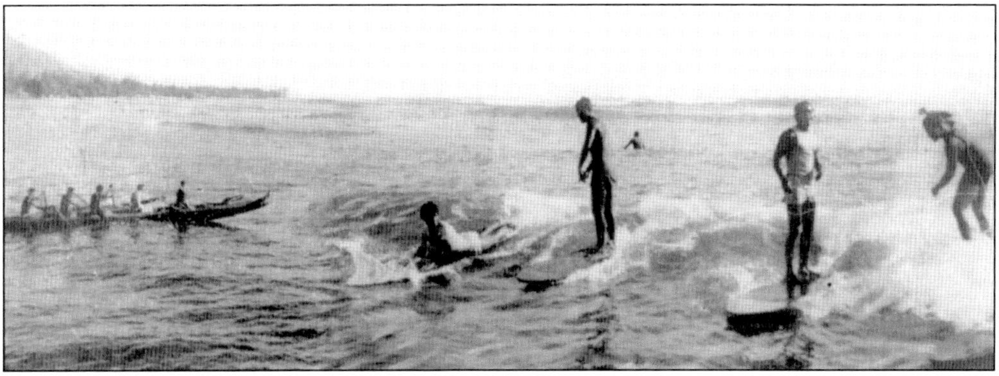

J.J. Williams' Photographs from the Beach in Front of the Moana Hotel, 1911. The image above was sold as a panoramic, and Williams manipulated it by shortening the area between the canoe and the far left surfer. The image below shows the surfers in a similar shot that same day. Both surfers are believed to be members of the Hui Nalu Club. J.J. Williams first came to Hawai'i in 1876 at the age of 24, and he became the leading photographer of his era and a friend to both King Kalakaua and author Robert Louis Stevenson. (Below, courtesy the Outrigger Canoe Club.)

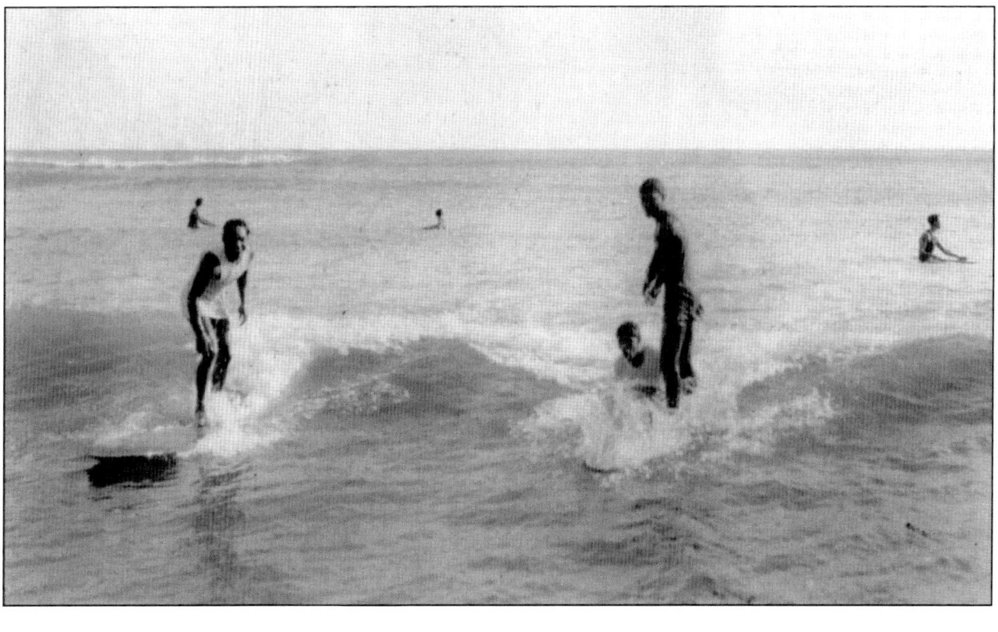

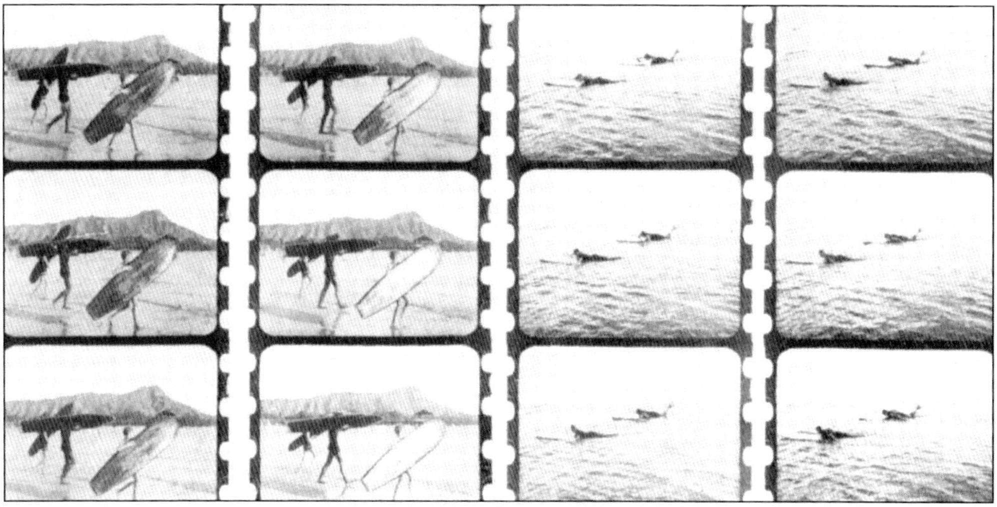

CINEMATOGRAPHER M. BOUVILLAIN, OF PATHÉ FRÈRES, FILMS THE SURF RIDERS, C. 1910. According to *Mid-Pacific Magazine* in 1914, "A great steel tripod was built for the representative of Pathé Frères, and this carried far out on the reef into deep water. Here it was erected and a platform, built just above the highest waves, and on this platform M. Bouvillain erected his motion picture camera. Here he caught the waves as they formed and the men and boys . . . may study the secrets of surfboard riding from the motion picture films." Below is a c. 1910 view from the Waikiki Villa Bathhouse looking east, with the Moana Hotel and Pier at the center and the Outrigger Canoe Club hidden between trees and the Moana Hotel. The tower at the end of the pier may be the structure built for Bouvillain.

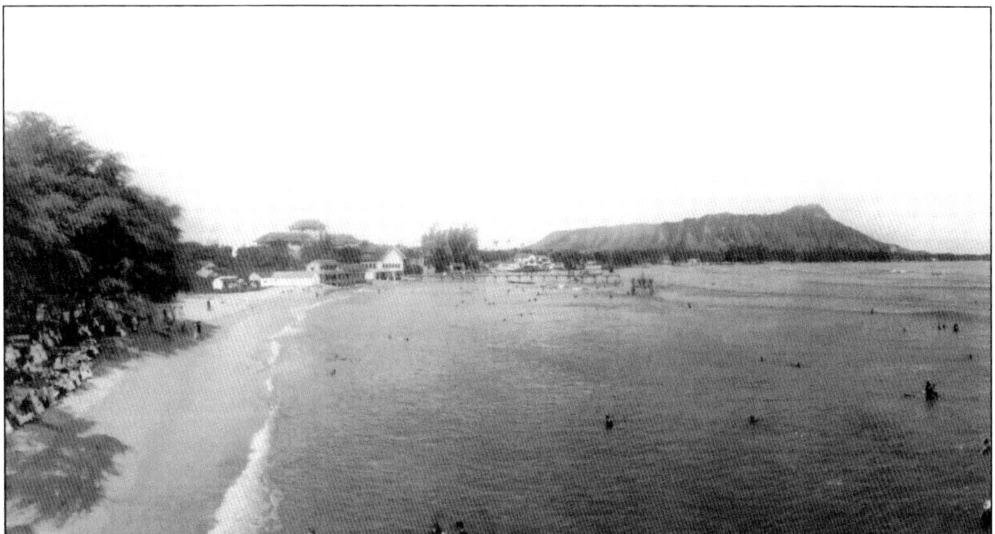

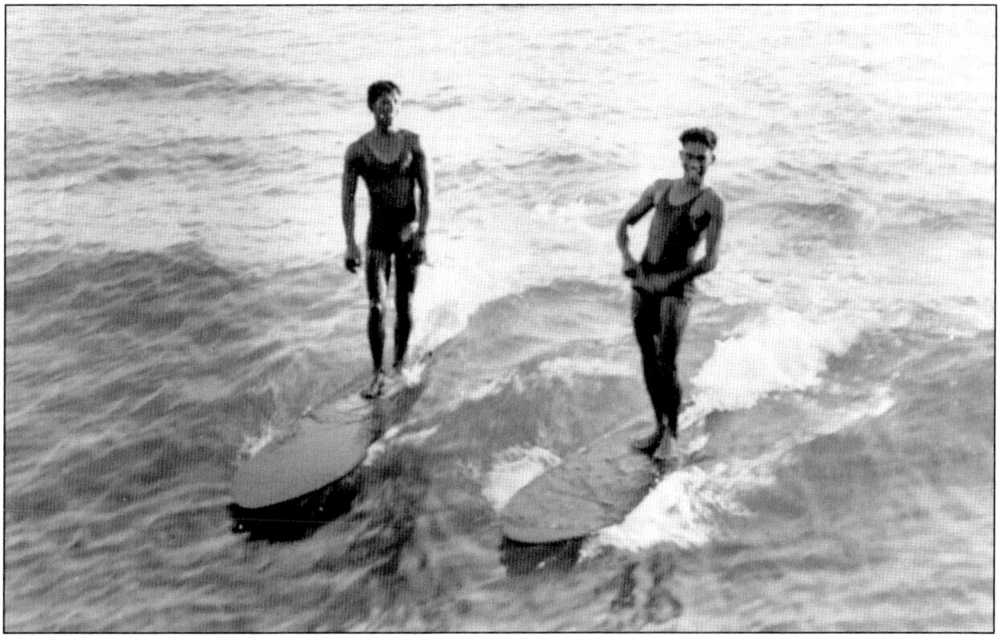

The Subject of Much Interest, the Dancing Beachboys of Waikiki. A July 1898 article in the *Advertiser* notes that "the first movie made in Hawai'i was done by Burton Holmes and his motion picture man, Mr. DePue. . . . The first of the new series of motion pictures will show that popular sport, surf riding in canoes." Then inventor Thomas Edison sent Robert A. Bonine in 1906 to make the world's first surf movie, *Surf Board Riders, Waikiki, Honolulu, Hawaiian Islands.* It was not until 1923 that the first drama featuring surfing was produced, Famous Players-Lasky's *White Flower,* released in March of that year.

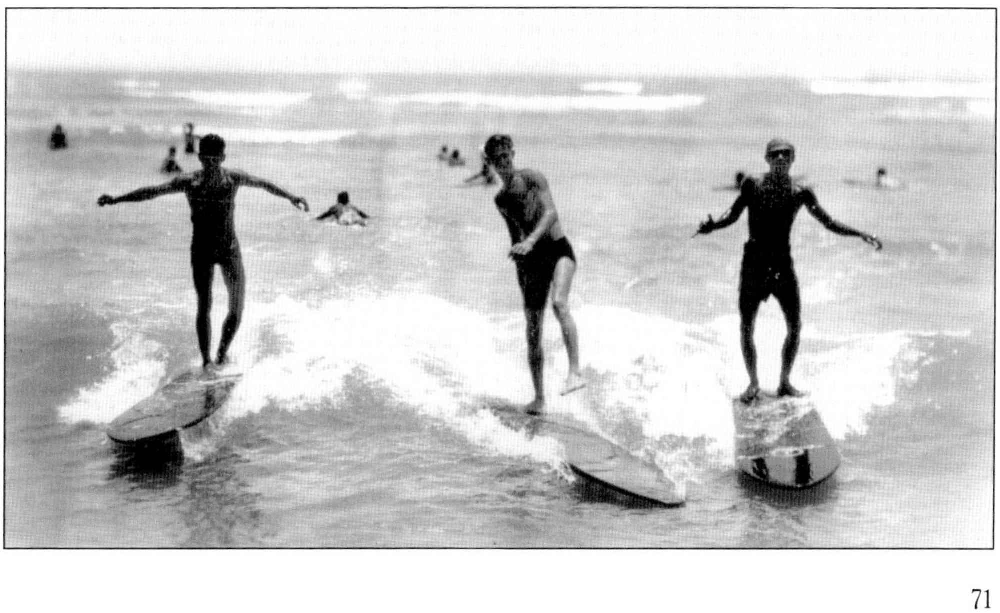

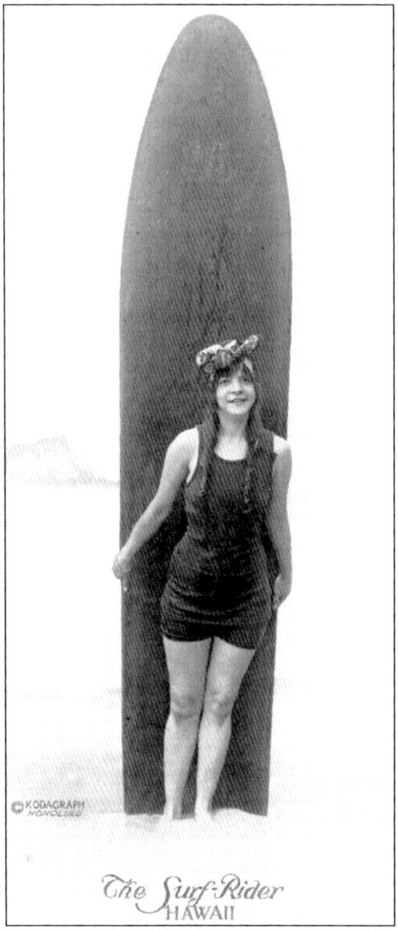

Maxie Mitchell in a Studio Photograph by Ray Jerome Baker, 1914. Maxie was part of the Jack Mcgee vaudeville troupe touring Honolulu. Below is the image used on the cover of "My Waikiki Mermaid" sheet music in 1916. In 1910, Ray Jerome Baker came to Hawai'i and opened a photographic studio. Besides being a photographer, he was a noted lecturer, and many of his magic lantern glass slides were hand painted by his wife, Edith. Baker's pioneering studies of the Hawai'ian people are considered some of the finest documentations available for the era. The music of the beachboys was called hapa-haole, which was a Hawai'ian melody with English lyrics. This style was introduced at the 1915 Panama-Pacific International Exposition in San Francisco by the Royal Hawaiian Quartet, led by George E. K. Awai, and was soon a musical craze that swept the Western world.

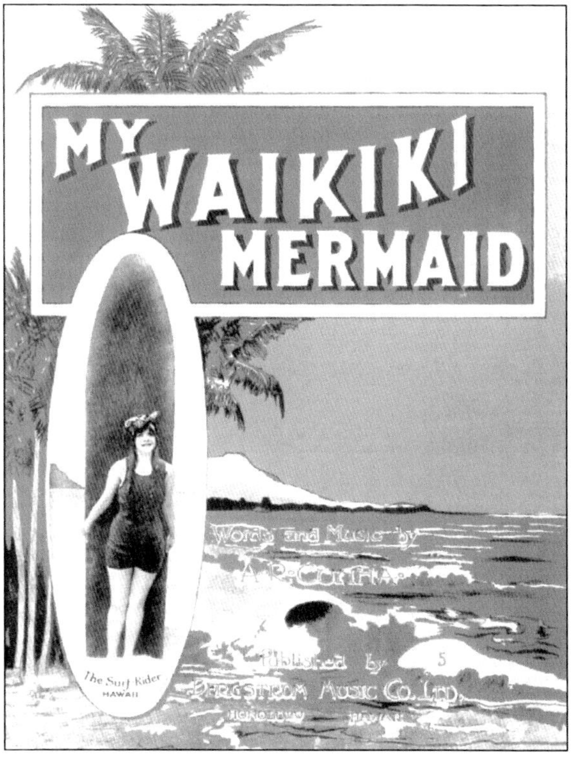

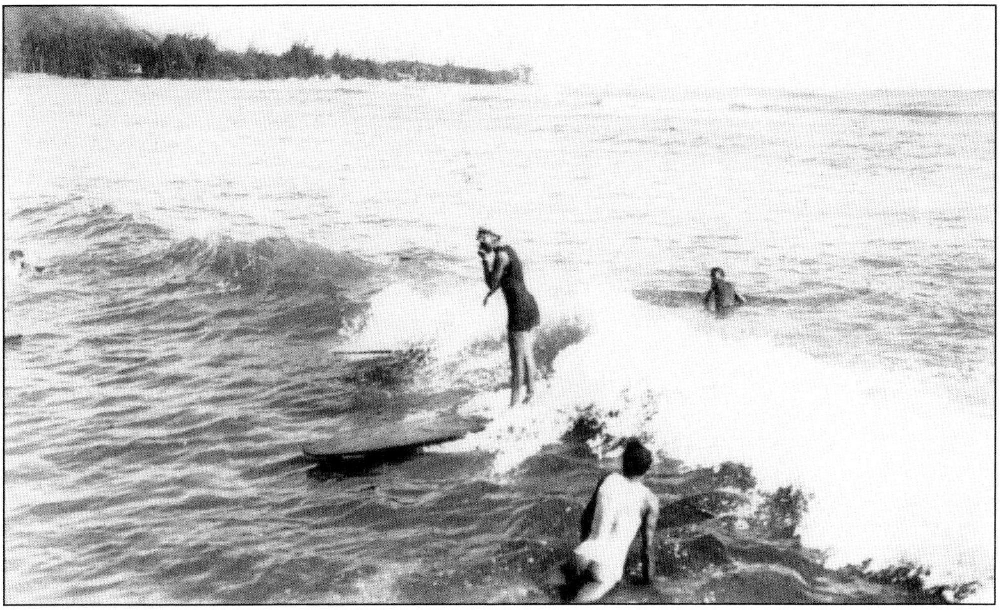

THE CHAMPION GIRL SURFER AT WAIKIKI IN 1915. The above photograph ran in a Sydney, Australia, newspaper, *The Referee,* in February 1915. The image was captioned, "This white girl is said to be the only girl surf-board expert in Honolulu." This was an erroneous statement, as countless girls and women surfed. The photograph is believed to be by James Williams and taken from the Moana Hotel Pier.

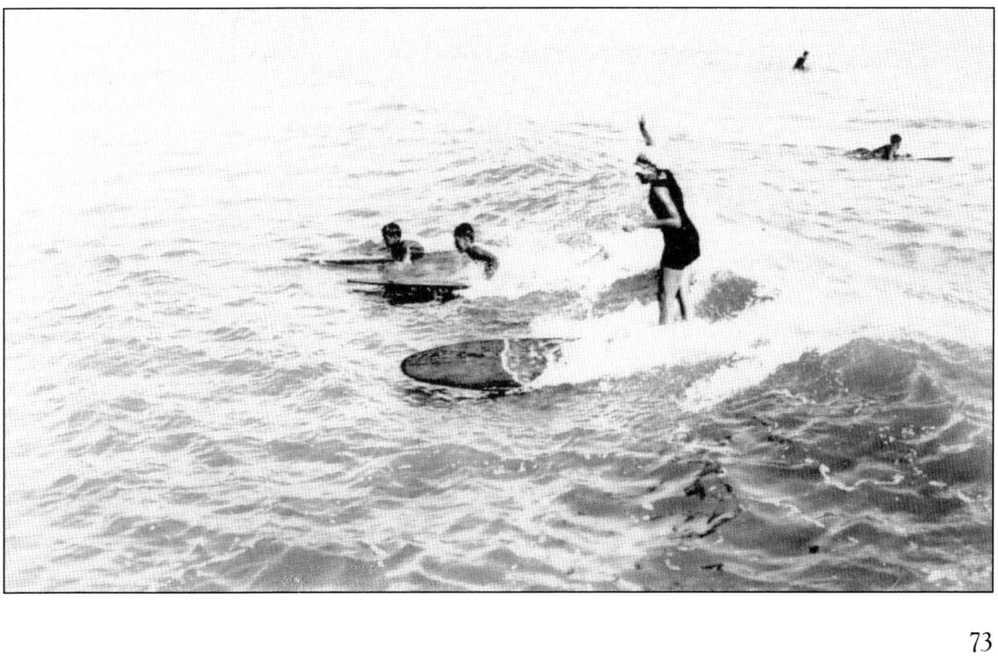

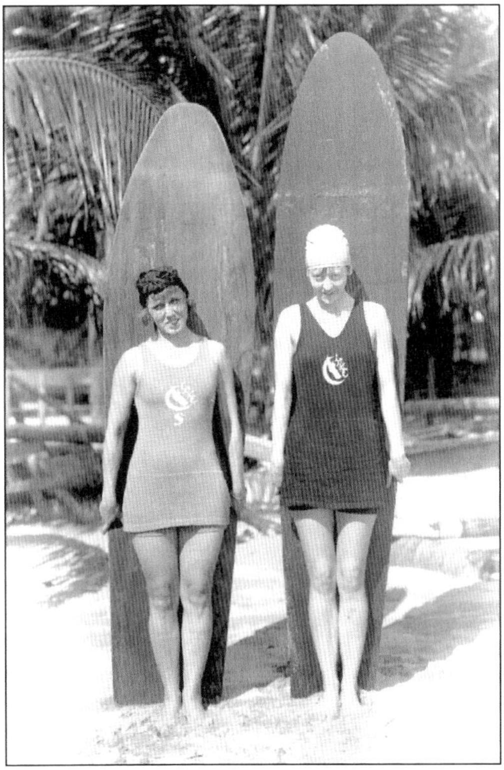

Los Angeles Athletic Club Swimmers and a Hui Nalu Surfboard. In *Surf-Board Riding in Hawaii*, Lorrin P. Thurston wrote, "A boy's surf-board is six to seven feet long, two feet wide and from an inch and a half to two inches thick. A regular man's sized surf-board is eight feet long by about two feet wide and two and a half or three inches thick, weighing from thirty to sixty pounds. The board is rounded off in front, being widest at a point two feet back, from here it tapers to the stern, where it is usually about eighteen inches wide, some of the newer boards are as narrow as six inches at the stern. The boards are all made of sugar pine, white pine or California redwood. They are shellacked or varnished with 'Valspar,' to keep them from becoming watersoaked."

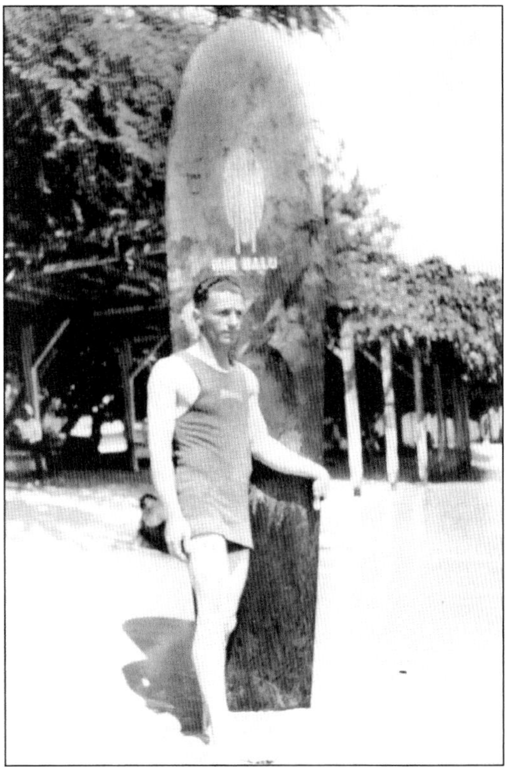

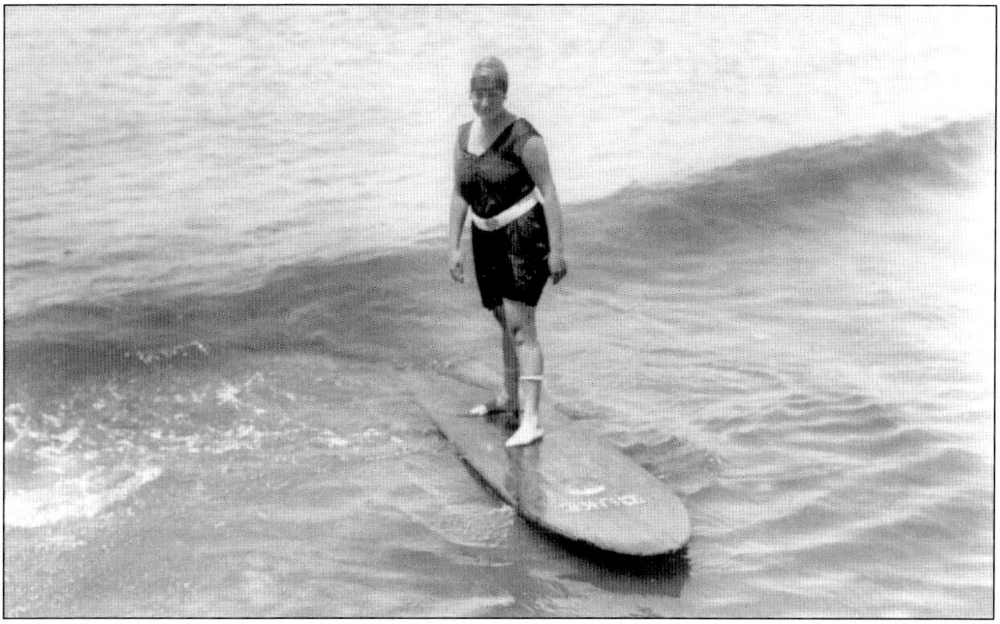

SURFING ON DUKE KAHANAMOKU'S SURFBOARD. With Duke's huge success in the Olympics, everyone wanted to try out the champion's surfboard, even if it meant surfing up onto the beach or simply standing next to his board. The image above was printed in *Mid-Pacific Magazine* with this caption: "Even the women of Honolulu now ride the surfboard and vie with the natives and youngsters on the waves that roll in at Waikiki."

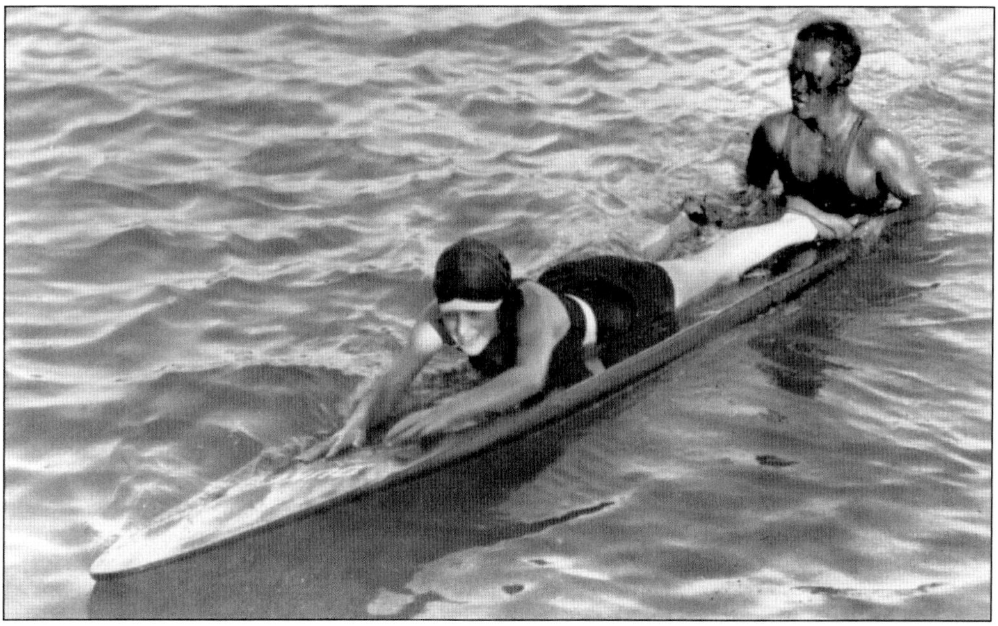

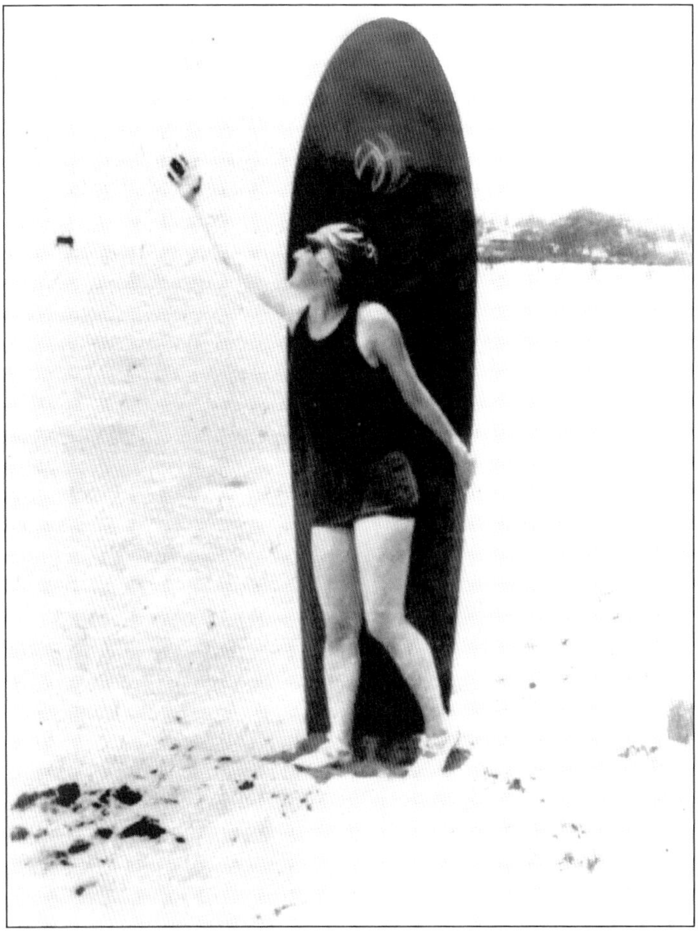

WAHINES SHOW STYLE ON THE BEACH OR IN THE WATER. Women's character and rights were going through some radical changes at the turn of the century. Previously, women's roles had centered on domestic labor, but the booming industrial society was drawing more and more women into the worlds of clerical work, industrial labor, and professional occupations. In 1920, the 19th Amendment to the Constitution was passed, granting women the right to vote.

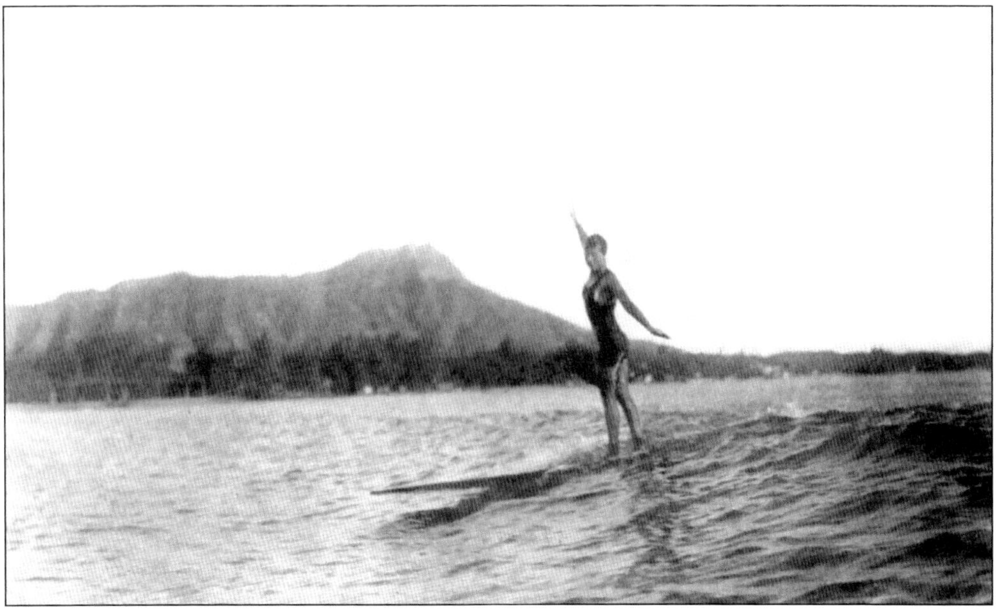

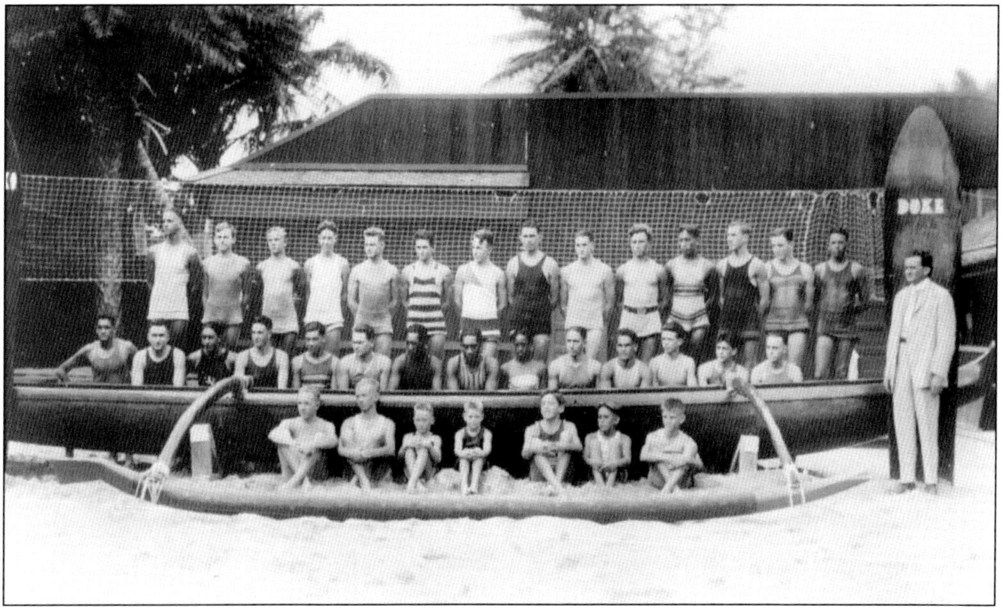

Outrigger Canoe Club Members Pose in Front of the New Volleyball Court. Dad Center is on the right, and Duke is in the center (striped shirt) with his brothers. In 1913, Dad took on the demanding role of club captain, overseeing the club's entire athletic program. He retained this position for nearly 20 years. (Courtesy Outrigger Canoe Club.)

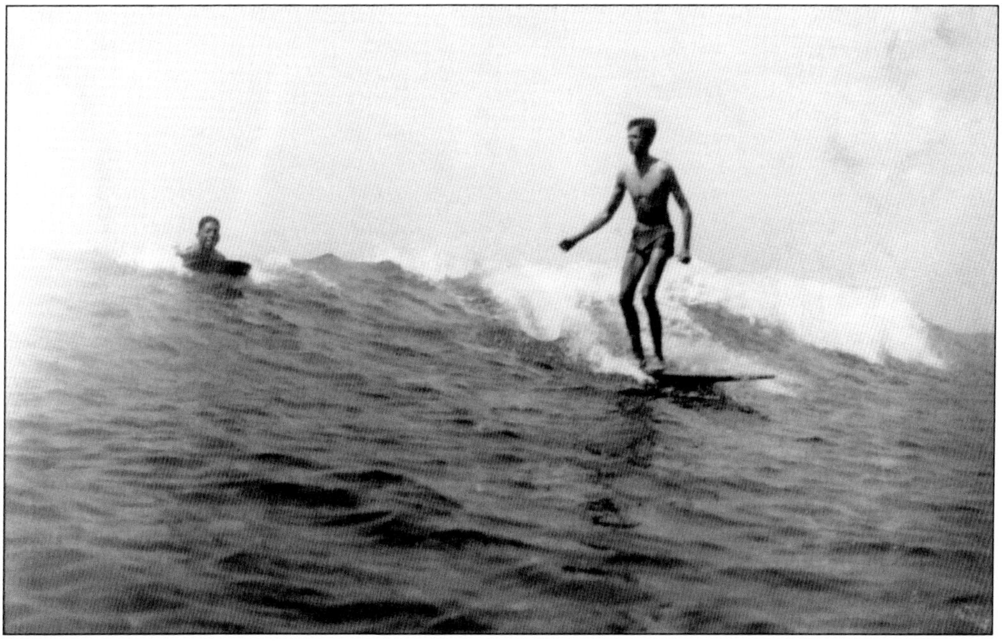

"Surfing at Waikiki." John M. Giles's poem "Surfing" appeared in *Mid-Pacific Magazine* in 1911, and it read, "Then you flash through space in a whirling race. / And a smother of salt sea spray, / And the sea laughs by and the great blue sky, / Both call their roundelay." The keiki photograph does not appear in the original article, but it feels appropriate. (Photograph by Roscoe W. Perkins, courtesy Hawai'i State Archives.)

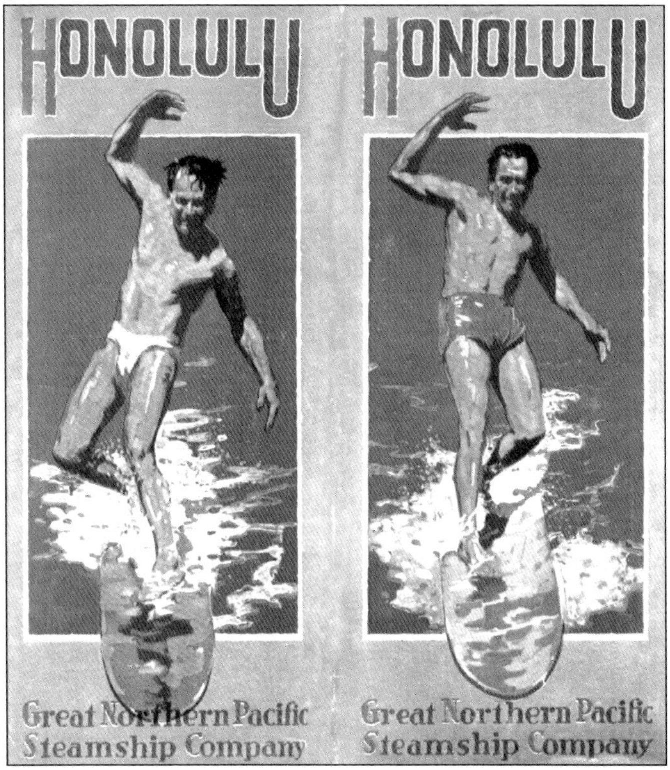

HONOLULU, GREAT NORTHERN PACIFIC STEAMSHIP CO., 1915. The Great Northern Pacific was formed in 1914 to compliment passenger train service from Oregon to San Francisco. During the winter season of 1915–1916, the company ran tours to Hawai'i. The business failed, and eventually the US government commandeered the ships for World War I. Note the subliminal message that what the native does on the left, a *malihini* (newcomer) can do on the right. (Courtesy Dan Pincetich.)

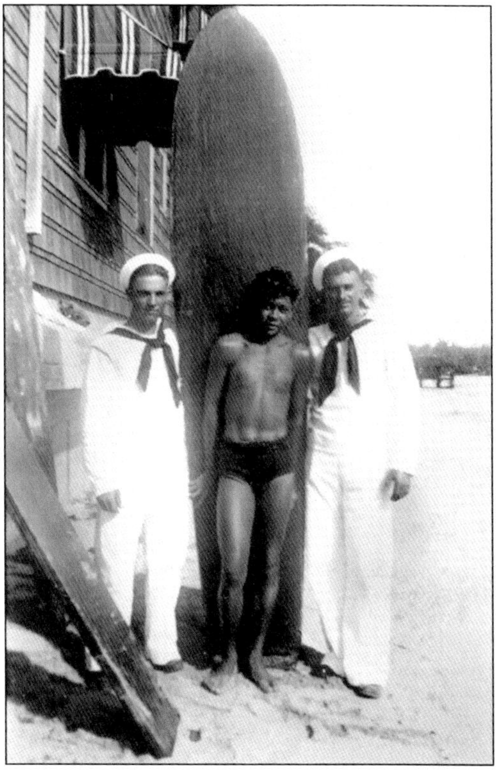

SAILORS STATIONED ON HAWAI'I ALWAYS FOUND TIME TO POSE WITH A REAL BEACHBOY. During America's involvement in World War I (1917 to 1918), tour boats were used in the war effort and tourism declined, but the fresh wave of sailors stationed at Pearl Harbor added a new element to the beach.

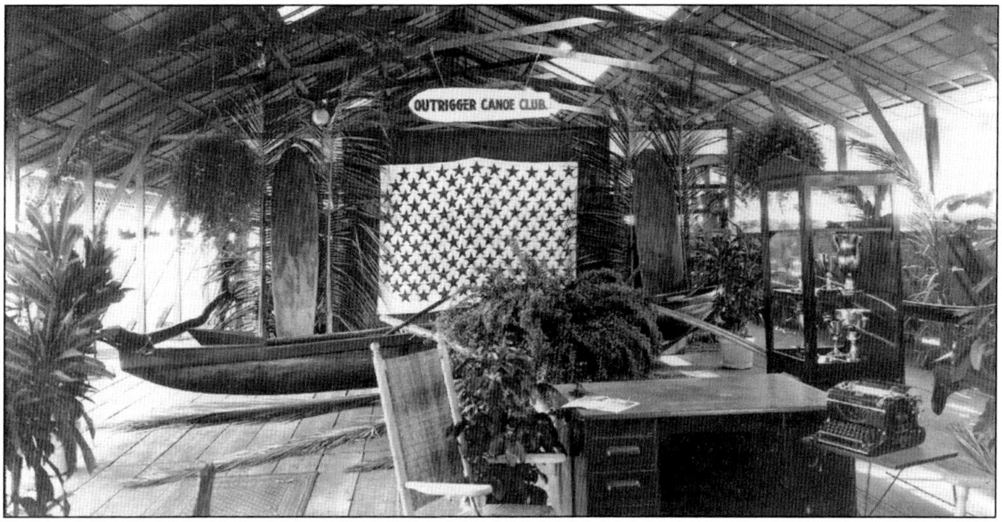

INSIDE OUTRIGGER CANOE CLUB DURING WORLD WAR I, 1917–1918. On the flag in the back, the stars represent members serving overseas in the war. A.H. Ford's typewriter is to the right. The desk is the one Ford used to sit at to write his many surfing promotional pieces and to work on his *Mid-Pacific Magazine*. (Courtesy Outrigger Canoe Club.)

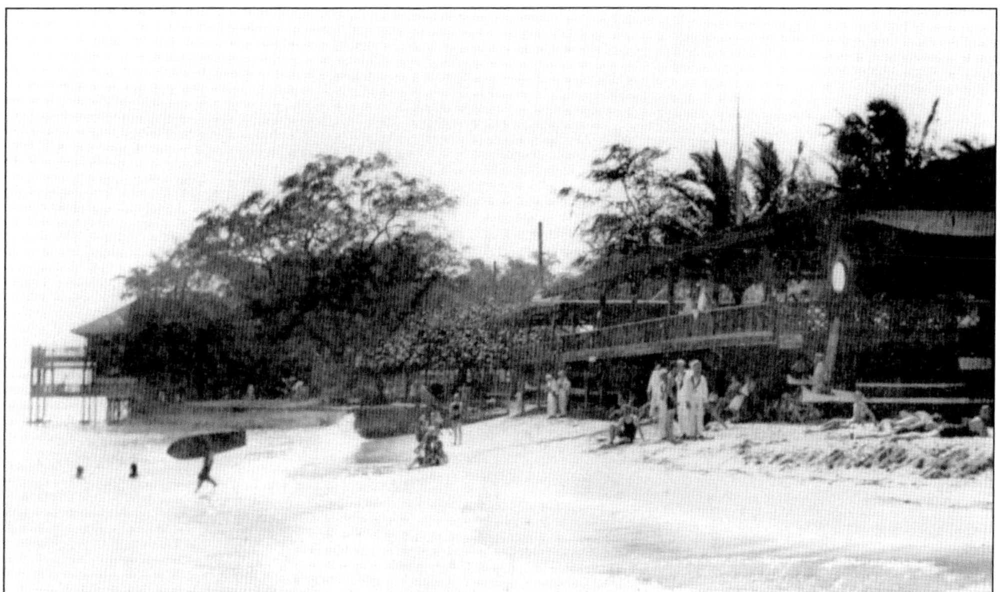

SAILORS ENJOYING REST AND RELAXATION AT THE OUTRIGGER CANOE CLUB. During World War I, according to the *Outrigger Canoe Club, The First One Hundred Years*, "Outrigger did its share of entertaining troops; service men were invited to use the Club's canoes and military units put together volleyball teams that played at the club." (Courtesy Cary Weiss.)

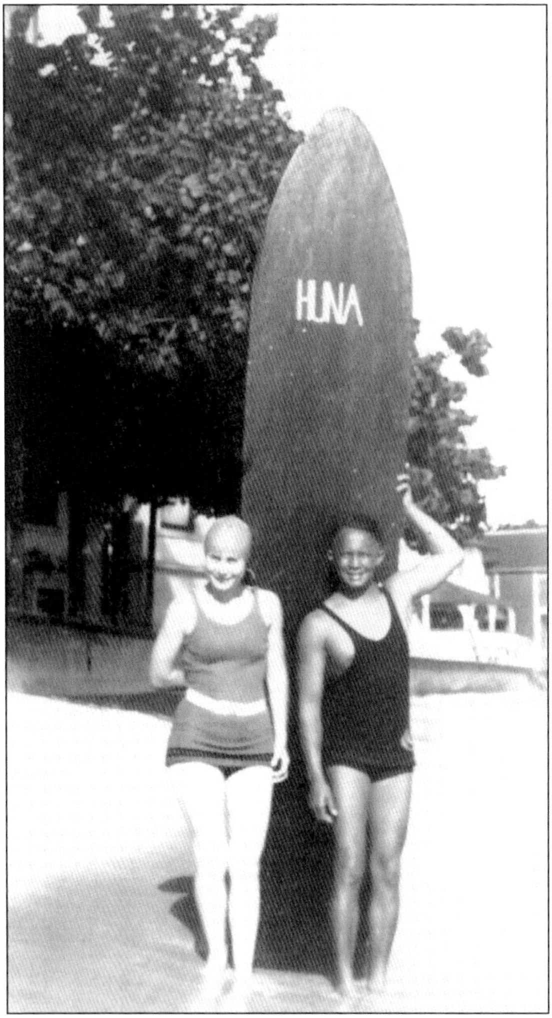

HUNA, C. 1919. With the end of the war, the growing middle class in America enjoyed an increase in leisure time, and Waikiki became the number one "Paradise destination," with the beachboys' notoriety spreading across the globe as a symbol of the idyllic Hawai'ian lifestyle. By 1921, the visitor count hit 8,000.

"EXPERT SURF RIDING, WAIKIKI, HONOLULU." This is a commercial stereoview of a surf-riding handstand taken at the Moana Pier by Underwood & Underwood Publishers, one of the largest makers of stereoviews. Stereoviews were extremely popular because they are able to re-create the illusion of depth by the use of two nearly identical images, each taken a few inches to the side of the other. When viewed through two lenses approximately the space between the eyes, the result is the illusion of a three-dimensional image.

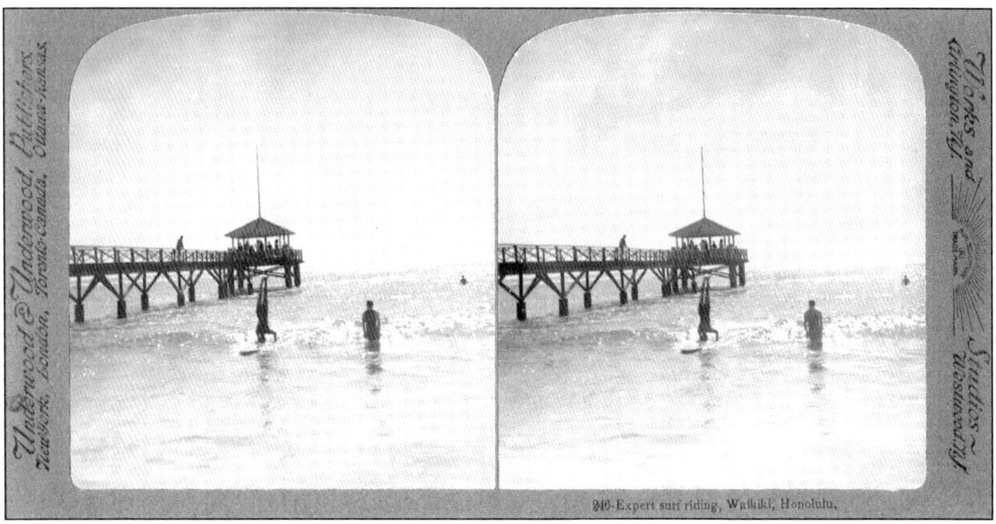

Daisy Potter in Front of the Outrigger Canoe Club. The surfboard belongs to one of her family members, William Potter. Originally from England, the Potters were highly skilled woodworkers, as evidenced by the fine carving detail on the surfboard. Daisy would marry Jason Froome, and they ran the renowned Froome Rooms at Waikiki. Daisy is Cindy Fragale's grandmother; Cindy is the wife of Mark Fragale, author of the introduction to this book. (Courtesy Cindy Fragale.)

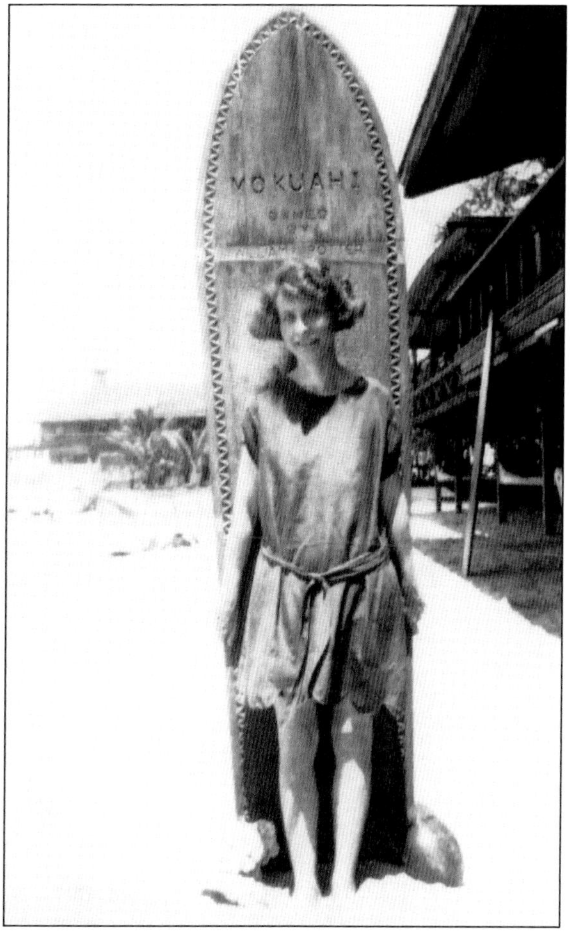

Dad Center (Left) and Cook, 1917. Dad rode one of the biggest swells in Waikiki's history with Duke in 1917. As Duke told Tom Blake, "They were running about thirty feet high. We were waiting off Castle Point . . . so far out that we recognized the captain of a passing steamer. . . . I went so fast the chop of the wave struck the bottom of my board like a patter of a machine gun . . . [we rode the waves for about] eight hundred yards."

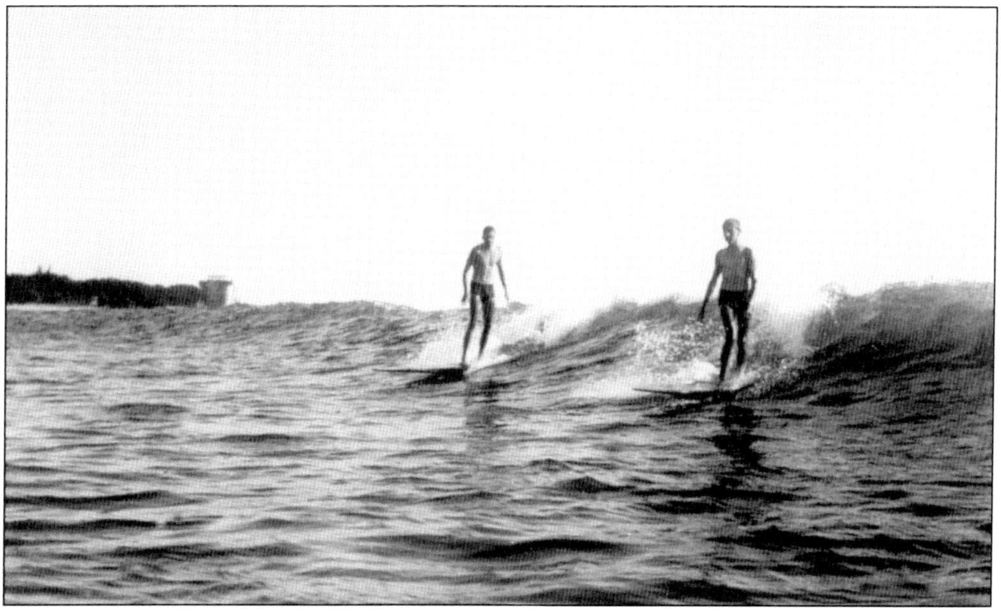

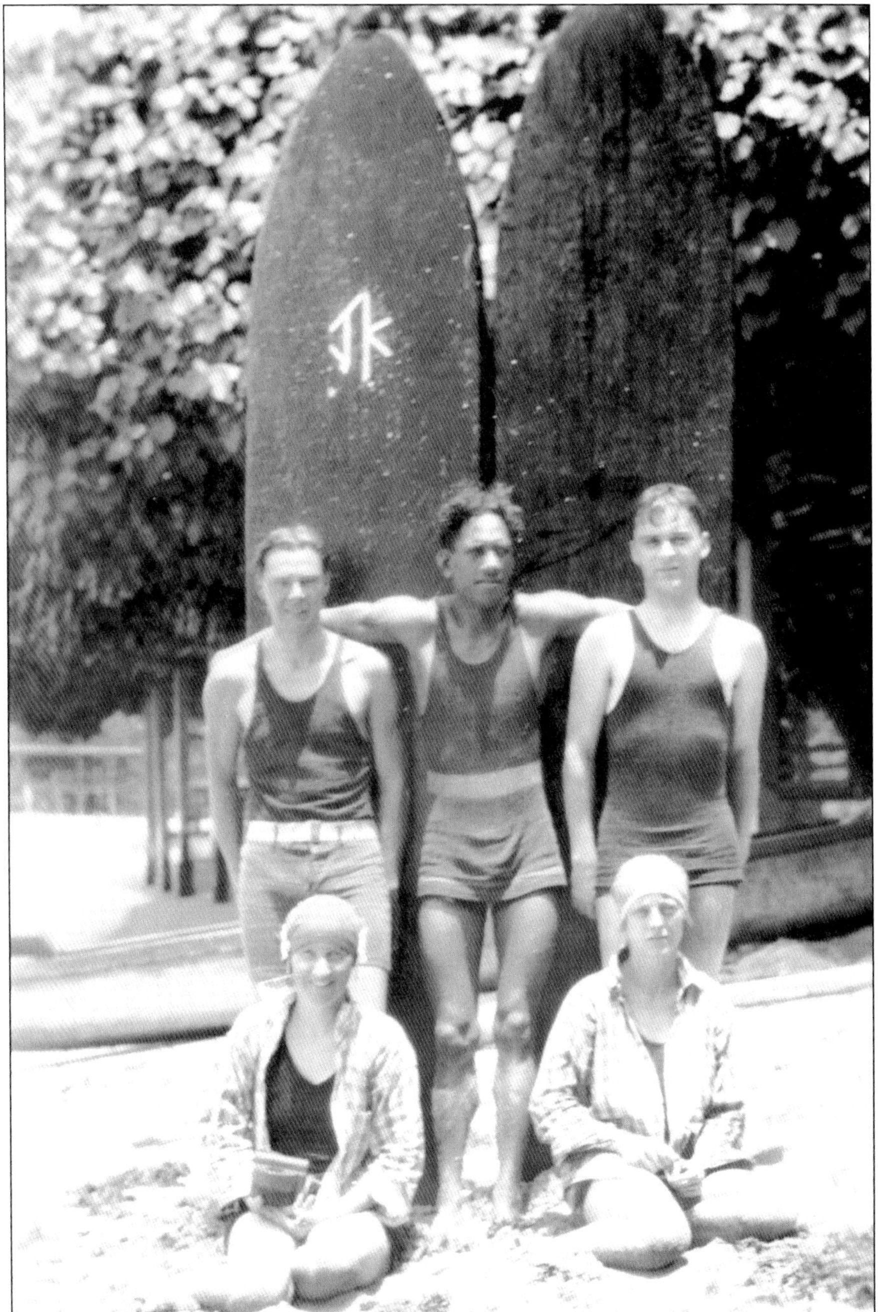

A Waikiki Vacation was Incomplete until One Met a Kahanamoku. Of the six brothers, Sam (center, at about age 14) was the mischief-maker. He would become an Olympic swimmer and a champion surfer and paddleboarder. Later, Sam gained notoriety as heiress Doris Duke's companion for many years. If no Kahanamoku was available to meet on a vacation, a good stand-in was a photograph taken with Duke's board and one of their dozens of cousins. Many of them were famous: Melvin, Malcolm, Fred "Boy" Paoa, and Olympians Warren Paoa Kealoha and Pua Kealoha.

Seven

Duke Paoa Kahanamoku
1890–1968

by Sandra Kimberley Hall

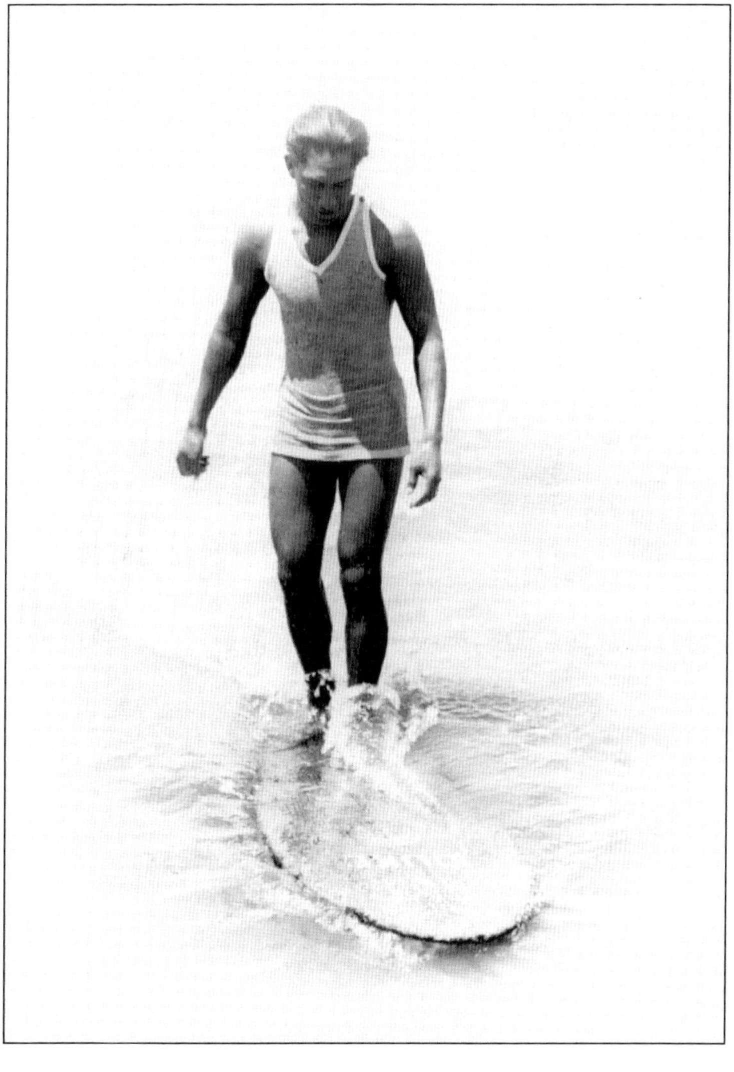

Everyone Called Him "The Duke." Duke displayed royal manners, a chiefly bearing, and he was the undisputed "King of the Ocean." He learned to swim when he learned to walk, and he learned to surf when he was in kindergarten. His niece Kamaka Clark Miyamoto said that Duke was born to "fulfill a prophecy." It had been prophesied that despite having their kingdom overthrown by *haoles* (foreigners) and their population diminished by disease, one day a Native Hawai'ian would bring international fame to Hawai'i. Duke fulfilled that prophecy.

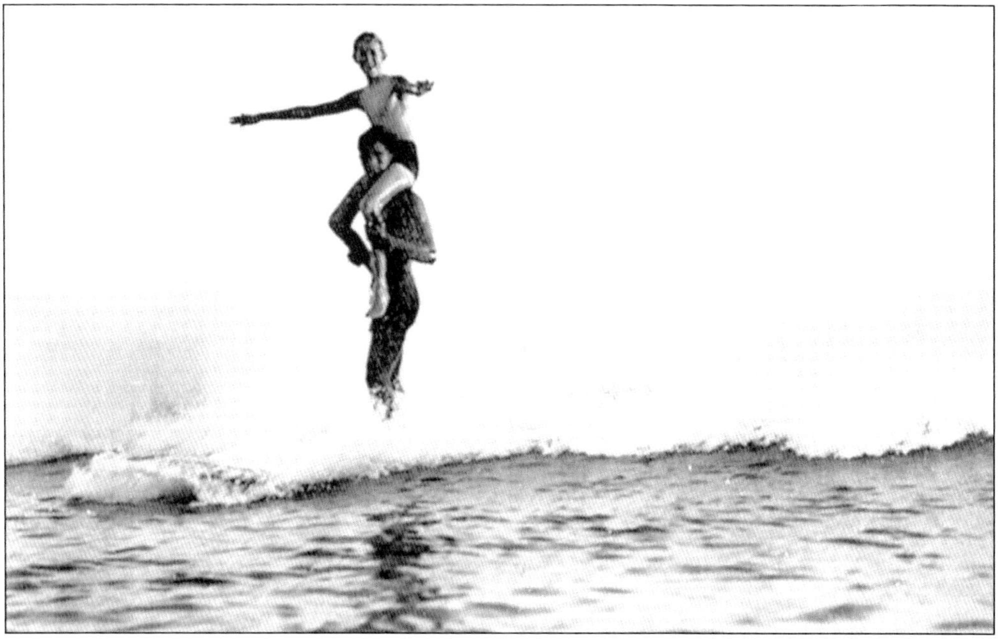

DUKE SURFING TANDEM AND DOING A HEADSTAND, C. 1912. "Duke was the greatest aquatic athlete the world has ever seen," so claimed the US Postal Service on release of the Duke stamp in 2002. He excelled in every water sport. Duke summed up surfing: "Let the ocean teach you. It will teach you everything you need to know." Duke was raised at Kalia, Waikiki, with a large extended family. He was taught to pass on what he had learned from his elders—whether how to make a surfboard by hand, how to steer an outrigger surfing canoe to victory in a race, or how to surf distant billows to shore a mile distant. He loved doing tricks for awed spectators, such as surfing on his head or surfing tandem with young Marston Campbell of the Outrigger Canoe Club. (Above photograph by A.R. Gurrey Jr., courtesy Joel T. Smith.)

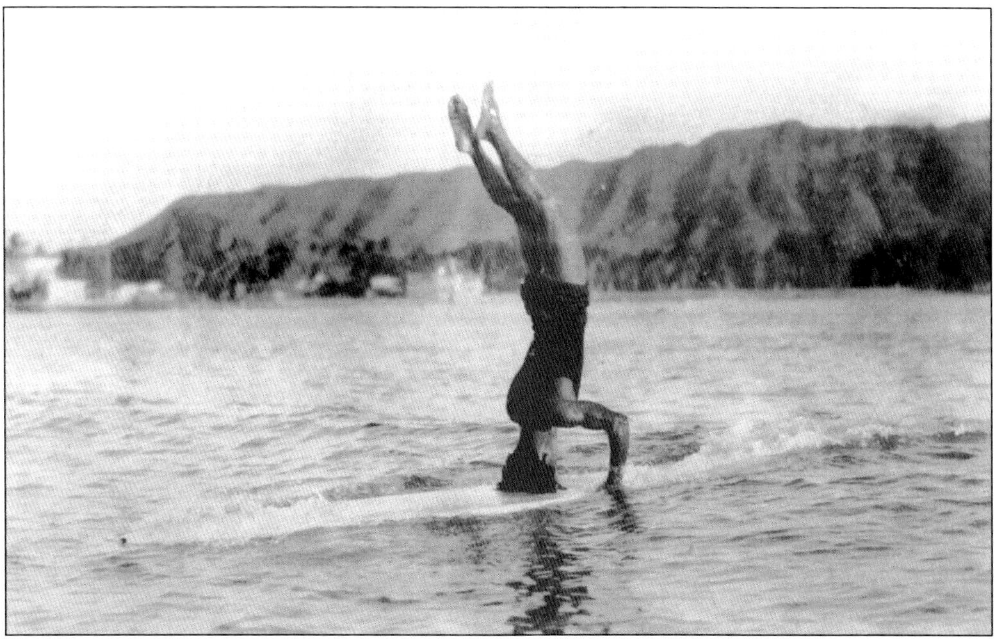

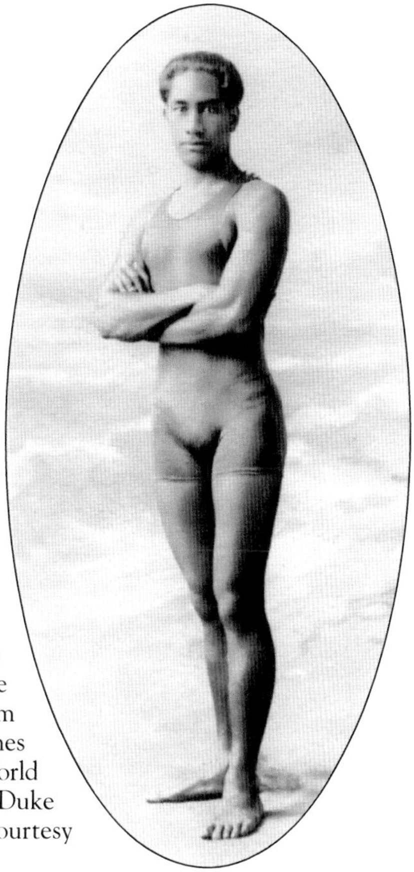

Duke Breaking Two World Swimming Records in Honolulu Harbor, August 1911. Duke was an unknown 20-year-old in Honolulu's first Amateur Athletic Union (AAU) meet. The AAU in New York City thought the Honolulu swim officials had measured the course incorrectly or they did not know how to use a stopwatch. So Hawai'i citizens raised money to send Duke to the mainland in 1912 to compete for the Olympic team. At first, he performed poorly in the short indoor pools, but with coaching he quickly learned how to make a clean start, turn, and improve his revolutionary freestyle stroke. He became the world champion at the Stockholm Olympics in 1912. He would compete in Olympic Games for an astonishing 20 years (1916 was cancelled due to World War I) and popularized freestyle swimming and surfing. Duke helped usher in the golden age of swimming. (Right, courtesy Outrigger Canoe Club.)

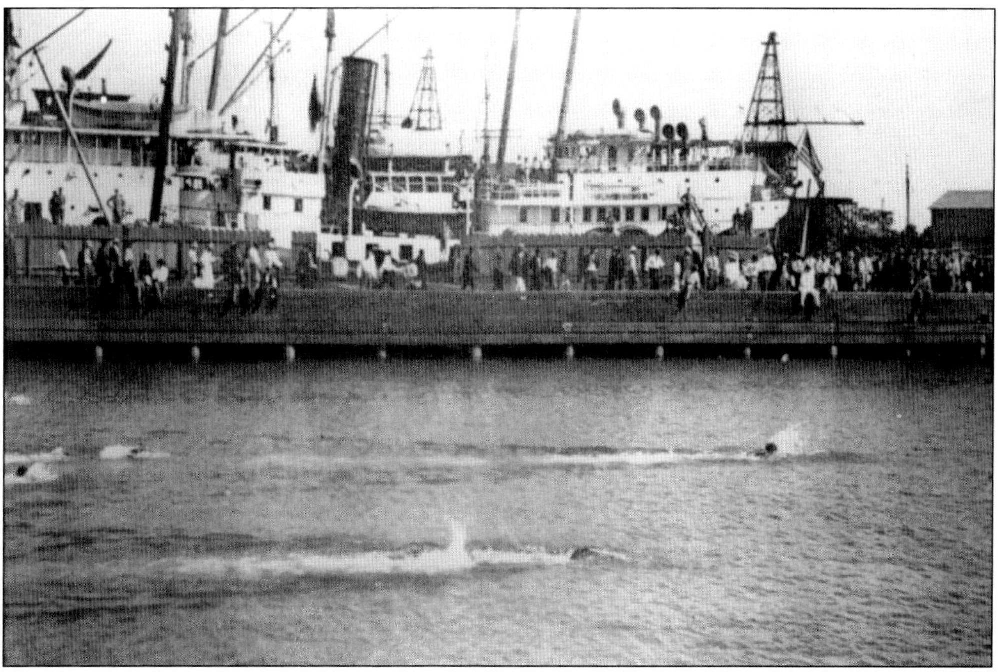

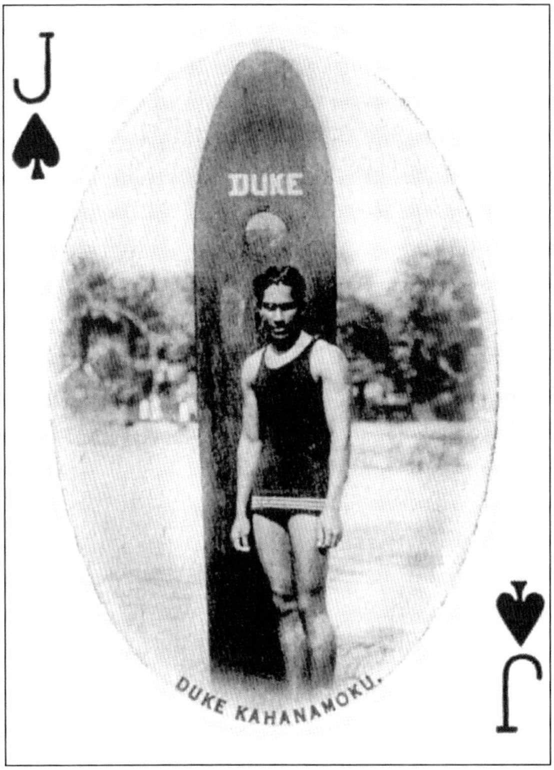

WITH DUKE'S OLYMPIC SUCCESS, HIS LIKENESS BECAME *THE* HAWAI'I SURFING IMAGE PROJECTED THROUGHOUT THE WORLD. At left is a Walls playing card, and below is a 1914 Mid-Pacific Carnival flyer. Today, Duke would be paid an enormous amount of money for his promotional efforts. During his career as an aquatic athlete, the AAU policy forbade payment for competitive events, swimming stroke demonstrations, or teaching swimming. Duke could have his expenses paid for, however, if he was competing on behalf of the AAU. He was often tempted by offers of up to $50,000 to turn professional. It was very stressful to compete for "just the love of the sport" as his financial contribution was needed to help support his eight siblings, especially after his father died in 1917. The AAU could not forbid his being paid for demonstrating surfing.

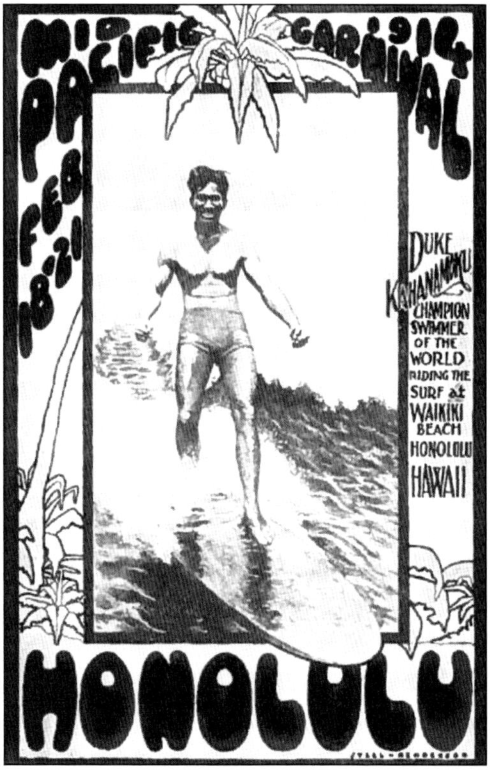

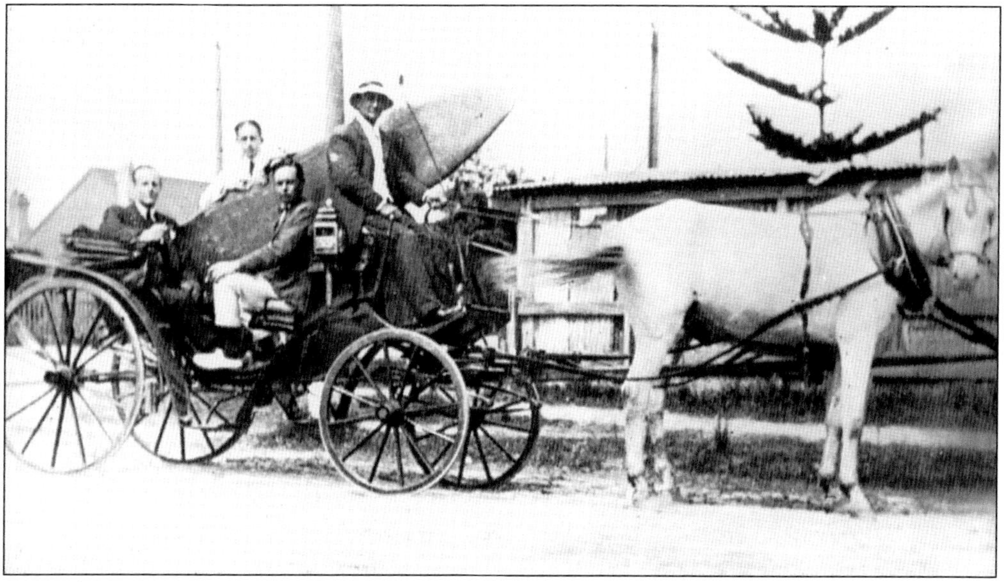

Duke Spreading the Gospel of Surfing and Aloha at Freshwater Beach, Australia, 1914. One of Duke's most memorable impacts on the sports of swimming and surfing was his visit to Australia for the National Swimming Championships of 1914–1915. The trip exceeded his Australian hosts' expectations; he showed them how to select a piece of wood and shape a surfboard before demonstrating some of his surfing tricks. Duke ignited a national passion for surfing, which is Australia's most successful international sport. He also demolished so many swimming records (over 30) that the organizers lost track. Wherever Duke traveled internationally, people wanted to see him. It was not unusual for crowds up to 40,000 to turn out to watch him. He promoted the Hawai'i tourism industry worldwide. (Courtesy Outrigger Canoe Club.)

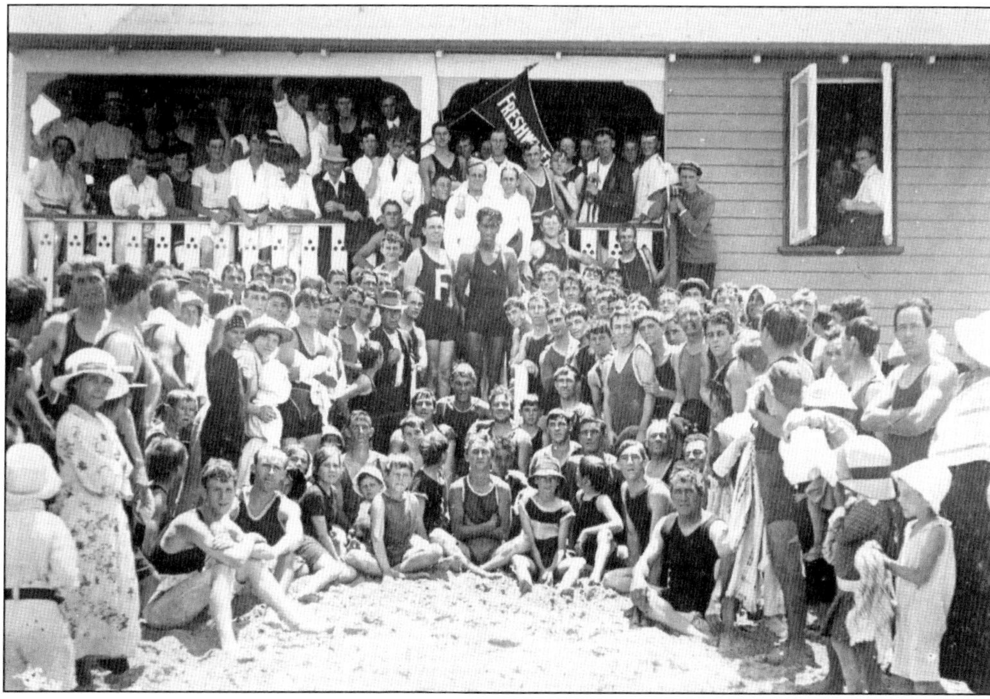

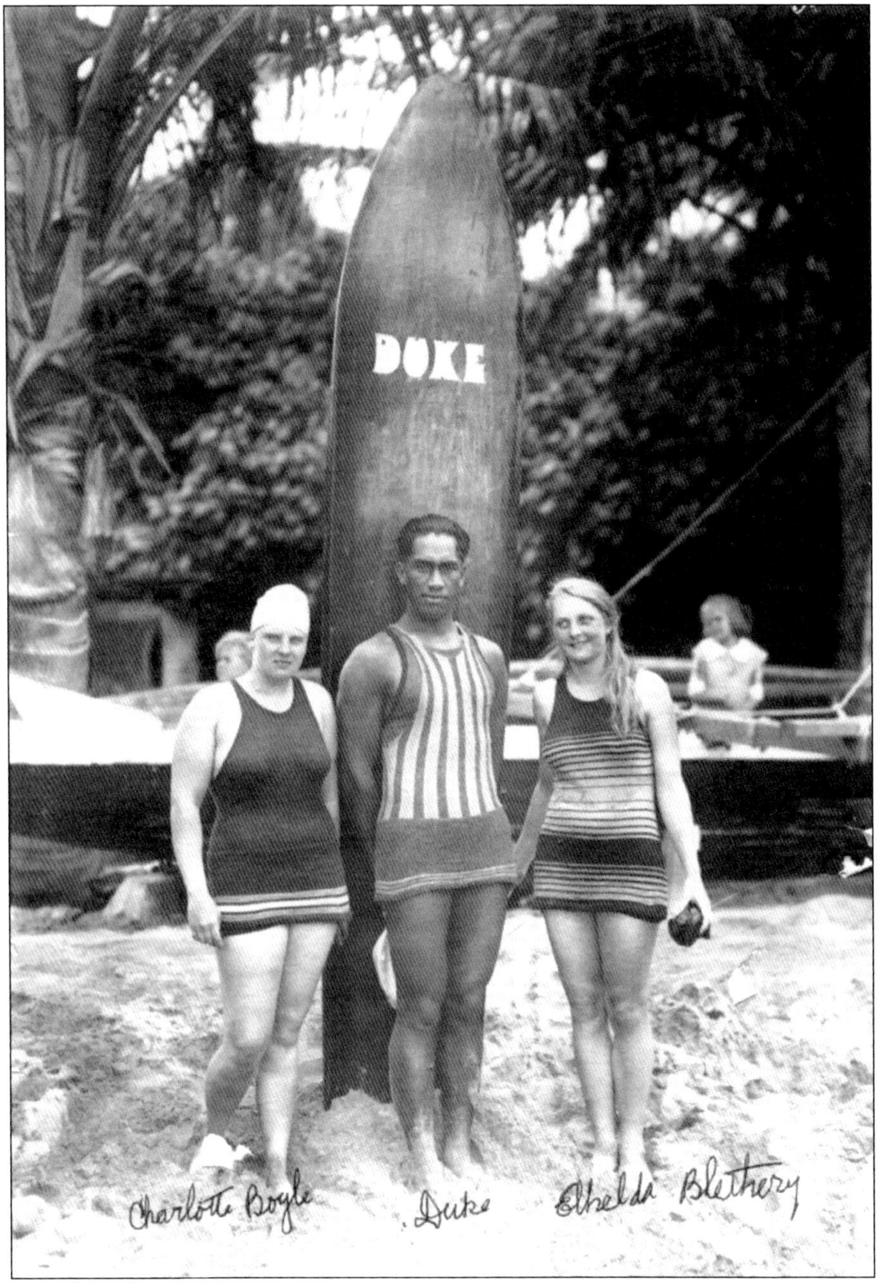

CHARLOTTE BOYLE (LEFT), DUKE, AND ETHELDA BLEIBTREY, 1920 OLYMPIC CHAMPIONS IN FRONT OF THE OUTRIGGER CANOE CLUB. Ethelda, who started swimming to help her recover from polio and took it up seriously to keep her good friend Charlotte company, was America's first female Olympic swimming champion and the only person ever to win all three of the women's swimming events at any Olympic Games. Charlotte won a bronze medal at the Antwerp, Belgium, Olympics. Amazingly, Duke turned in a faster time than he had at the 1912 Olympics. He won two golds at Antwerp and six Olympic medals in all: three gold, two silver, and 1 bronze. He believed in the Olympic motto of "Citius, Altius, Fortius" (Faster, Higher, Stronger), which was achieved by consistent practice and a healthy lifestyle. (Courtesy Outrigger Canoe Club.)

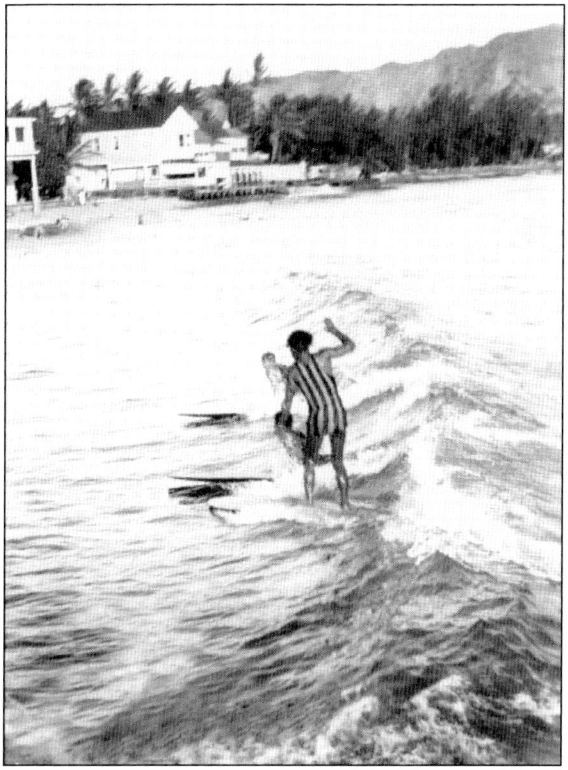

DANCING ON WATER OFF THE MOANA PIER IN 1922. Images of the Duke surfing are rare, as he was generally captured in his swimming attire or posing with admiring celebrities. These images capture Duke in a playful mode, surfing off the east side of the Mona Pier, dazzling the gathering crowd on another perfect day in paradise. The photographers, Lucile Hughes and Mildred Schwartzhaugh, were students from Toledo, Ohio, mentioned by an article in the *Los Angeles Express* as "two pretty maids studying as they travel."

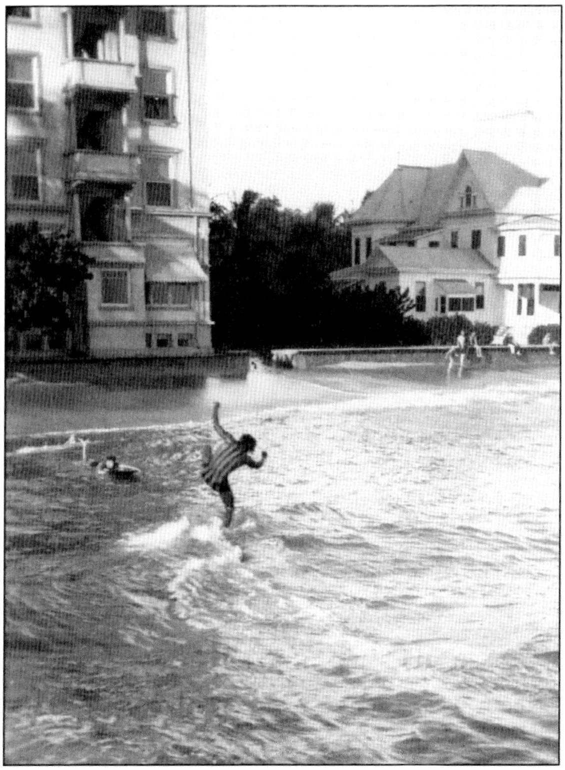

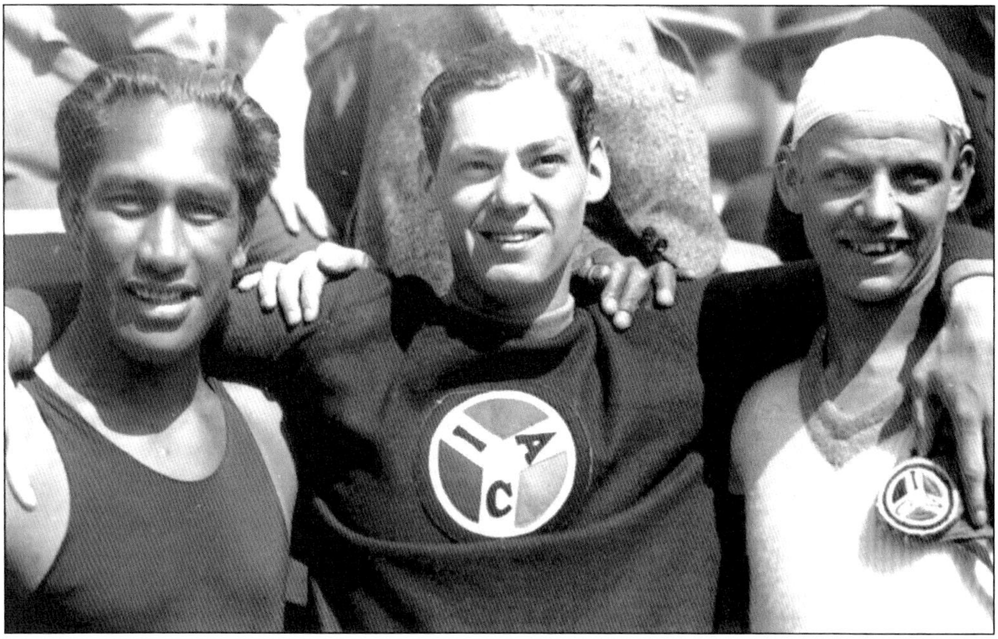

One of the Most Famous Swimming Trios Ever. At 34, Duke (left) is definitely the "old man" at the 1924 Paris Olympics. Johnny Weissmuller (center), sporting an Illinois Athletic Club logo, had just beaten Duke to become world champion. Weissmuller, who later became famous as Tarzan, is seen here at age 20. Champion long-distance swimmer Arne Borg, the "Swedish Sturgeon," is 23 here. Borg and Weissmuller were lifelong friends of Duke.

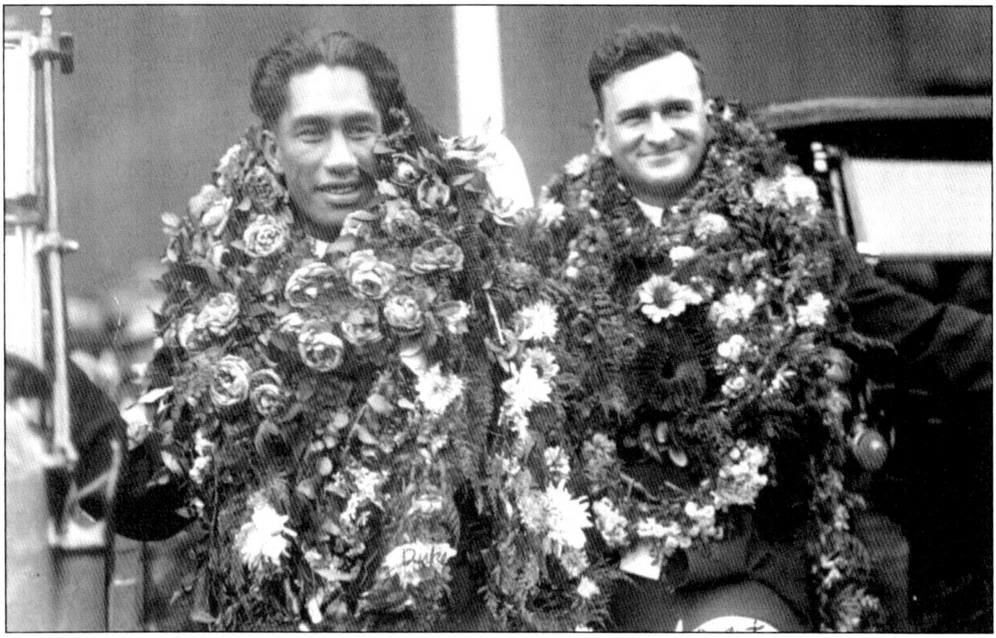

Duke and George Dad Center (Olympic Coach) after the 1920 Olympics. Center was Duke's close friend, and they often surfed and paddled together. Center chose 10 Hawai'ians to be part of the greatest Olympic swimming team Hawai'i has ever sent to an Olympics. At the games, Duke suggested that surfing should be an Olympic sport. (Courtesy Outrigger Canoe Club.)

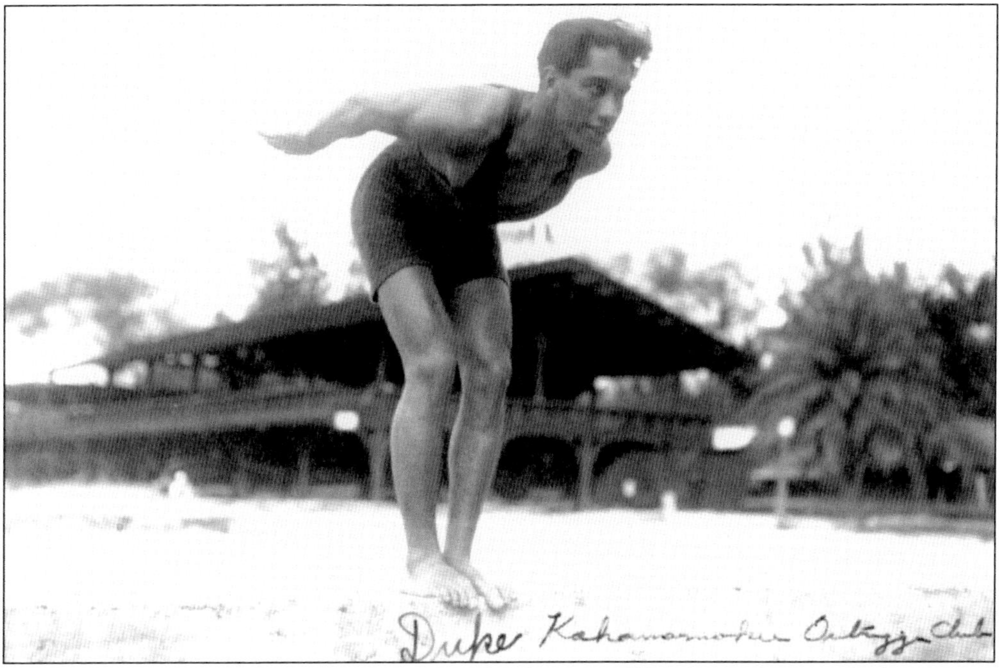

HOLD THAT POSE, PLEASE. Duke obliges a fan by showing off his diving form on the breakwater in front of the new Outrigger Canoe Club. An OCC member since 1919, he was steersman for innumerable outrigger canoe championship victories, was a fearsome volleyball player, and relaxed at the club with some of the world's most famous people from movies and the military. (Courtesy Outrigger Canoe Club.)

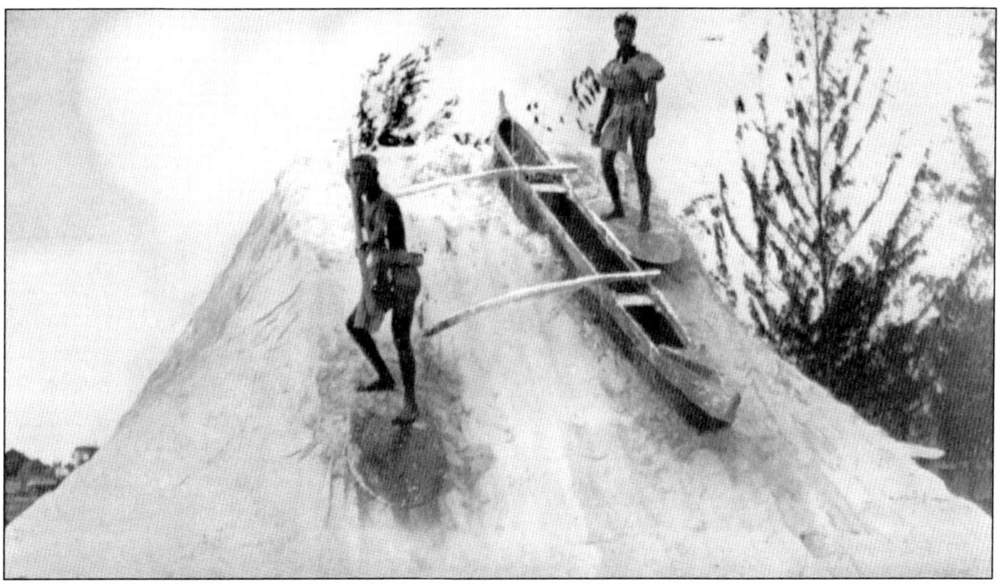

KING OF THE CARNIVAL IN THE 1917 WASHINGTON DAY PARADE. There was no better way to represent Hawai'i than with a float featuring surfing. Beachboy "Steamboat" Keaweamahi is "surfing" on the left, holding a blunted spear, a weapon used in *lua*, the ancient Hawai'ian martial art. Duke is wearing a malo, the traditional surfing breechcloth. Soon after this, he refused to be exploited by wearing traditional clothing. (Courtesy Dan Pincetich.)

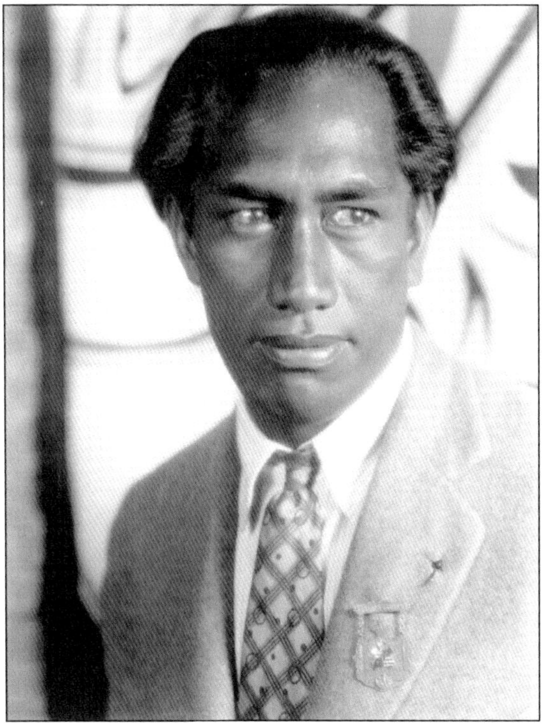

Duke's Saves Eight. When the *Thelma* was broadsided by a wave and capsized at Newport Beach Breakwater in 1925, Duke, Gerald Vultee, and Owen Hale reacted immediately with their surfboards and rescued 12 people; sadly, 5 drowned. Duke paddled out and back to the beach three times, rescuing eight in the water. The three men were honored by the Los Angeles Athletic Club (LAAC) and the Hawai'ian Society of Los Angeles with gold watches and the medal shown here.

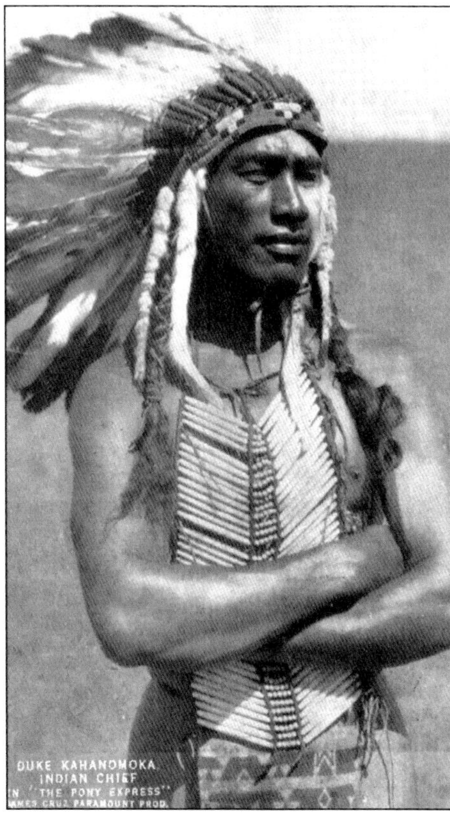

Duke as Indian Chief in *The Pony Express*. Los Angeles was *the* place to be in the 1920s, and the LAAC wanted Duke. Movie mogul Douglas Fairbanks and the LAAC made the proverbial "offer he could not refuse." Duke worked in movies, and between auditions and roles he worked as a mechanic, LAAC spokesman, and lifeguard. He appeared in over 30 movies, mostly black and white silent films.

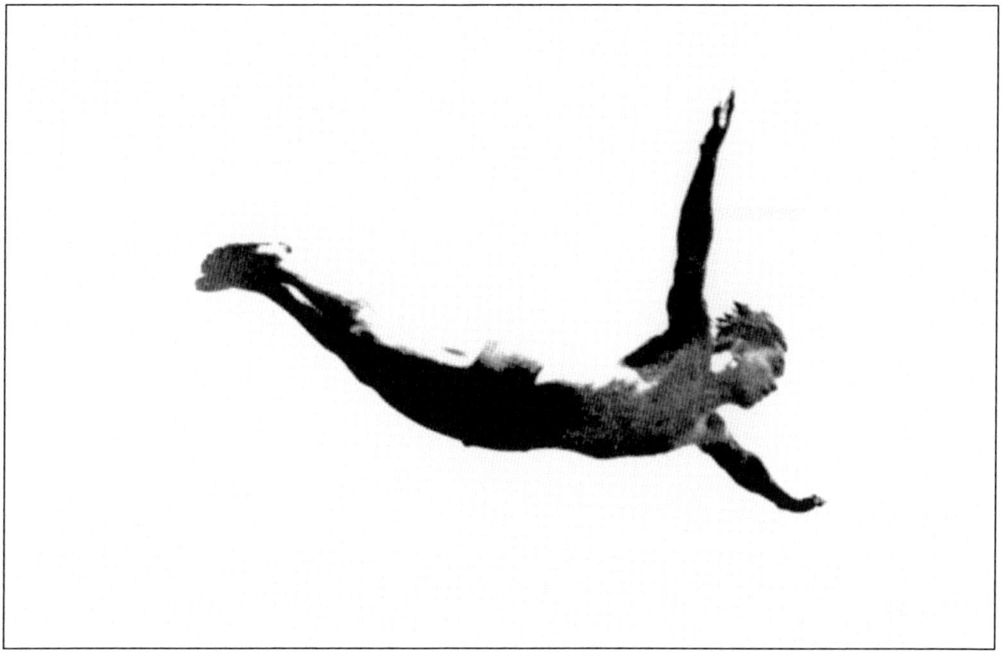

THE ANCIENT HAWAIʻIAN WORD FOR SURFING MEANS GLIDING. A.R. Gurrey Jr. captured Duke's exquisite glide through the air, in a swan dive from the mast of a ship, 100 feet above the surface of the Honolulu Harbor. The above photograph was used in many mainland newspapers in new Sunday rotogravures featuring photographs from around the world. Although Duke competed in the Olympic Games in two sports, water polo and freestyle swimming, it is unfortunate that Honolulu lacked appropriate diving towers as he may have been an Olympic diver also. Gurrey was a swimmer and surfer himself and appreciated Duke's abilities. He captured some of the most exquisite images of the young Duke. (Both courtesy Outrigger Canoe Club.)

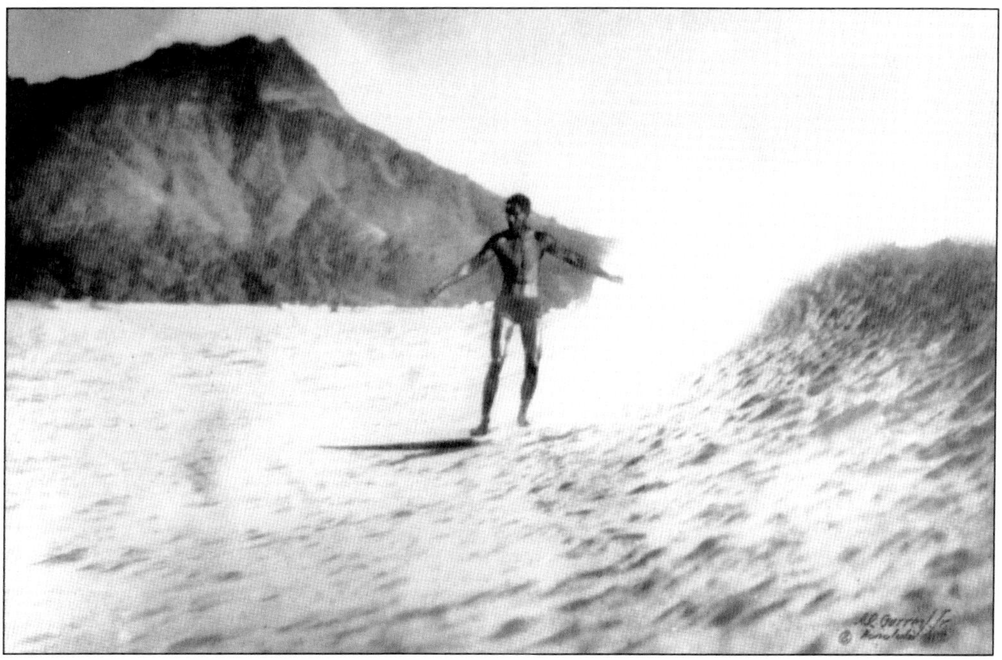

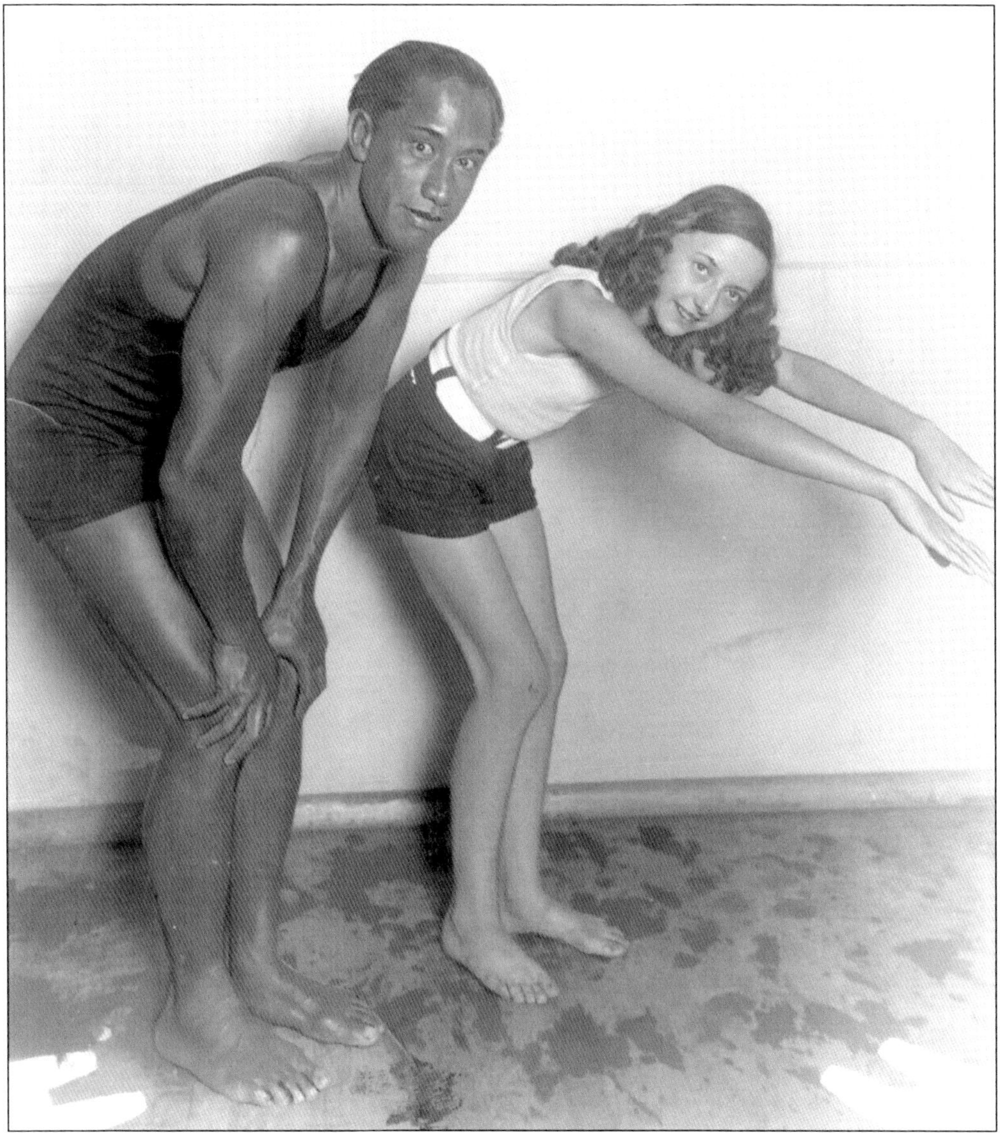

Duke Teaching Edna Lucille Harvey Swimming on a Stage. In 1927, at age 37, just before Duke sailed from Los Angeles to Honolulu for the dedication of the Natatorium, he starred in a vaudeville show at the Hillstreet Theater at 801 Hill Street. The theater was built by RKO Pictures in 1922 and was one of the most opulent in Los Angeles. His act was called "The Greatest Swimming Champion" and was a precursor to later swimming aquacades, like Billy Rose's. Tickets sold for just 50¢ each, and the *Los Angeles Times* gave Duke front-page coverage. A tank was erected on stage, but it is unclear what the program consisted of. It was followed by an LAAC tribute to Duke that proclaimed, "The one and only Duke as a [LAAC] swimmer has won more championships than any other swimmer in the West. He holds the world record for the fifty-yard swim with the time of 22 3/5sec and unofficially holds the records for the 120 and 200-yards swims over the long course and the 75-yards swim over the short course." Note that the image has been edited to move Duke closer.

Eight

On Solid Ground
1920–1930

BY TIMOTHY T. DELAVEGA AND SANDRA KIMBERLEY HALL

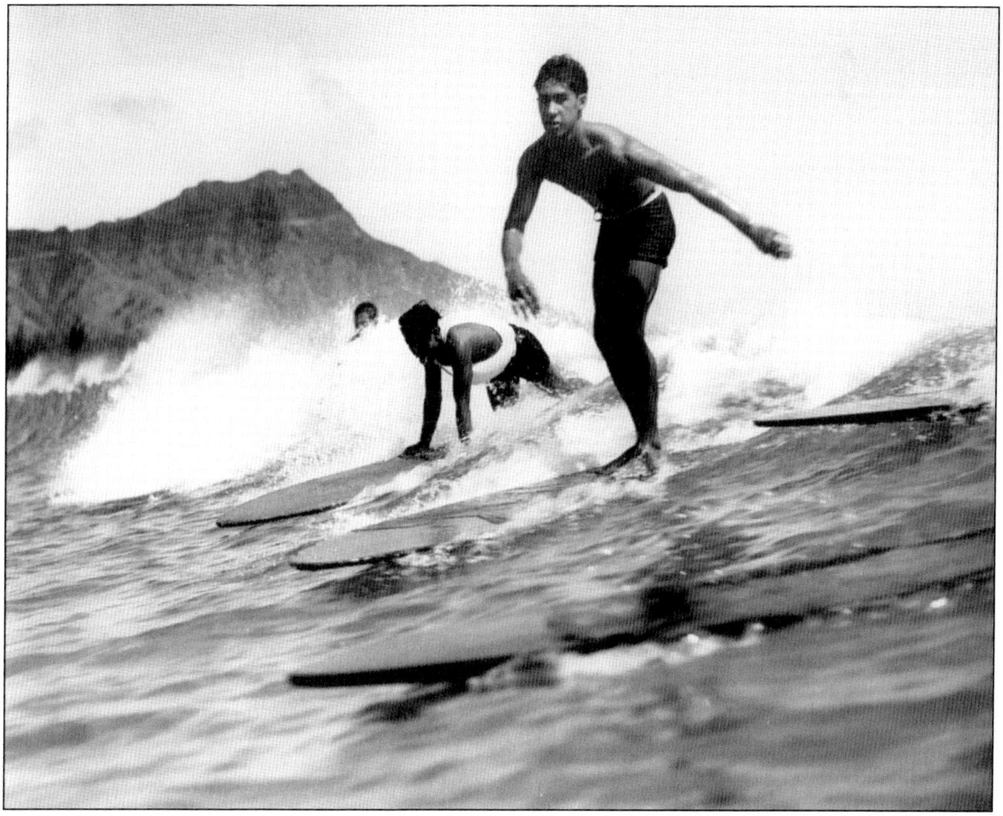

THE DYNAMICS OF SURFING ON WOOD PLANKS AT QUEENS. "The beachboys who ruled Waikiki before 1930 probably came closest to the romantic ideal. They led a conspicuously languorous existence. The job of the beachboy was not really a job at all but something they did during their off hours for little or no money," writes Grady Timmons in *Waikiki Beachboy*. After 1930, as tourism flourished, being a beachboy became more of a career, patronized by well-heeled repeat visitors like Art Linkletter, who had the beachboys supervise his children.

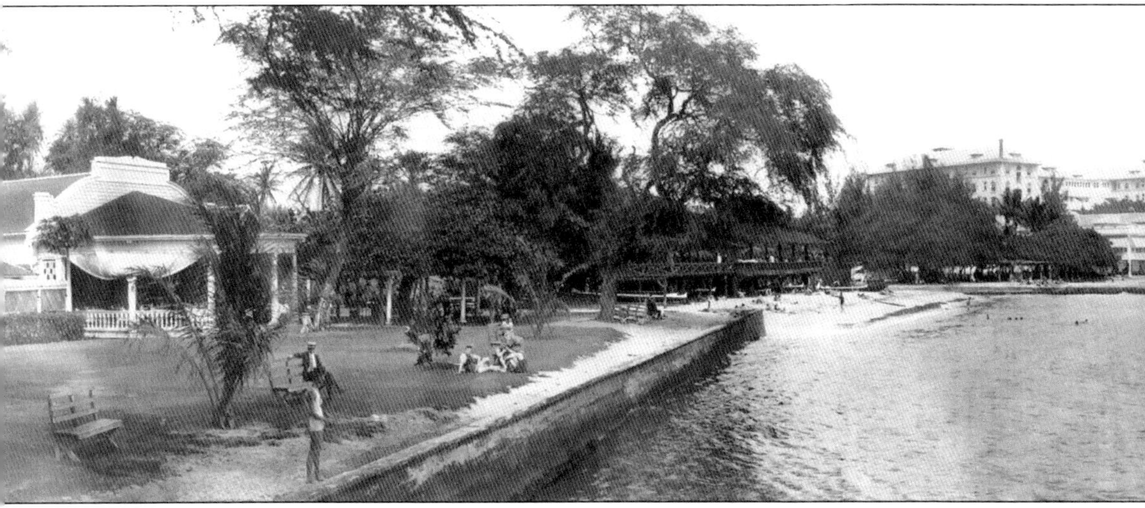

A PANORAMIC PHOTOGRAPH OF WAIKIKI, c. 1920. Taken from the decks of the Waikiki Villa Bathhouse, this view looks east towards Diamond Head, with the Moana Hotel and Pier in the center. To the left, the Seaside Hotel, where Jack London stayed, would soon be razed to make way for the palatial Royal Hawaiian hotel. Waikiki would change drastically every decade afterward.

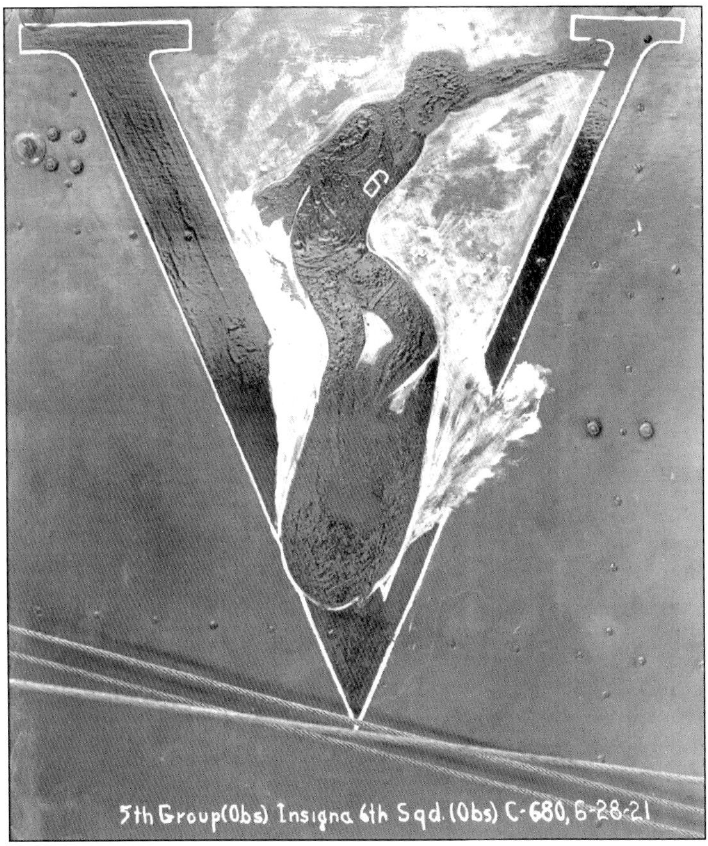

SURFING INSIGNIA ON AN OBSERVATION PLANE, 1921. The US Army Air Corps was based at Luke Field, Ford Island. The insignia is on a DeHavilland DH-4 plane of the 5th Group of the 6th Squad Observation. Despite heavy gunfire, the 5th Group was the first in the air after the 1941 Pearl Harbor surprise attack.

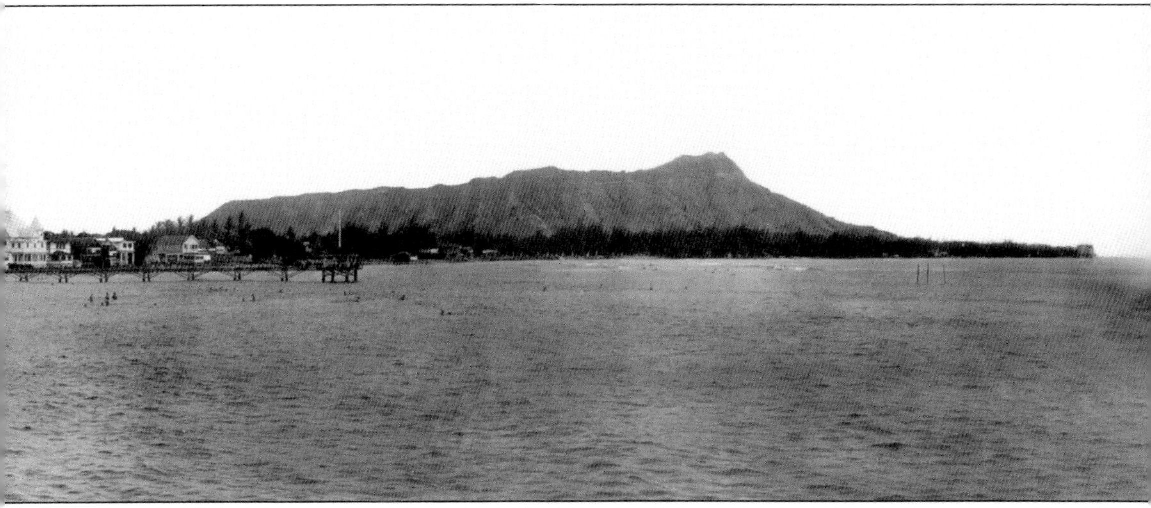

This included the surfing breaks, the construction of the Ala Wai Canal, and the beach areas, which would undergo realignment, widening, and sand replenishment. Rates at the hotels ranged from $4.50 a day at the Moana to $10.00 a week at the Waikiki Inn.

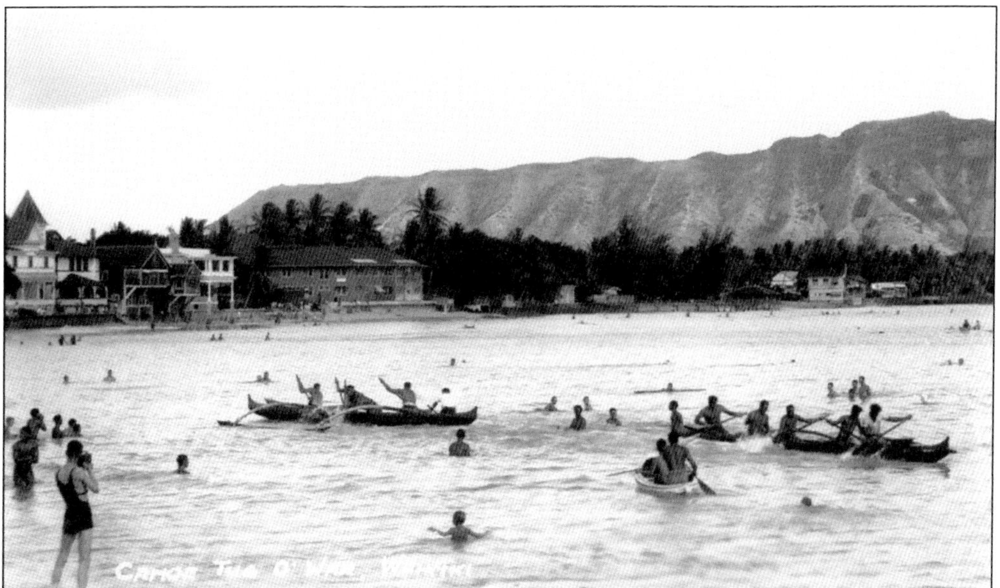

CANOE TUG-OF-WAR, WAIKIKI. The beachboys competed in everything and anything. Some would not only bid passengers good-bye at the docks but would also stay on board the ocean liner and then dive off the ship as it passed by Waikiki to swim miles to shore. Note the photographer with an early Kodak Brownie camera at the water's edge on the left.

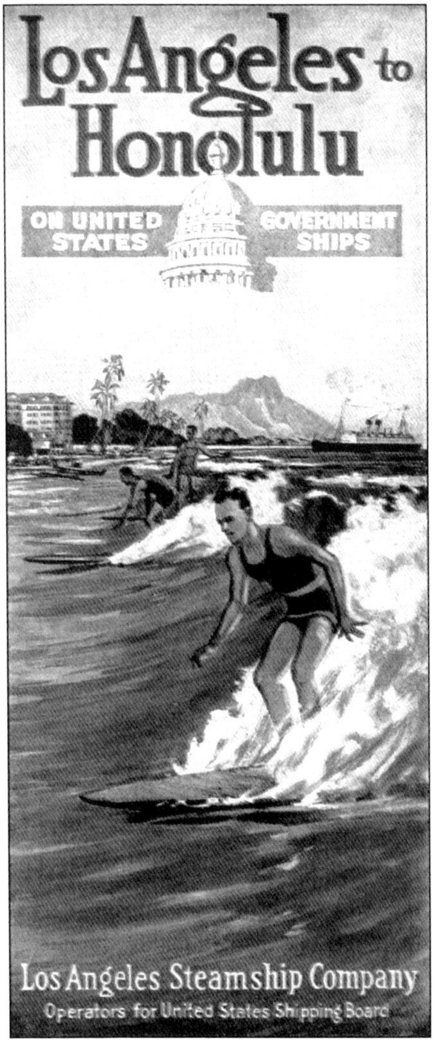

The Los Angeles Steamship Company (LASSCO). This was the first passenger line to originate in Los Angeles and was in competition with the San Francisco–based Matson Navigation Company. LASSCO used two former German Lloyd liners that had been seized during World War I. Note how the advertisement reads, "On United States Government Ships." Throughout the 1920s, LASSCO was famous for its stylish ships, artistic advertisements, and well-heeled movie stars. It even had authentic Hawai'ian sand next to the swimming pool, and notice the entertainment listed on the menu from 1925. In 1927, LASSCO ships carried more passengers to Hawai'i than rival Matson, but by 1931 Matson bought LASSCO after its stock crashed in the Great Depression. (Both courtesy Dan Pincetich.)

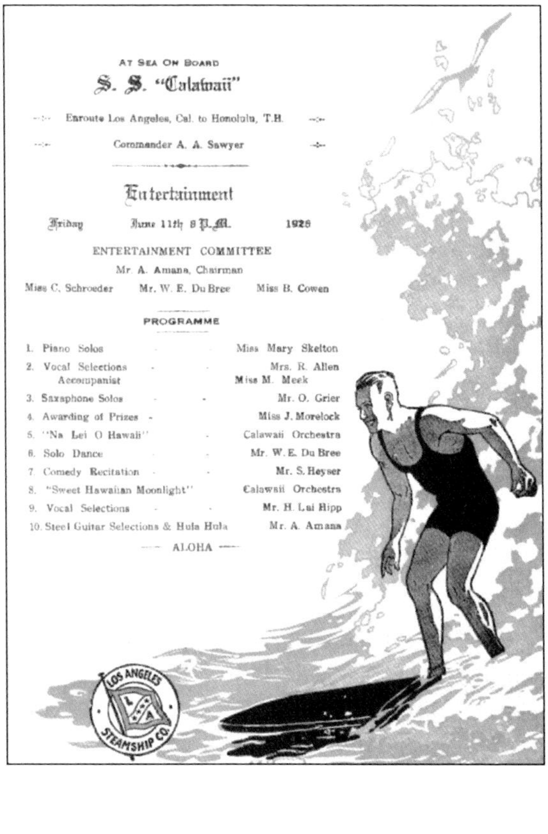
At Sea On Board
S. S. "Calawaii"
Enroute Los Angeles, Cal. to Honolulu, T.H.
Commander A. A. Sawyer

Entertainment
Friday June 11th 8 P.M. 1925

ENTERTAINMENT COMMITTEE
Mr. A. Amana, Chairman
Miss C. Schroeder Mr. W. E. Du Bree Miss B. Cowen

PROGRAMME

1. Piano Solos - Miss Mary Skelton
2. Vocal Selections - Mrs. R. Allen
Accompanist Miss M. Meek
3. Saxaphone Solos - Mr. O. Grier
4. Awarding of Prizes - Miss J. Morelock
5. "Na Lei O Hawaii" - Calawaii Orchestra
6. Solo Dance - Mr. W. E. Du Bree
7. Comedy Recitation - Mr. S. Heyser
8. "Sweet Hawaiian Moonlight" Calawaii Orchestra
9. Vocal Selections - Mr. H. Lai Hipp
10. Steel Guitar Selections & Hula Hula Mr. A. Amana

— ALOHA —

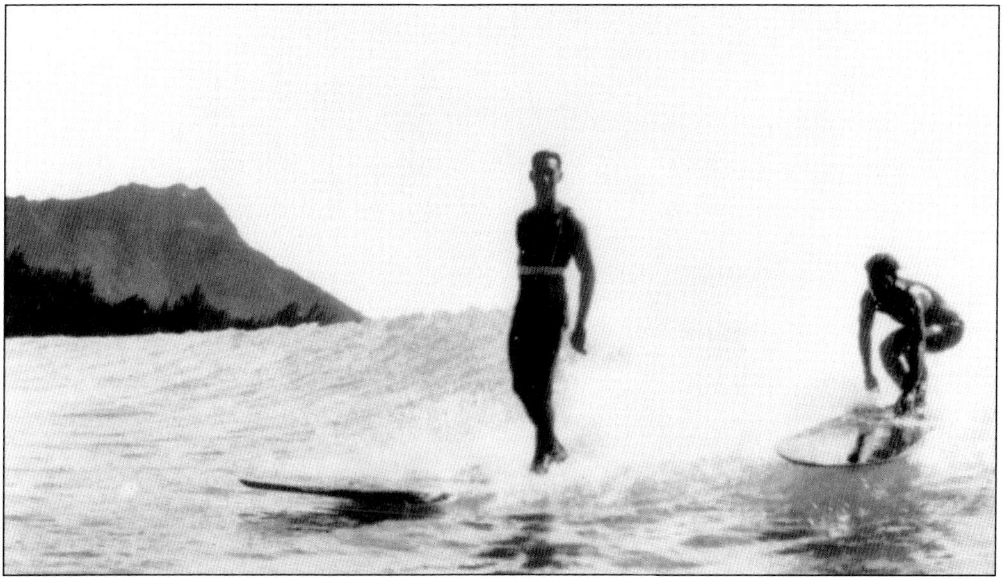

Beachboys and Keiki Playing Around at Waikiki. The Keystone View Company's *On the Sands of Waikiki Beach* states, "Waikiki is the only place in the world where successful surfboarding has been practiced to any great extent. The reason for this is that the contour of the ocean bottom at Waikiki coupled with the location of the protecting coral reefs is such that it supplies just the right kind of continuous surf crests to propel the boards for as far as two miles shoreward on one wave. When one knows how, surfboarding is one of the most thrilling of all water sports." (Above, courtesy Cary Weiss.)

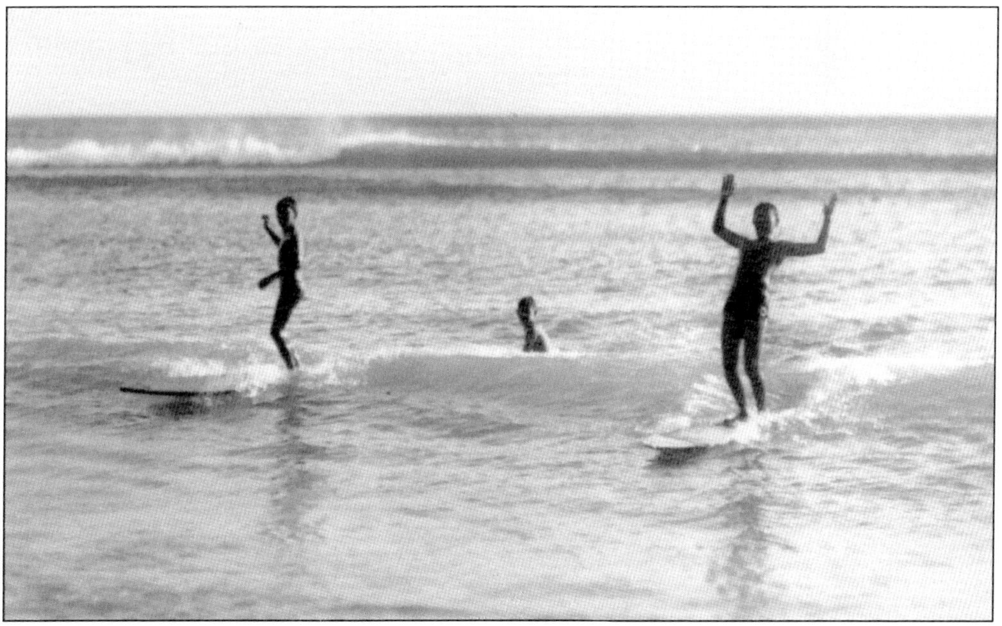

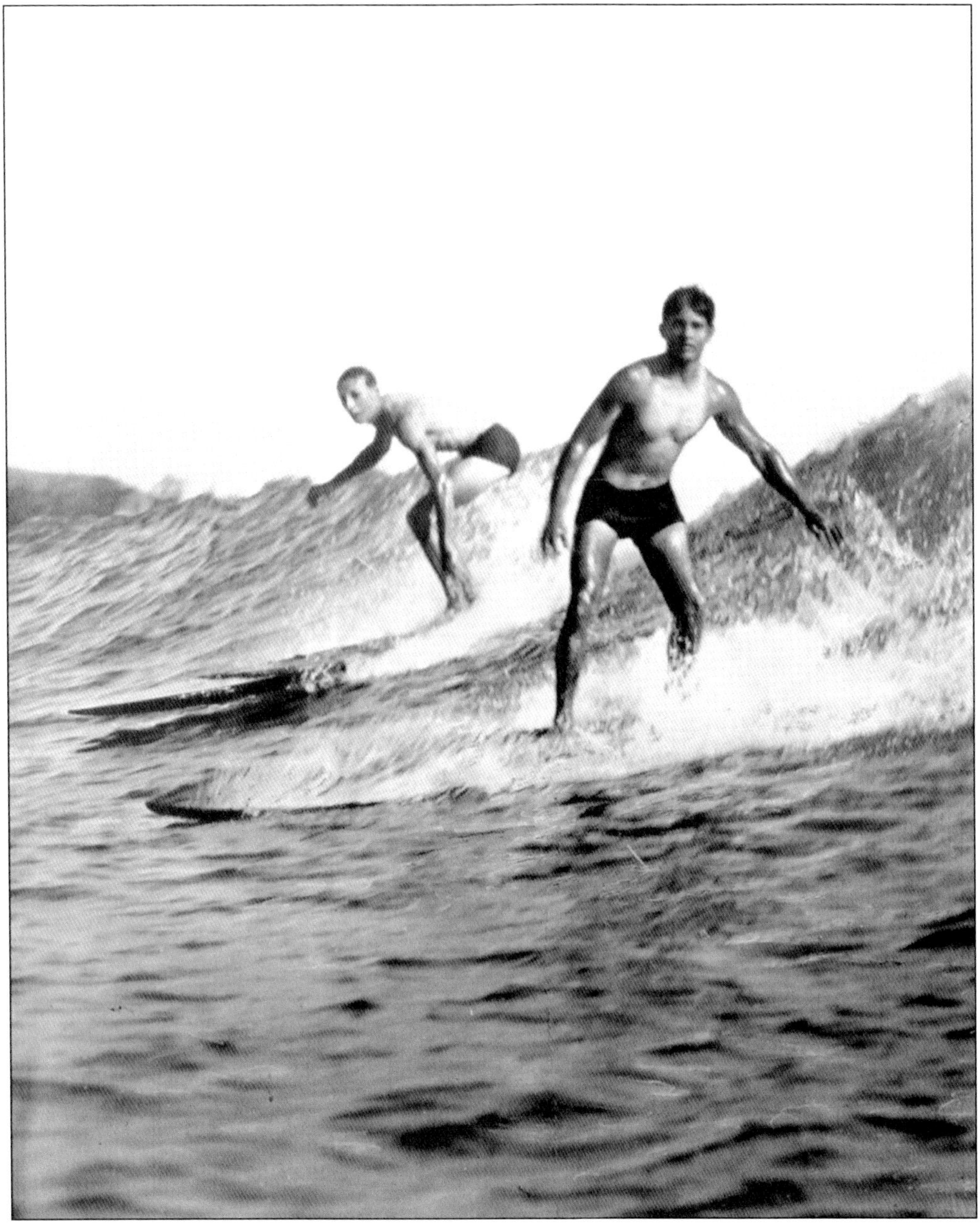

Surfing at Honinou, Hawai'i, July 1924. Iowa native Edward P. Irwin captured this image, and it appeared on the cover of a local publication, possibly the *Crossroads of the Pacific*, a Honolulu weekly of which Irwin was the editor. He was a notorious scrapper. In *Presstime in Paradise: The Life and Times of The Honolulu Advertiser, 1856–1995*, George Chaplin wrote that Irwin "had a fist fight in the Territorial Legislature chamber with Senator David K. Trask, who had demanded an apology for an article that appeared in Irwin's weekly." (Courtesy Hawai'i State Archives.)

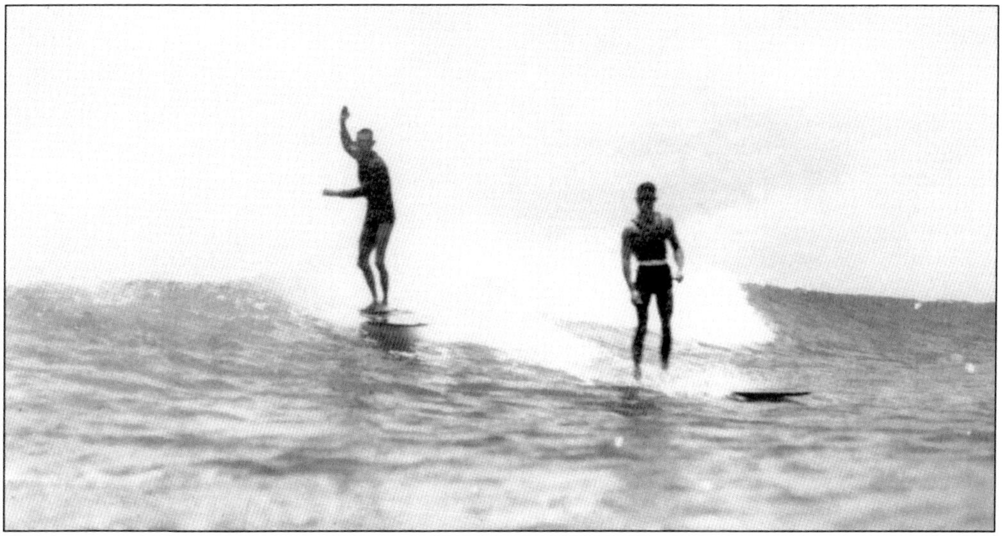

Far Out at Sea, the Expert Guides his Board with Ease. A 1919 *Mid-Pacific Magazine* write-up stated, "Sometimes the wave is caught a mile out at sea and a skilled surfer may hold his wave, standing on his board, until it touches the beach and he steps ashore." According to Tom Blake, Lorrin Thurston introduced the 12-foot surfboard in 1924.

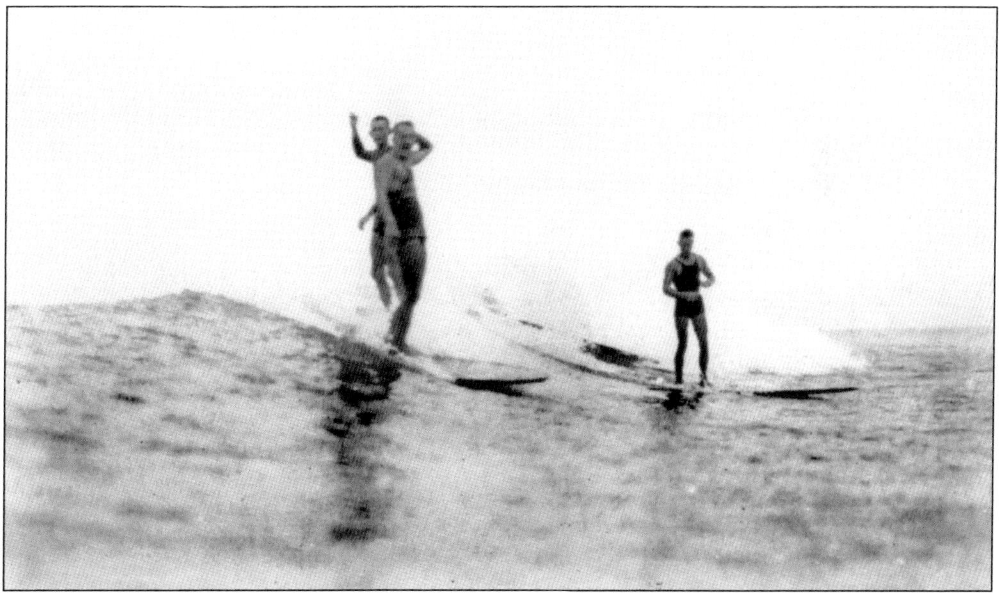

The Beachboys Are at Home Even in the Most Difficult of Surf. "The trick of standing on the surfboard as its is hurled before the wave is the quick lightning-like agility necessary to rise to the feet at perfect balance," stated a 1919 article in *Mid-Pacific Magazine*. Both photographs on this page appear to have been taken the same day and of the same surfers. Notice the loose surfboard behind the surfers.

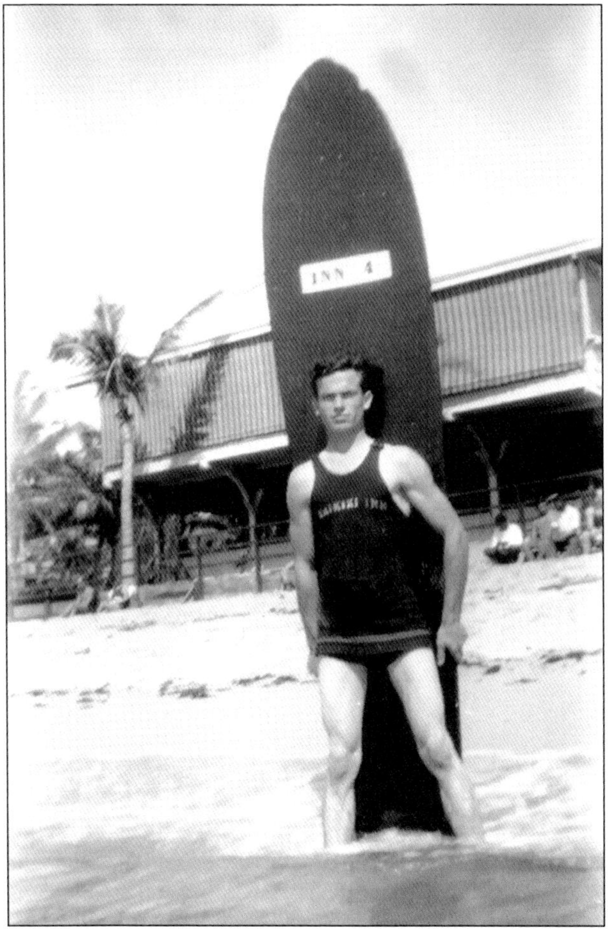

Visitor and a Rental Board from the Waikiki Inn. The inn adjoined Queen Liliuokalani's summer residence facing Queen's Surf, a renowned fast-breaking wave over a shallow reef. Compared to the photograph on page 37, the inn's rental surfboard and style had changed with the times. This unidentified man's swimsuit is probably rented from the inn, along with a robe, a towel, and other beach gear.

Lewis Edwin Capps Captured Surfing in Prose and on Film, 1920. *A Song of Hawai'i*, by Capps, contains two surfing poems and this photograph of a surfer. "The Surf Rider," starts with "Like a sea-bird he rests in the far away / Then suddenly rises with arms outspread / While the spray at his feet in a silver shower / Curves like the wings of the Gull overhead." (Courtesy Joel T. Smith.)

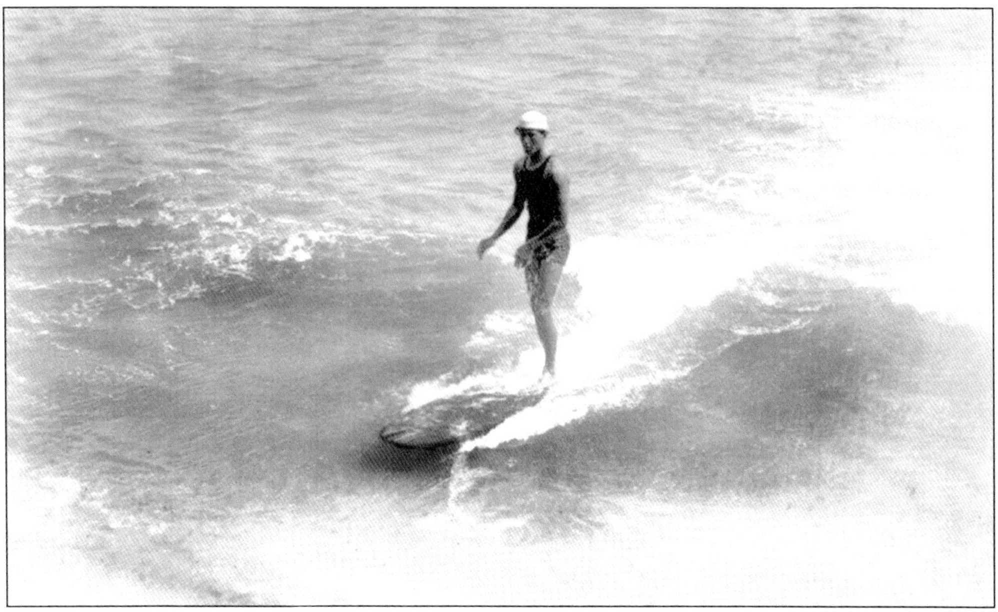

A STREET GUIDE TO THE CITY OF HONOLULU, 1922. Honolulu had grown astronomically because of the flourishing sugar and pineapple plantations. Its population in 1922 had reached 127,000. In 1930, the *Traveler's Guide to Honolulu* remarked, "A day scarcely passes in Hawai'i without sunshine, though there are nearly always scattered clouds over the mountains. Honolulu has, during an average year, 118 clear days, 178 partly cloudy days, and 69 cloudy days." (Courtesy Dan Pincetich.)

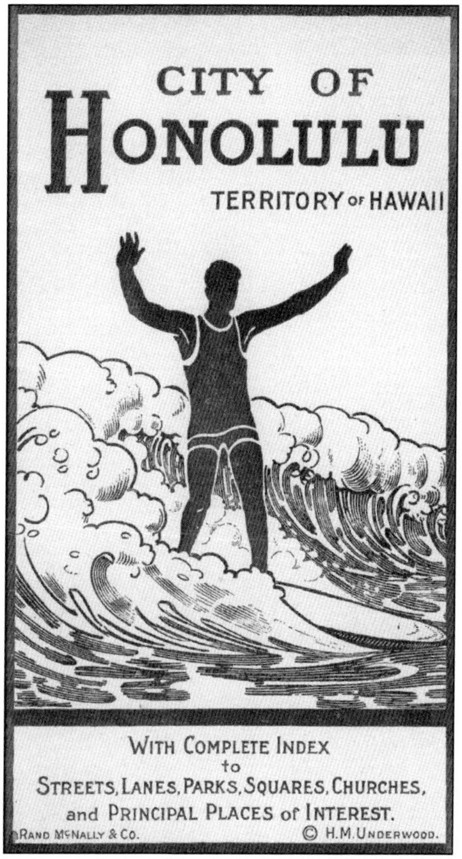

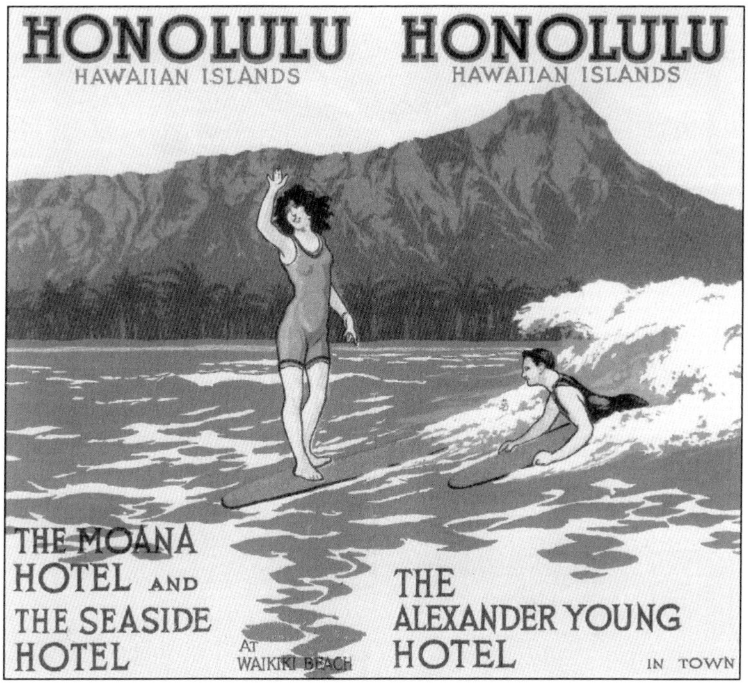

MOANA HOTEL AND THE SEASIDE HOTEL BROCHURE, 1920. The Moana Hotel, located at the world's heart of surfing on Waikiki Beach, quickly capitalized on surfing images to entice tourists. With the Roaring Twenties just ahead, Hawai'ian tourism grew from just 8,000 in 1921 to a pre-Depression peak of 22,000 in 1929 before it crashed. Many tourists never surfed, but they enjoyed watching. (Courtesy Dan Pincetich.)

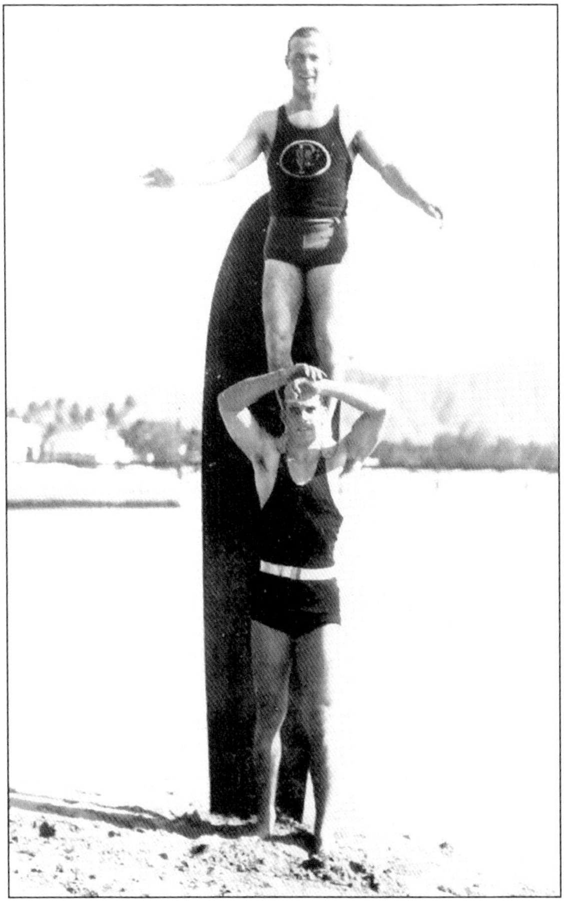

Beach Acrobatics in the 1920s. Visitors and beachboys were always trying out antics while hanging around the beach whenever the surf went flat. (Courtesy Dan Pincetich.)

Beachboy Style. The beachboys by the 1920s had become an institution. They were adored for their water skills, musical ability, playfulness, and willingness to please. With quick smiles and a funny nickname, the beachboys appeared to be relaxed and easygoing; but in reality, they took their jobs very seriously. Without beachboys, Waikiki would be just another beautiful beach.

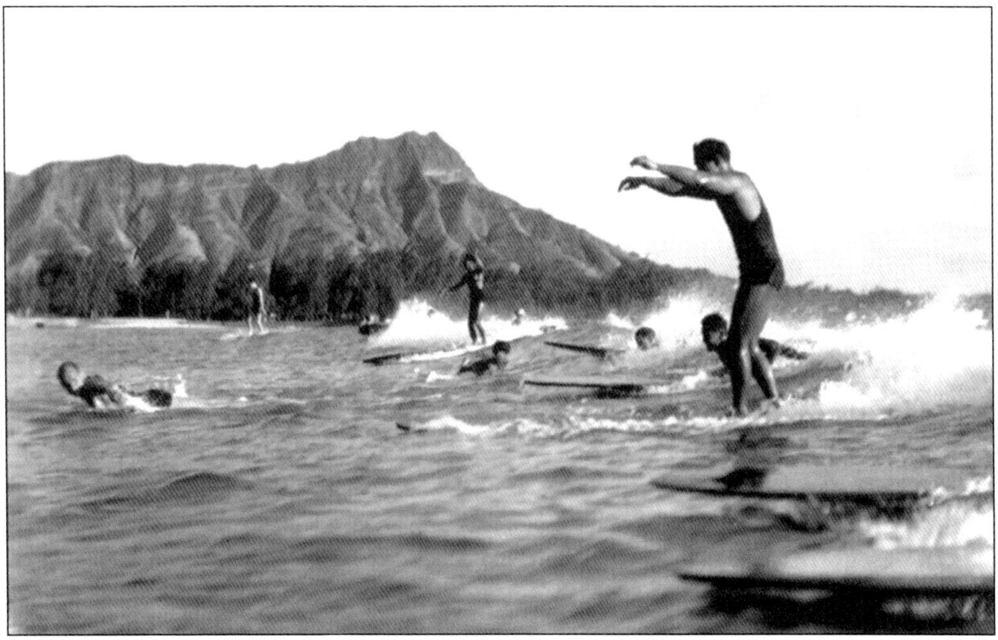

Modeling the "Page Bob," "Dutch," or, Simply Said, the Bob Haircut, Ever So Much the Rage. The bob haircut was created in World War I by female ambulance drivers who, for convenience and sanitation, had their hair lopped off, documented here as three unidentified people pose for the camera. In 1918, Irene Castle, the renowned ballroom dancer (with her husband, Vernon), launched the cut in the United States. The revolutionary short cut was easier for female swimmers and surfers as well.

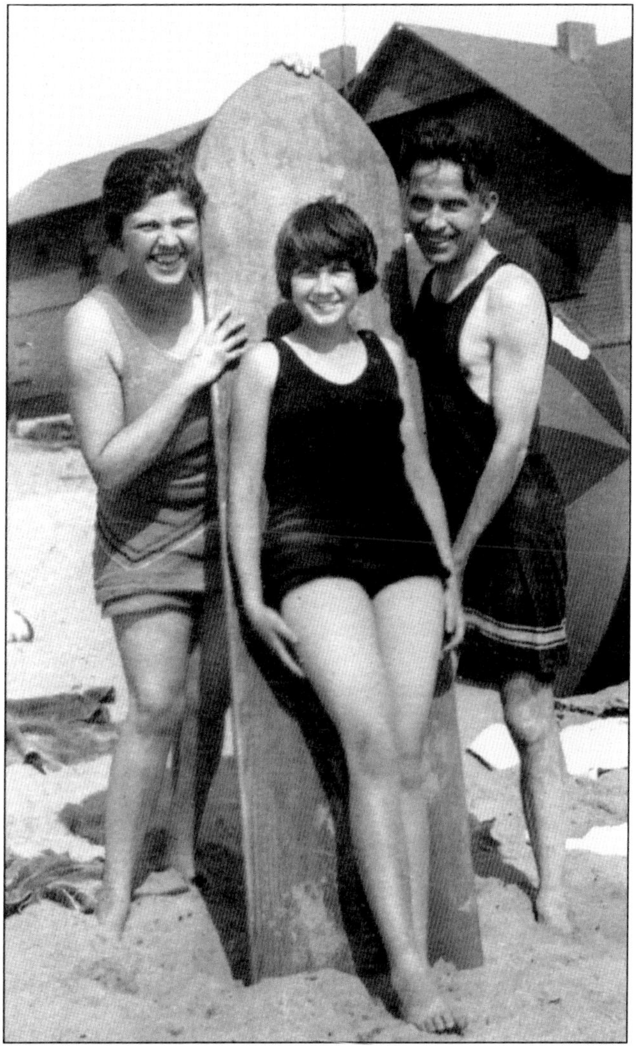

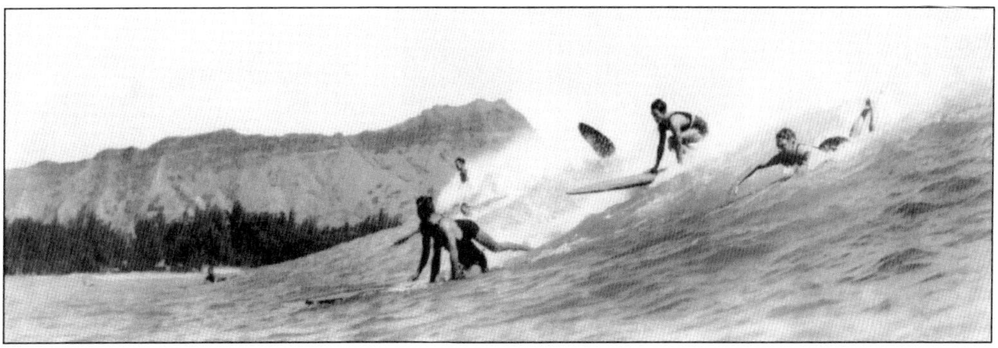

James Williams Captures the Drama of a Perfect Day at Queens Surf, 1924. James Williams took this popular image while he worked for the *Honolulu Advertiser* newspaper. Williams had been the *Advertiser*'s chief photographer until 1920, when he left to take over his father's business, J.J. Williams Studio. James Williams continued to freelance as an *Advertiser* news photographer for many years. He pioneered the use of the sophisticated Graflex camera in Hawai'i.

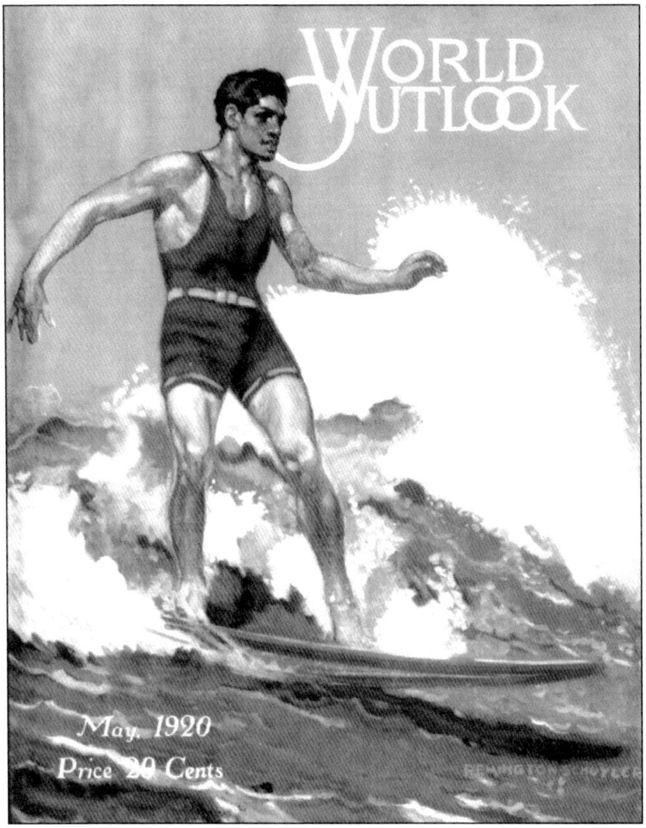

WORLD OUTLOOK MAGAZINE, MAY 1920. This illustration is by Remington Schuyler of Buffalo, New York. A relative of the famous Frederic Remington, Schuyler was classically trained in Europe. His art appeared on many magazine covers, including the *Saturday Evening Post*. Schuyler taught art and was an artist-in-residence at Missouri Valley College in Marshall, Missouri. There is no record the he surfed, but this image shows the latest early-1920s swimsuit fashion.

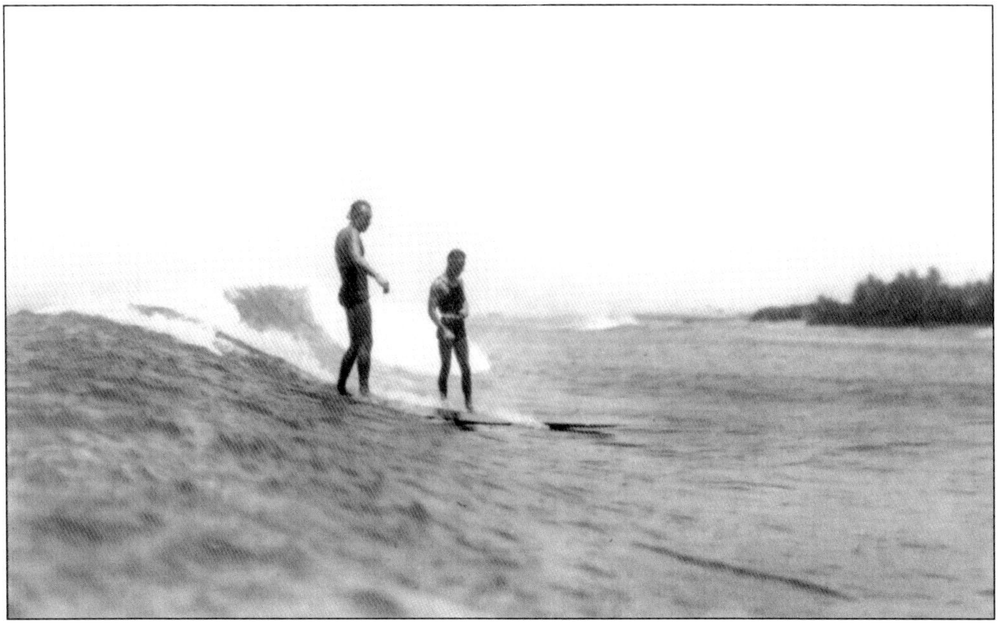

A PERFECT DAY OUTSIDE AT WAIKIKI. This photograph shows that the style of bathing suit shown in the painting by Remington Schuyler was rapidly gaining popularity with the Waikiki crowd. (Courtesy Hawai'i State Archives.)

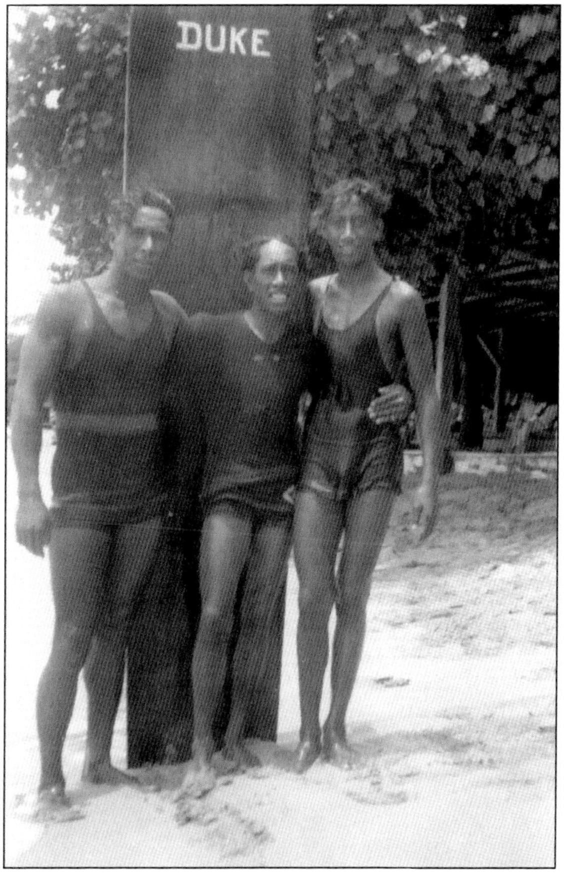

From left to right, a Duke Look-A-Like, William Kahanamoku, and Sargent Kahanamoku Pose. The nine Kahanamoku siblings were very close. Duke was born in 1890, Bill in 1899, and Sarge in 1910; all were champion sprint swimmers. Bill had two nicknames, "Ollofella" and "Tarball." Sarge was given his name when his father was promoted to sergeant with the Honolulu Police Department. (Courtesy Outrigger Canoe Club.)

Keiki Practice Their Style at Malihini Surf. Malihini means "newcomer" in Hawai'ian. Here it refers to the easy, or baby, surf where keiki and tourists first began surfing. *Mid-Pacific Magazine* in 1919 stated, "Children of five and six years of age own and operate their surfboards at Waikiki. They begin in the small surf that sweeps up to the beach and later tackle the big big rollers on the reef." (Courtesy Cary Weiss.)

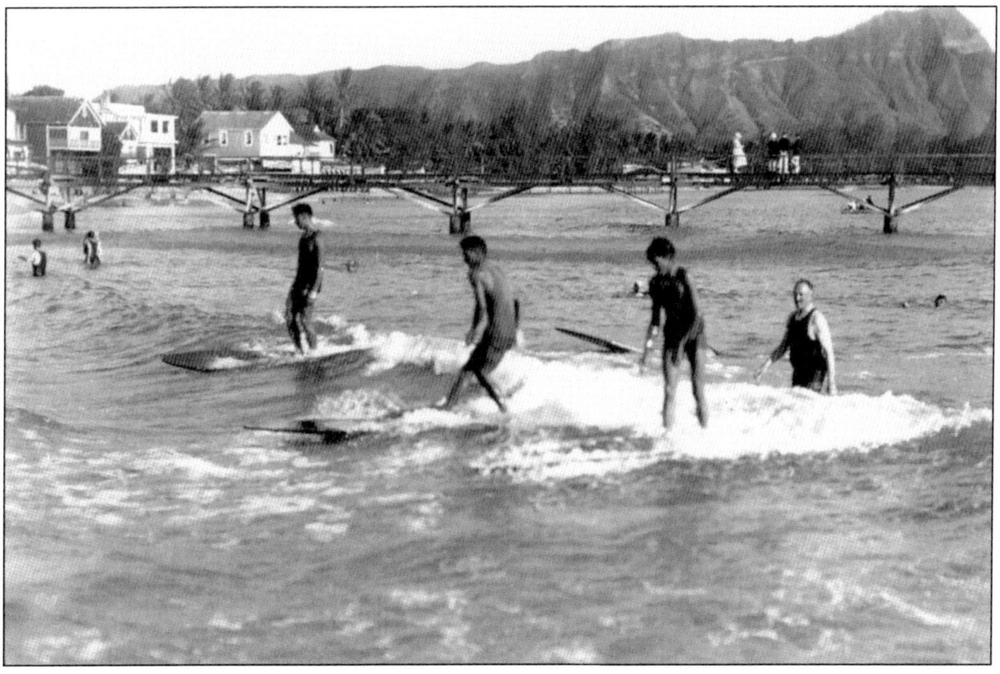

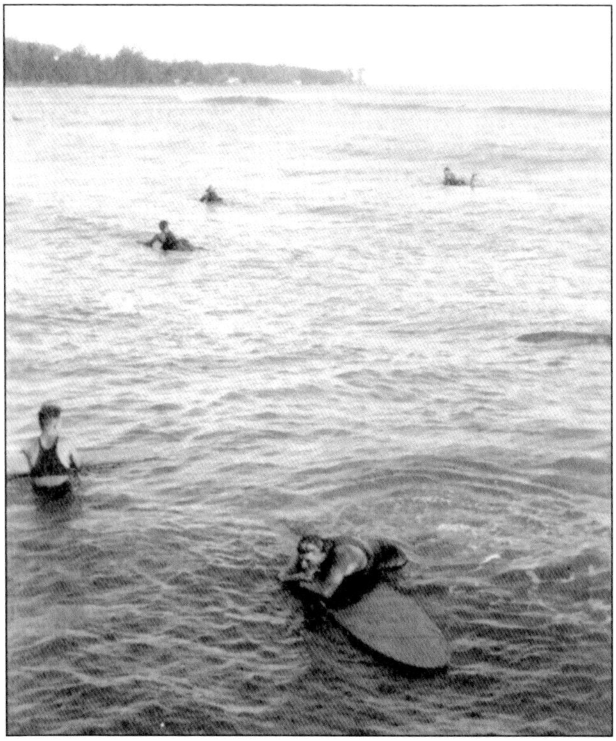

A Zen Moment. This view from the Moana Pier shows how surfing teaches meditation by the act of waiting for the next set of waves, allowing contemplation on the meaning of life, on how to master a newly learned surfing move, or simply checking out the surfing babes.

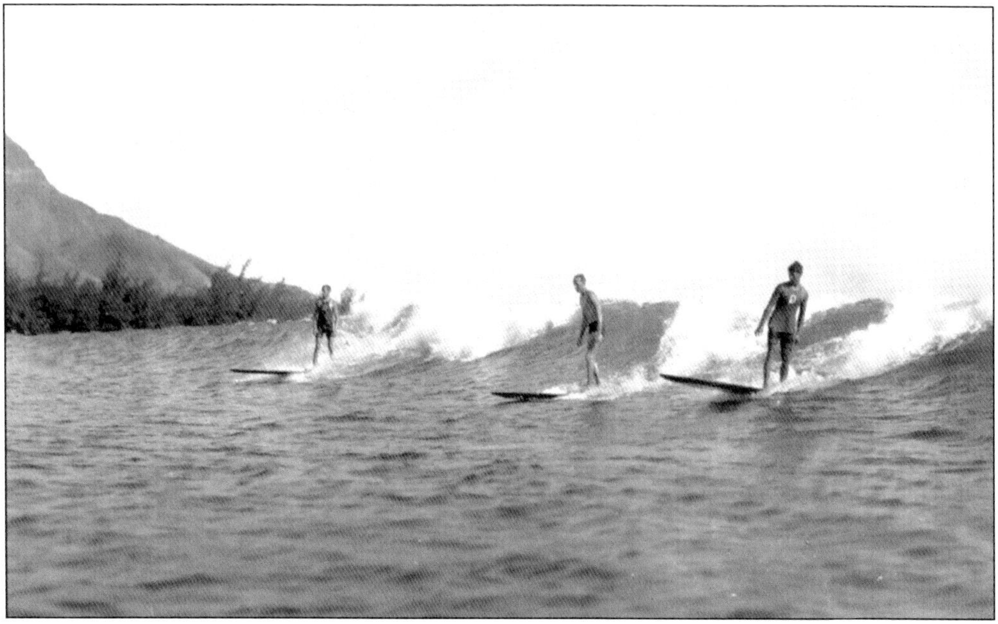

"Riding the Surf at Waikiki, Honolulu." A 1924 article in *National Geographic Magazine* states, "The swimmer with his surfboard . . . works his way out to where the high rollers rise. Selecting his wave, he gets his boat underway by paddling furiously with his hands and feet, and at the proper moment, mounting a high wave, throws himself on the board just as it is seized by the force of the onrushing water, which carries him with race-horse speed toward the beach." (Photograph by R.K. Bonine.)

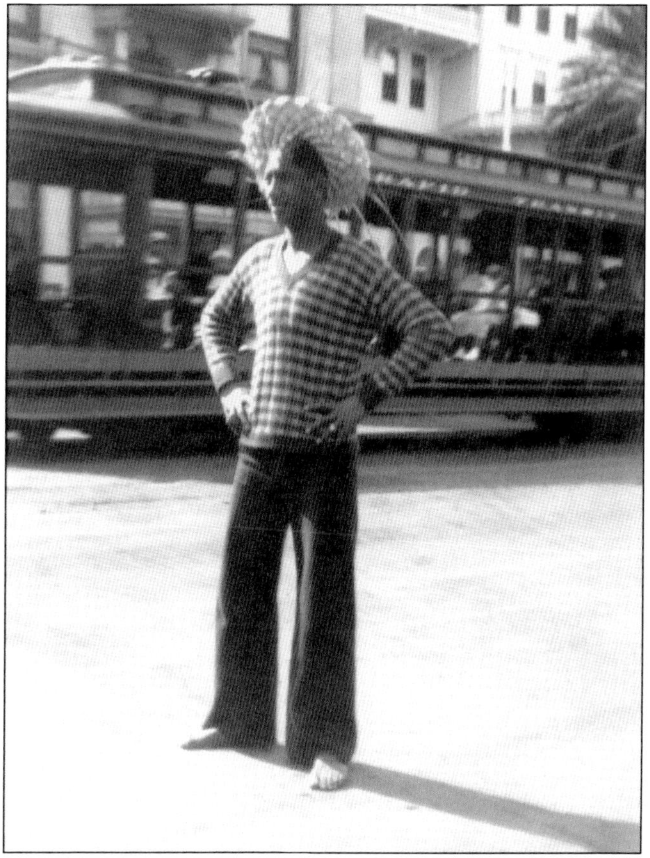

George "Tough Bill" Keaweamahi on Kalakaua Avenue in Front of the Moana Hotel. Tough Bill got his name by popping the cap off beer bottles with his thumbs in the days when most people thought a bottle opener was necessary. A person would have to be a beach regular to know why he was called Bill, as well as why fellow beachboy Louis Hale was called "Sally." (Courtesy Cary Weiss.)

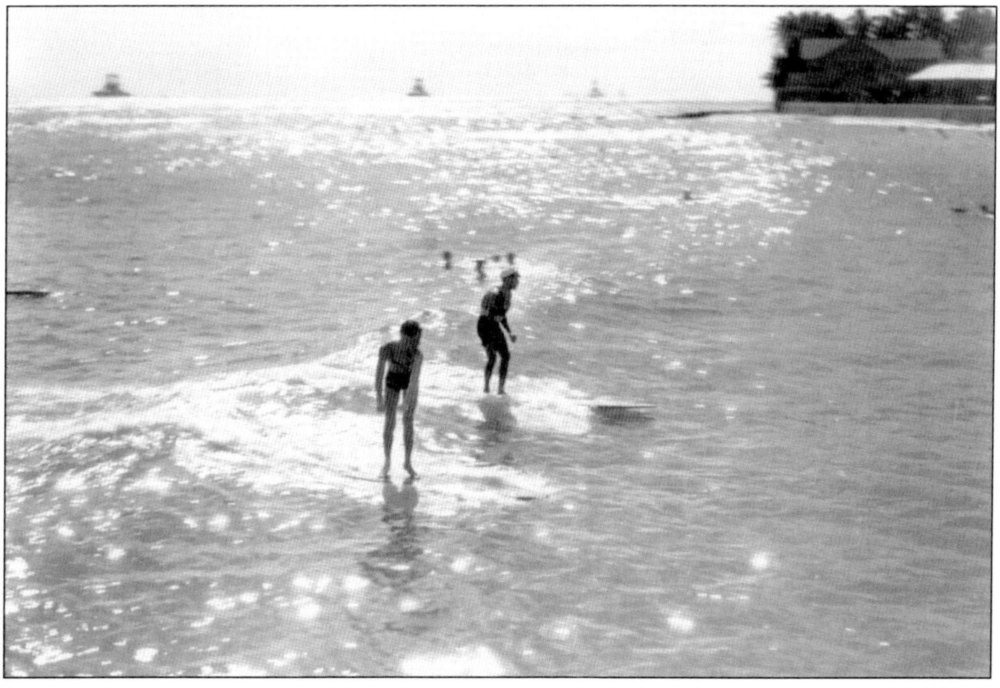

Surfing to the West of Moana Pier. The surfer with the captain's hat probably is beachboy Sally Hale, who would eventually in 1934 become the "captain" of the Outrigger Canoe Club's beach services and guest amenities, the Waikiki Beach Patrol. The photographer for the SS *Resolute* captured this photograph on the ship's world cruise in 1928.

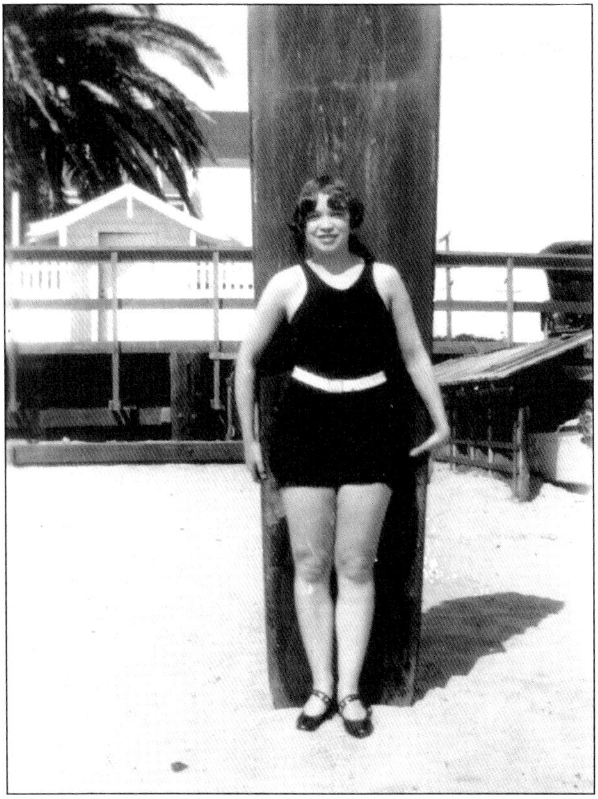

A THOROUGHLY MODERN WOMAN AND HER SURFBOARD. With her bob hairdo, stylish white belt, and polished shoes, this unidentified girl would turn heads at the beach. (Courtesy Cary Weiss.)

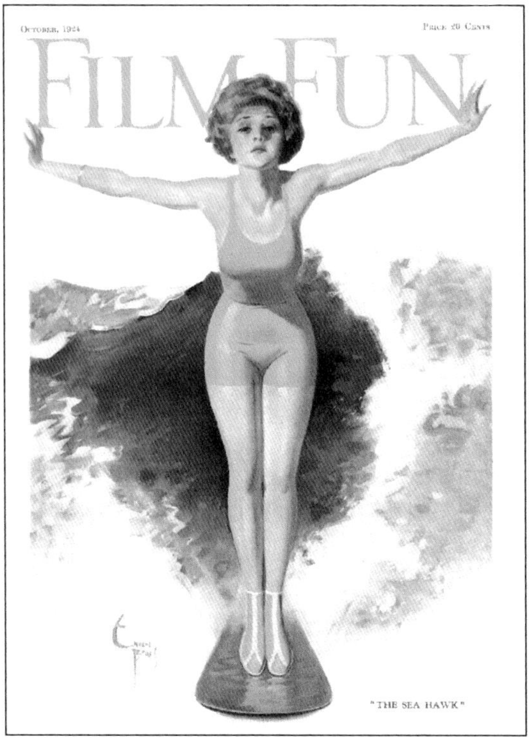

THE SEA HAWK, 1924. Florida-born Enoch Bolles was renowned for his "Bolles girls" in *Film Fun Magazine*. In 1923, he became the cover artist for *Film Fun* and drew over 200 covers until *FFM*'s demise in 1943, when the magazine was declared "salacious" by the Post Office Department.

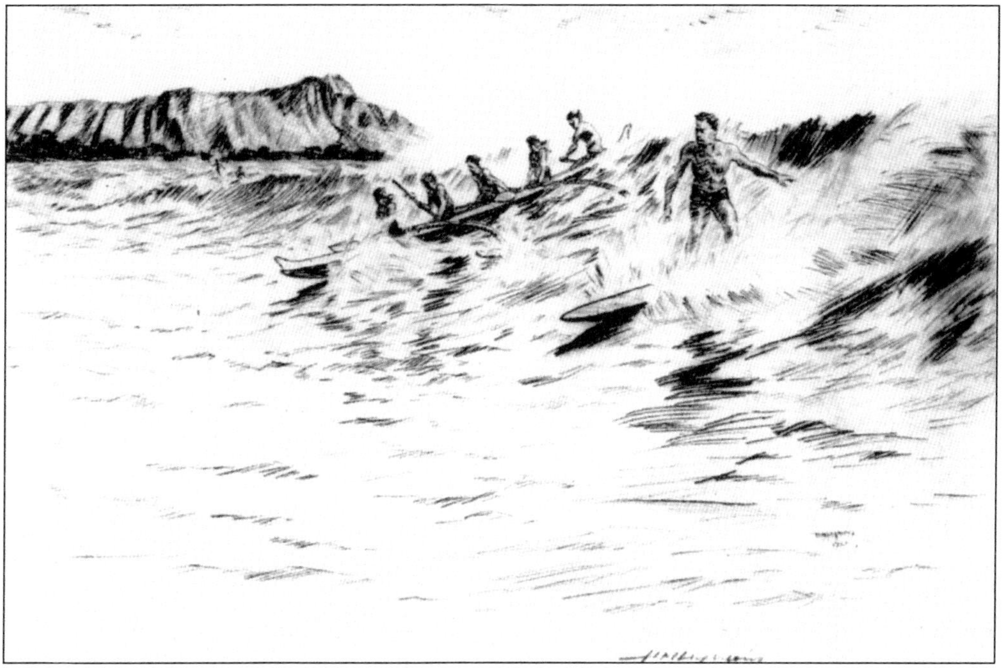

THE FIRST FINE ART SURFING IMAGES CREATED AND SOLD BY ESTABLISHED ARTISTS. Huc Luquiens's *Surfer* (above) is a drypoint etching on paper done in 1921. Luquiens was a successful portrait painter in New England before he came to Hawaii in 1917. His major focus was on drypoint etching, drawing lines into a copper plate with shading, and images produced from black ink falling into the carved lines in the plate. *A Single Surfer, Duke Kahanamoku* (below) was done in 1921 by Charles W. Bartlett. Bartlett was 57 when he arrived in Hawaii in 1917. An artist classically trained in Europe, he was working with Shozaburo Watanabe of Tokyo in woodblocks. Of the over 50 color woodblock prints that Bartlett and Watanabe produced from 1917 to 1928, only three subjects were Hawai'ian, and two of these were of surfing. (Both courtesy Dan Pincetich.)

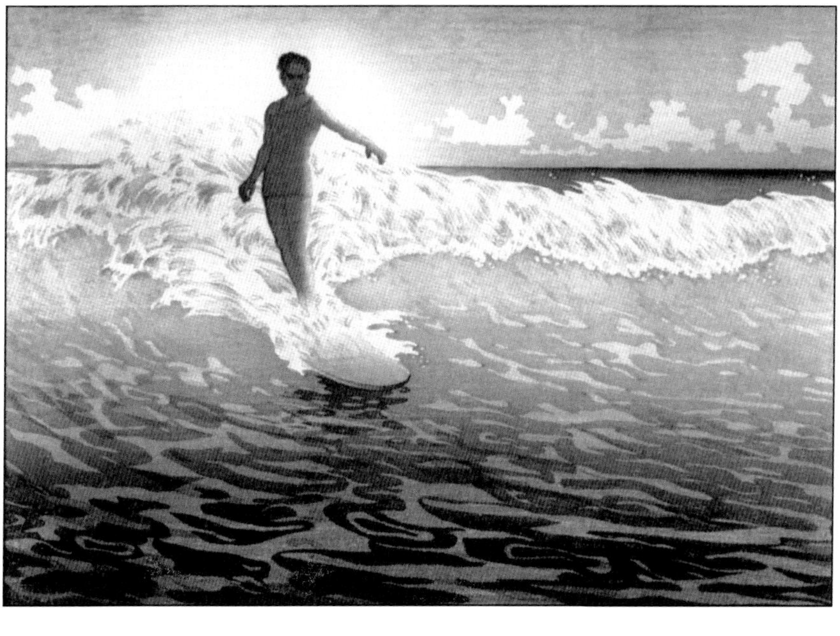

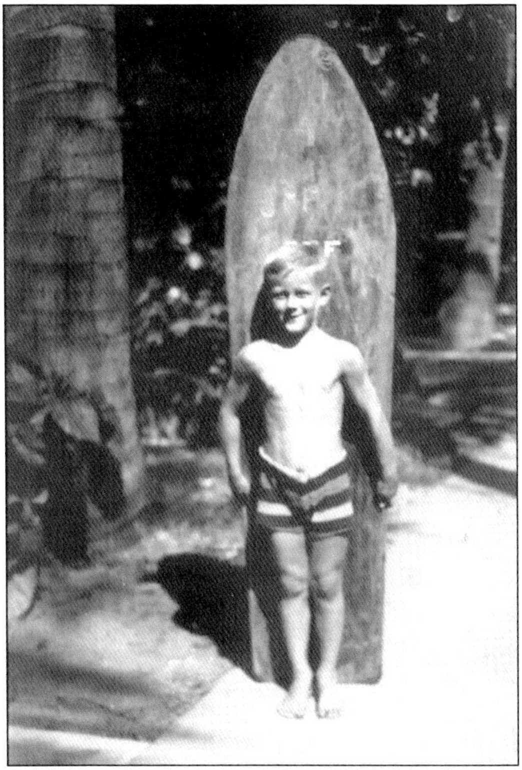

J.T.F.'s Surfboard, Honolulu. Probably nobody knows who J.T.F. was, but he stands proudly in front of his most prized possession. Boards sported names, initials, and even elaborate paintings in the days of wood. To surf is an ageless experience, with devotees ranging from little children to nonagenarians.

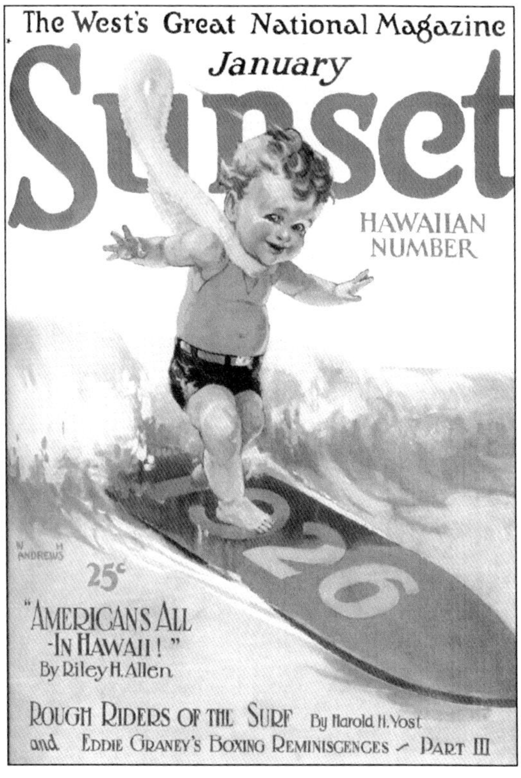

The New Year Baby *Surfing into* 1926. This illustration by W.H. Andrews gave *Sunset* magazine its perfect icon for the January "Hawai'ian Number." (Courtesy of Sunset Publication Corporation.)

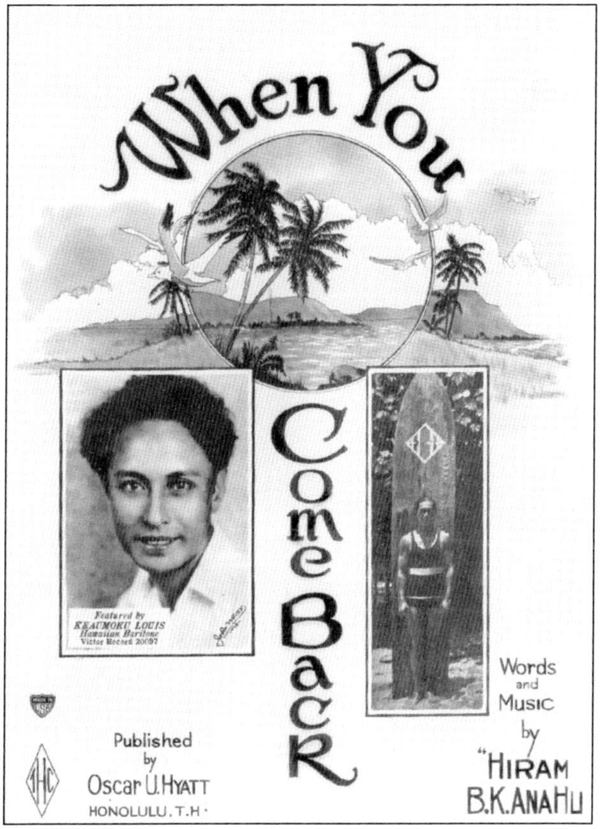

"When You Come Back," Words and Music by Beachboy Hiram B.K. Anahu, 1925. Hapa-haole music was "good, fun kine music" as the beachboys would say in pidgin. Beachboys flirted with and serenaded adoring wahine when they played under the Moana Pavilion or on the Moana Pier. (Courtesy Dan Pincetich.)

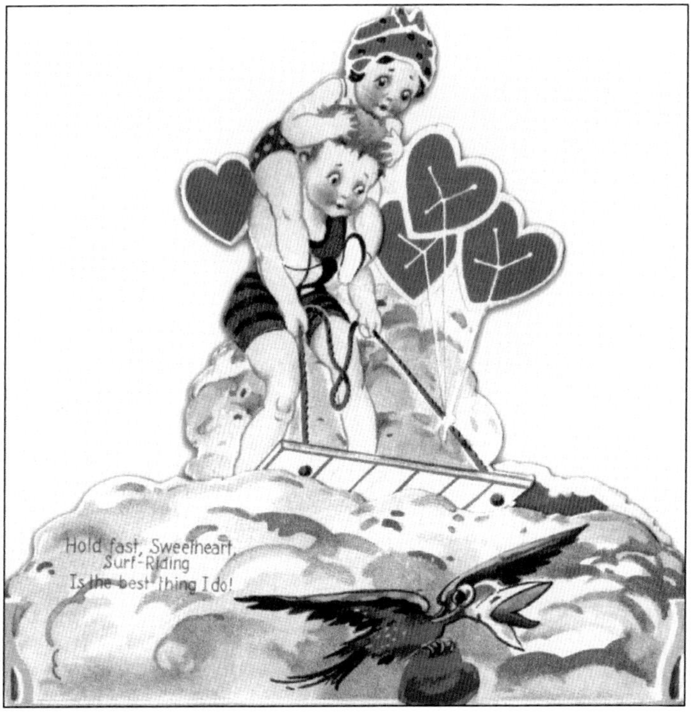

Hold Fast, Sweetheart, Surf Riding Is the Best Thing I Do. This novelty c. 1924 Valentine's Day card was made in 3-D. Around 1920, a new surf-riding fad began—even on lakes with no waves—pulling a modified surfboard behind a motorboat.

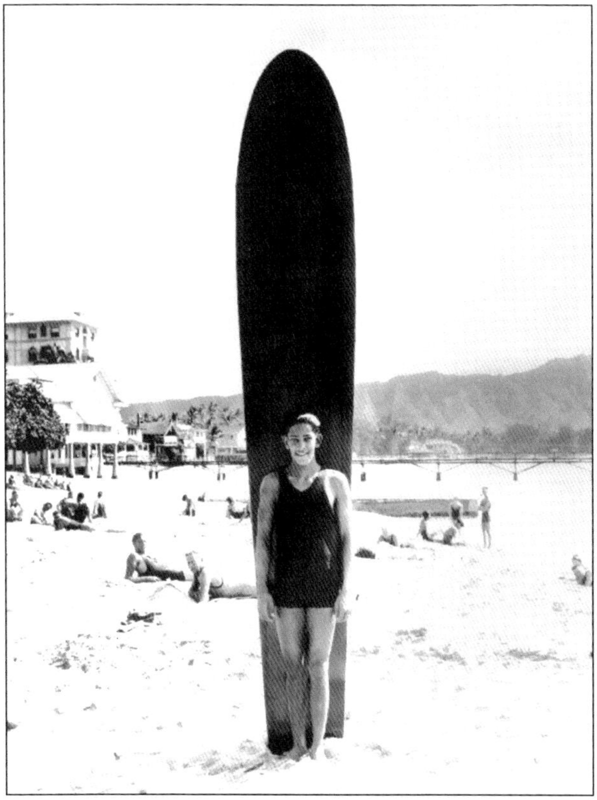

Paddleboard Champ Tom Keakona. L.E. Edgeworth snapped Outrigger Canoe Club's Keakona, who was the world record holder until Tom Blake won on the Ala Wai in 1929. In that race, Blake introduced his hollowed-out paddleboard. Keakona refused to compete, declaring it was unfair to use such light equipment against the solid wooden surfboards. (Courtesy Outrigger Canoe Club.)

Outrigger Canoe Club Paddlers in Surfboard Races on Ala Wai Canal, January 1927. They are, from left to right, Gordon Corson, Dorothy Waters, Hans Bahr, Fred Steere, ? Gillis, Helen Moses, Gay Harris, Whitey Hess, Edric Cook, and Tom Keakona. OCC member Corson won the Boys 16 and Under Division and continued to compete in swimming races into his 60s. (Photograph by L.E. Edgeworth, courtesy Hawai'i State Archives.)

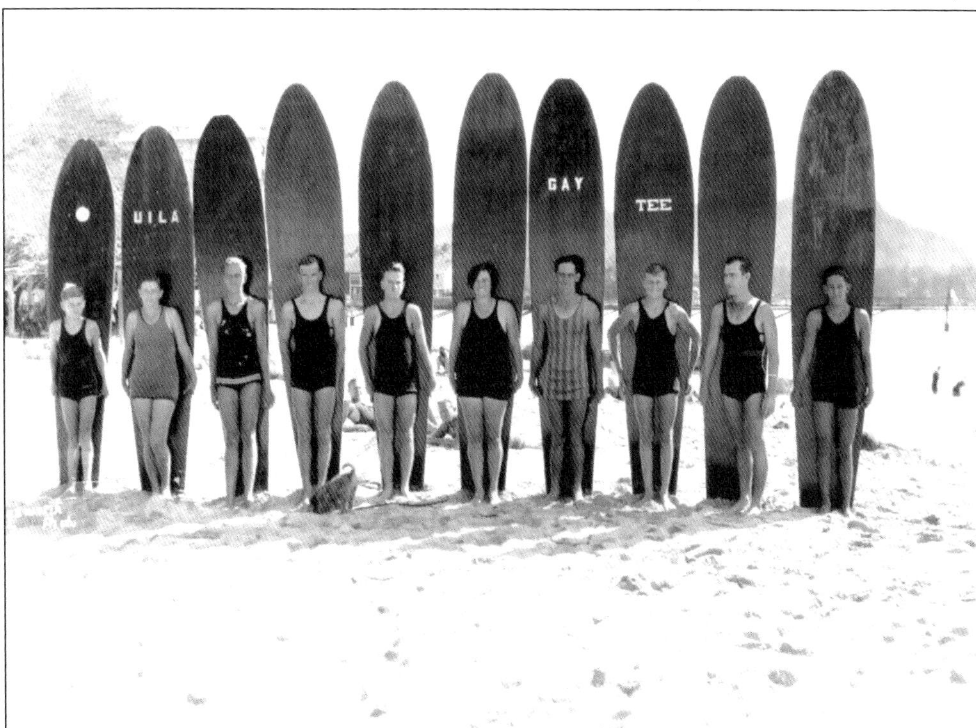

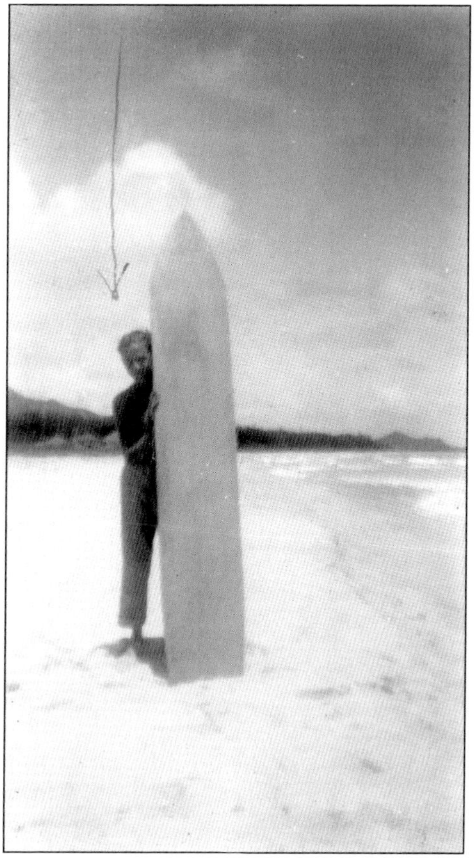

"ME AT 14." A young, unidentified surfer's pride is evident. This is countryside compared to town, as Waikiki was and is called. Kaneohe, Oahu, around 1925 was quite remote. Hawai'ian surfing photographs pre-1930 are extremely rare outside of Waikiki, as are even other "country" photographs. Images from neighbor islands are even more unusual.

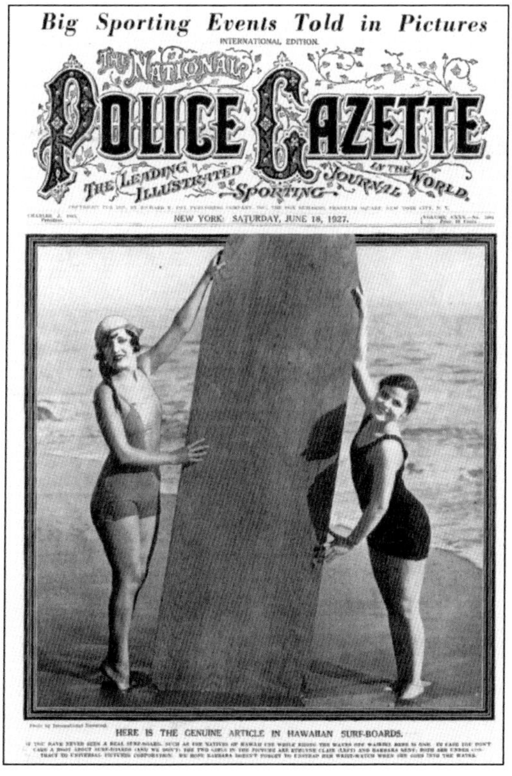

Big Sporting Events Told in Pictures

INTERNATIONAL EDITION.

THE NATIONAL POLICE GAZETTE

THE LEADING ILLUSTRATED SPORTING JOURNAL IN THE WORLD.

NEW YORK, SATURDAY, JUNE 18, 1927.

HERE IS THE GENUINE ARTICLE IN HAWAIIAN SURF-BOARDS.

"HERE IS THE GENUINE ARTICLE IN HAWAI'IAN SURFBOARDS." In a 1927 *National Police Gazette*, the caption reads, "If you have never seen a real surf-board, such as the natives of Hawai'i use while riding the waves off Waikiki, here is one. In case you don't care a hoot about surf-boards (and we don't) the two girls in the picture are Ethlyne Clair (left) and Barbara Bent." (Courtesy Cary Weiss.)

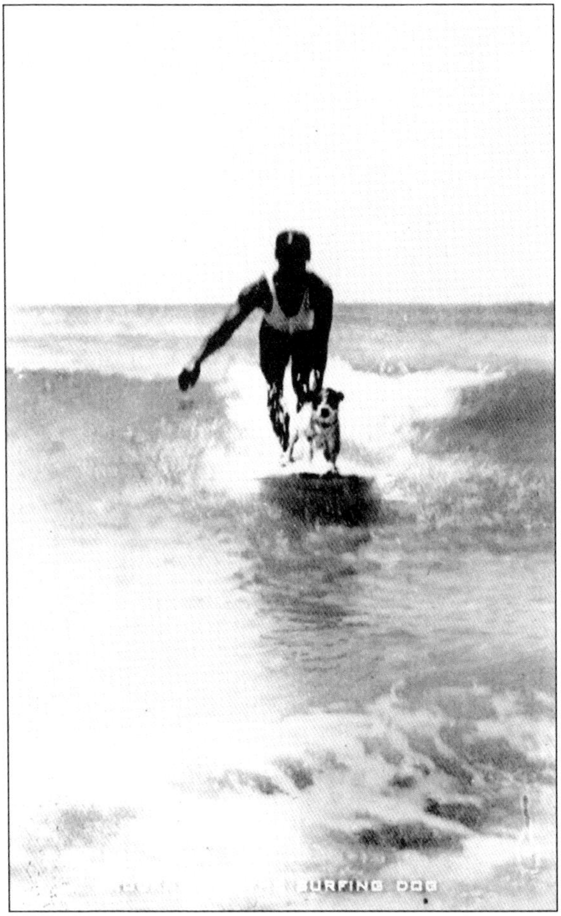

Surfing Dog Rockne and His Beachboy. There have always been surfing dogs—and even a pig or two. Another famous surfing dog from this era was Night Hawk. Of course, they only went surfing with a human aboard. This popular postcard was sent back home by an amazed tourist.

The Most Dangerous Moment in Surfing. While paddling back out to where one catches the big combers, many a time the most dangerous part is making it past the charge of incoming surfers. It appears that the surfer on the left is pondering doing a "turtle dive," where he will roll over the surfboard and hang on underwater, hoping not to get clobbered. (Courtesy Outrigger Canoe Club.)

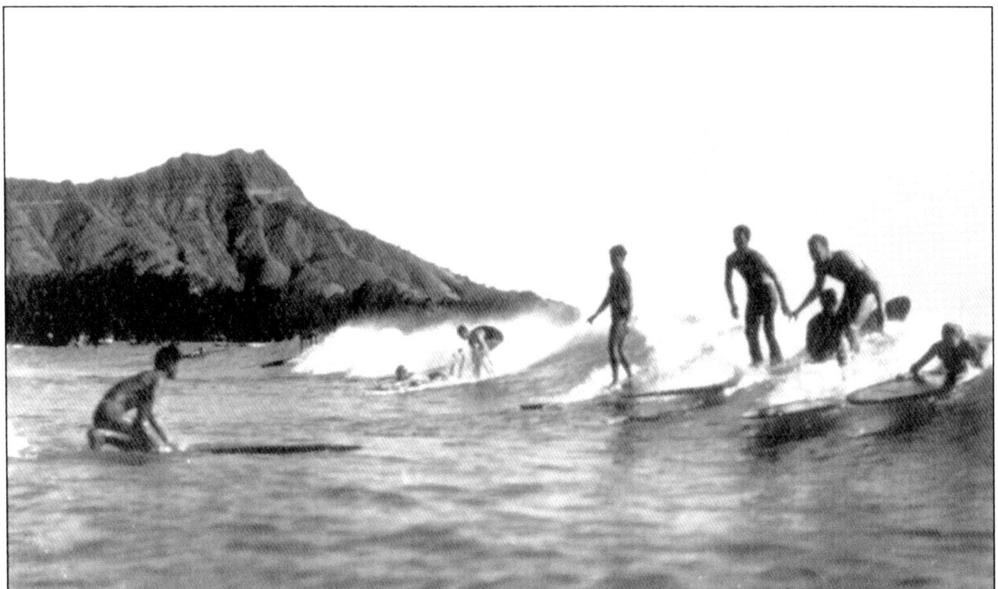

SS *Matsonia* Souvenir Passenger List. The menu text inside reads, "Waikiki Beach, Honolulu, is the home of surf-riding. Surfboards are anywhere from six to ten feet long, made of oiled or varnished redwood, and weighing from forty pounds up. With a good surf running, the rider will be carried shoreward at twenty-five to thirty miles an hour, just ahead of the wave."

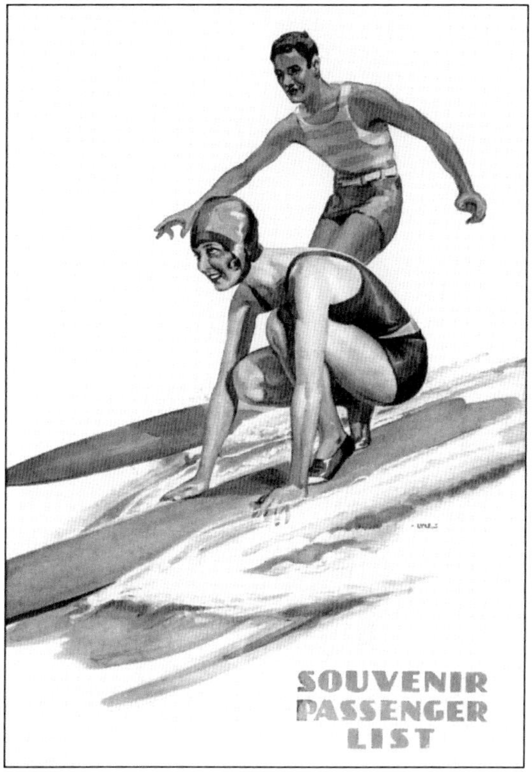

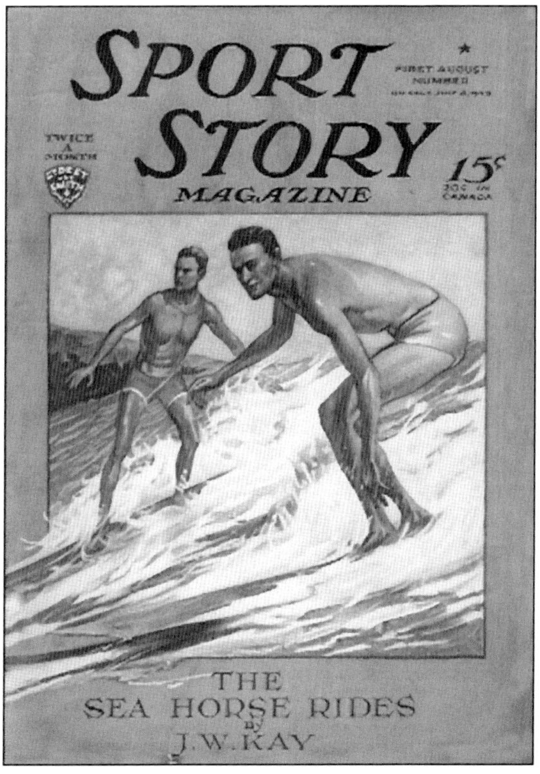

"The Sea Horse Rides." Surfing became mainstream when major sports publisher Street & Smith put out enticing issues such as this. *Sport Story* ran from 1929 to 1943. Once a major publishing house, Street & Smith may be best known for its American sports bibles—the Street & Smith's sports annuals. The company's range of publications also included comics, magic and adventure books, and *Mademoiselle* magazine. Ocean waves were often compared to galloping horses with flying manes.

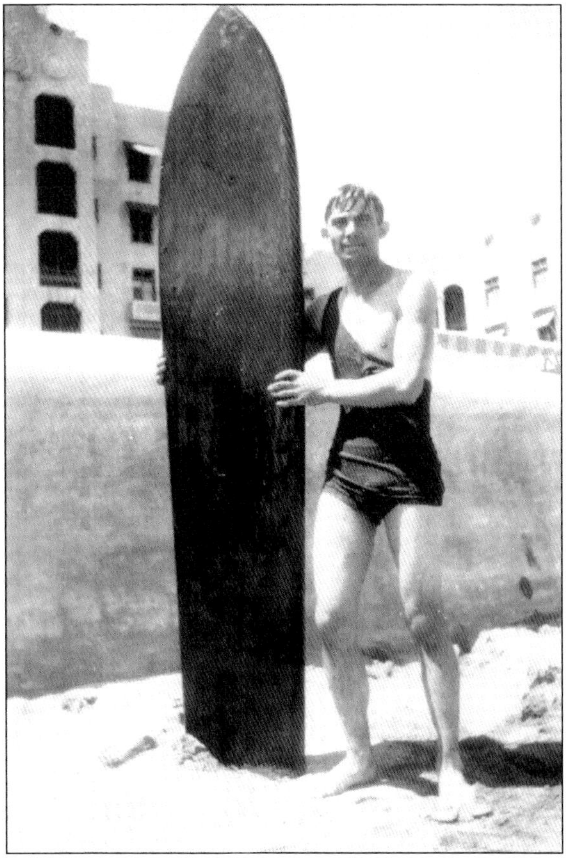

A Tourist Wants to Remember These Moments. The luxurious Royal Hawaiian, owned by Matson Navigation Lines, had 400 rooms. This doubled the number of available rooms for tourists at Waikiki and spurred more growth. It was called "royal" because the hotel was on the site of a former king's summer home. Some of the original coconut trees were still there. (Courtesy Cary Weiss.)

An Unknown Surfer Shows Some Classic Style. In the 1926 book *My Dear! He Says Hawaii is American!!*, Samuel G. Blythe writes, "All you have to do is paddle out atop the surf board . . . wait for a wave and come in a-whooping, riding on the crest of the wave like whatever it is that rides atop wave crest—like a Kanaka beach boy, let us say—a picture of grace, of daring, of muscular beauty."

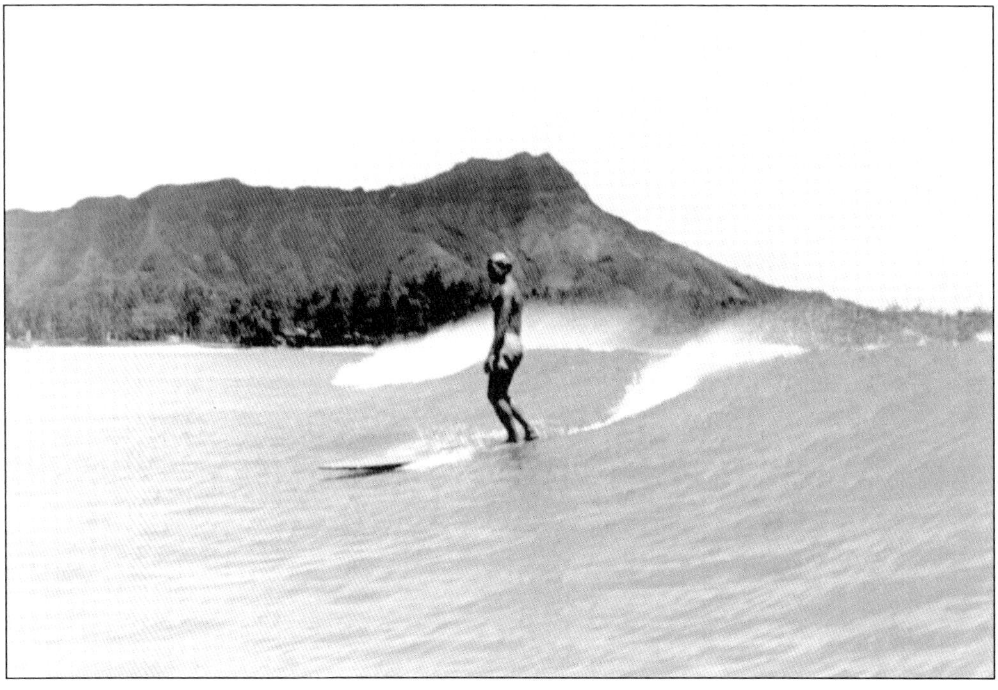

A Good Ride, 1930. Armstrong Sperry's drawing of a wahine enjoying the surf at Waikiki appeared on the cover of *St. Nicholas* magazine in September 1930. The popular children's magazine was published from 1873 to 1940. Sperry loved Polynesia and was an assistant to Bishop Museum head Kenneth Emory. Sperry won the 1941 Newbery Medal for *Call It Courage*, a children's classic.

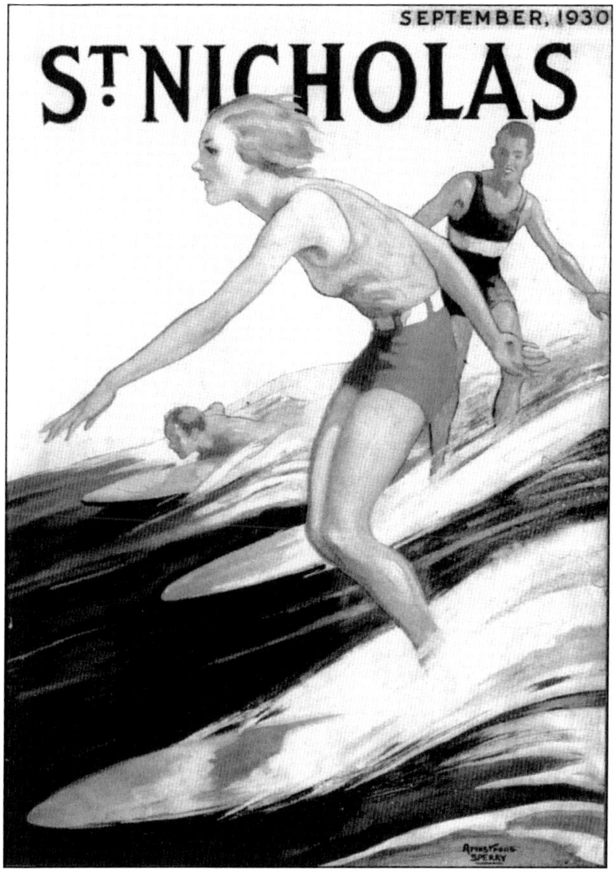

The Lineup Included a Wahine Hanging on for Dear Life to a Beachboy. "I turned my attention to surfing, to riding in atop the glistening breakers that scatter their pearls on the golden sands of the beach at Waikiki, as the advertisements say: riding in on a surfboard as the bronzed and graceful beachboys ride in," stated Samuel G. Blythe in *My Dear! He Says Hawaii is American!!* (Courtesy Outrigger Canoe Club.)

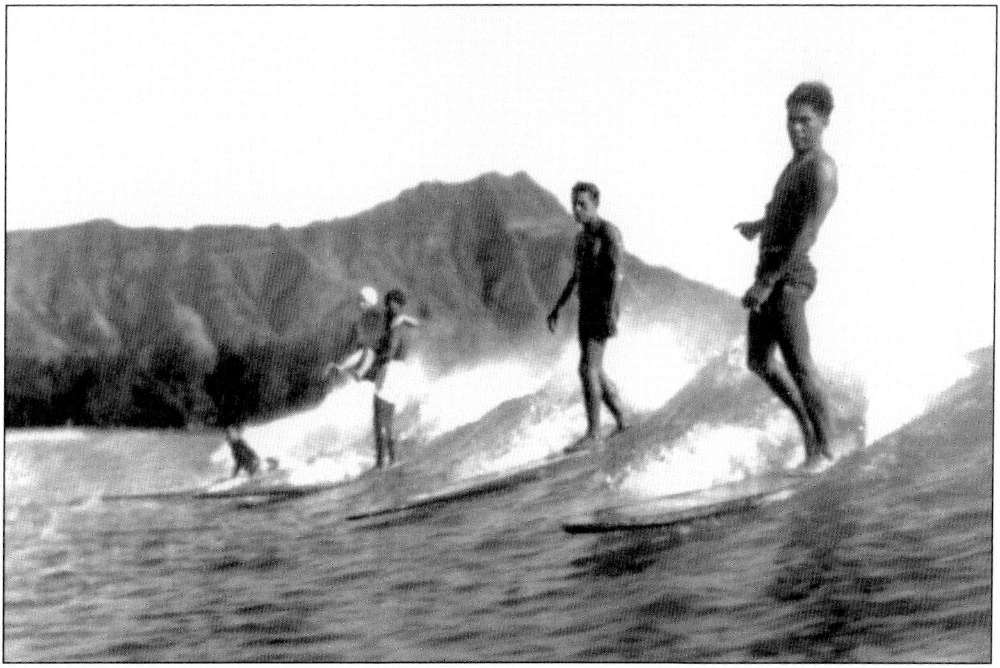

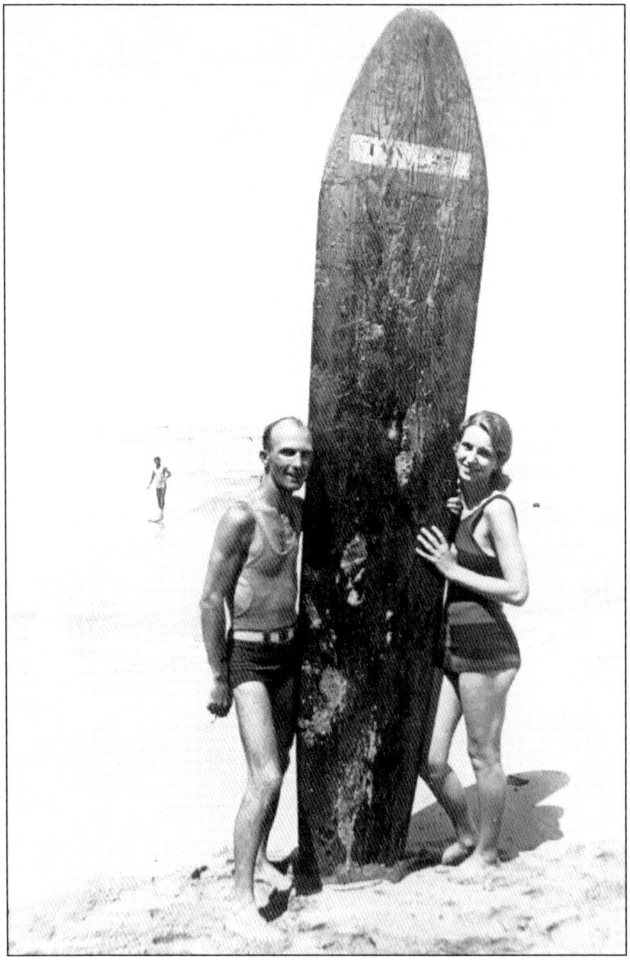

After Battling the Waves, a Happy Couple Displays Their Redwood Plank. For so many malihini, surfing was *the* Hawai'ian experience. In the background a beachboy glides ever so casually onto the beach, ready to step onto the sand. He makes it look so easy. (Courtesy Cary Weiss.)

A Swing-Era Couple Poses with Their New Ford Model A, Papa Li'ili'i Boards, and Ukulele at an Unknown Beach, c. 1930. As the Roaring Twenties came to an end, the United States was at the peak of an economic boom, with more young people emulating the laid-back beachboy lifestyle. It would all crash in the Great Depression.

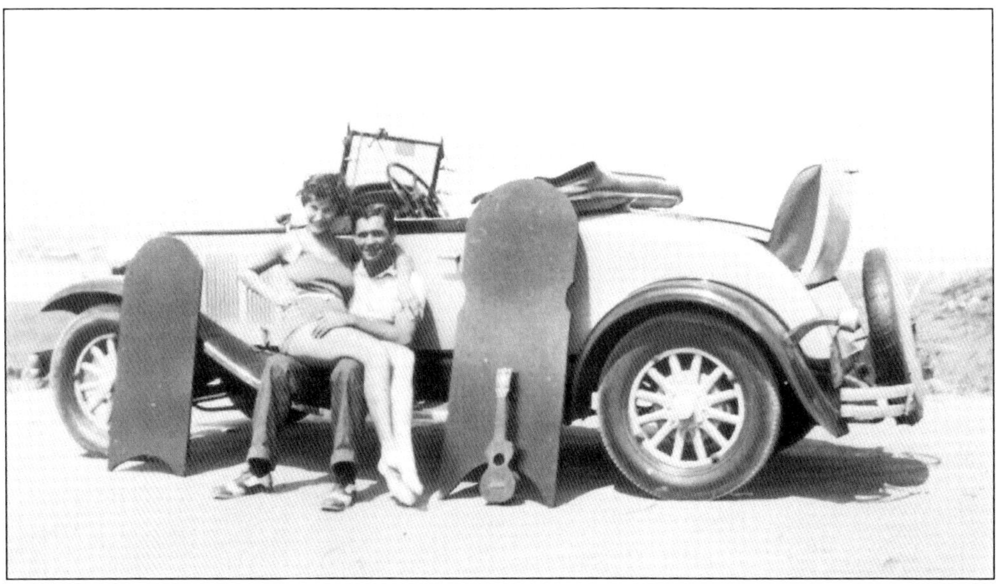

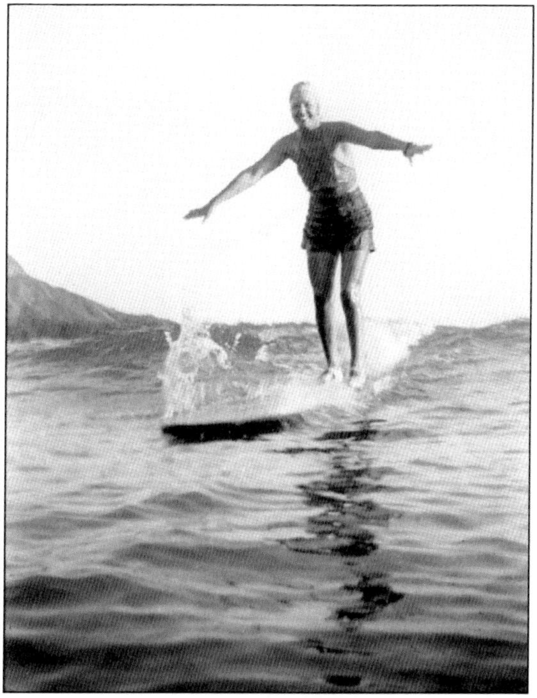

A Sport without Equal. Donald Gillies wrote in "Riding Waikiki's White Horses," an article in *The Sportsman Magazine* in 1929, "But the excitement that awaits the proficient a half mile or more at sea cannot be greater than that felt by the novice who rides his first little roller, near shore, in the *Malihini* surf. Here I learned the rudiments of the sport: a sport, I think, that is without an equal." (Courtesy Cary Weiss.)

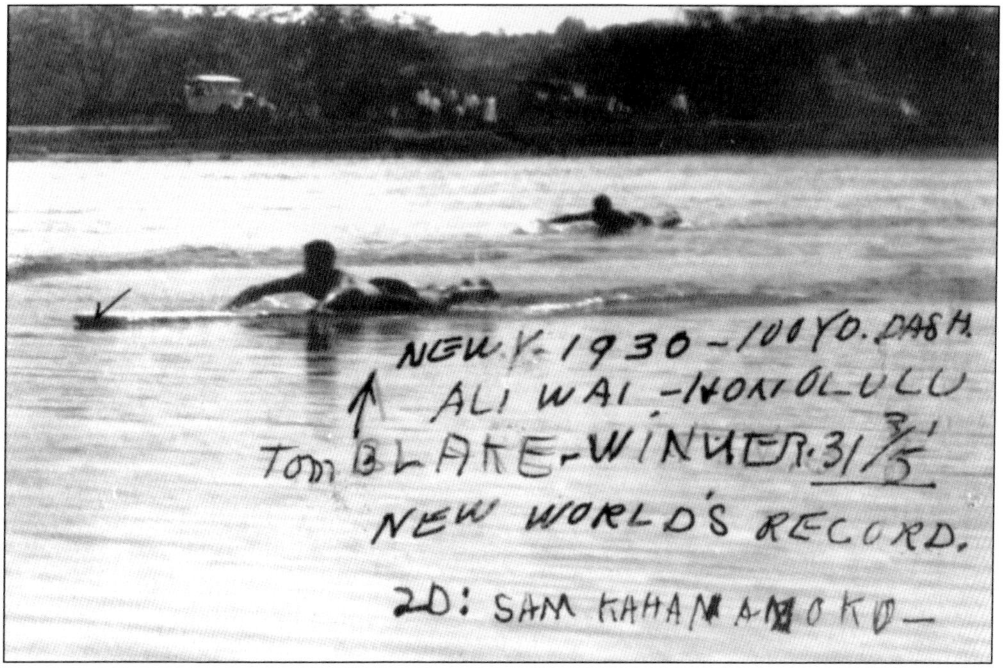

Tom Blake Notes. Scrawled on the photograph is this message: "1930—100 yd. Dash, Ali Wai, Honolulu. Tom Blake, winner—31 3/5, New World Record." Wisconsin-born Blake began studying Bishop Museum's ancient surfboards in 1926. While experimenting, he discovered he could lighten a surfboard by drilling holes. With the hollow surfboard known as "Blake's cigar," he revolutionized surfing and paddling. The cigar was one of the most successful water safety devices ever. (Courtesy Gary Lynch.)

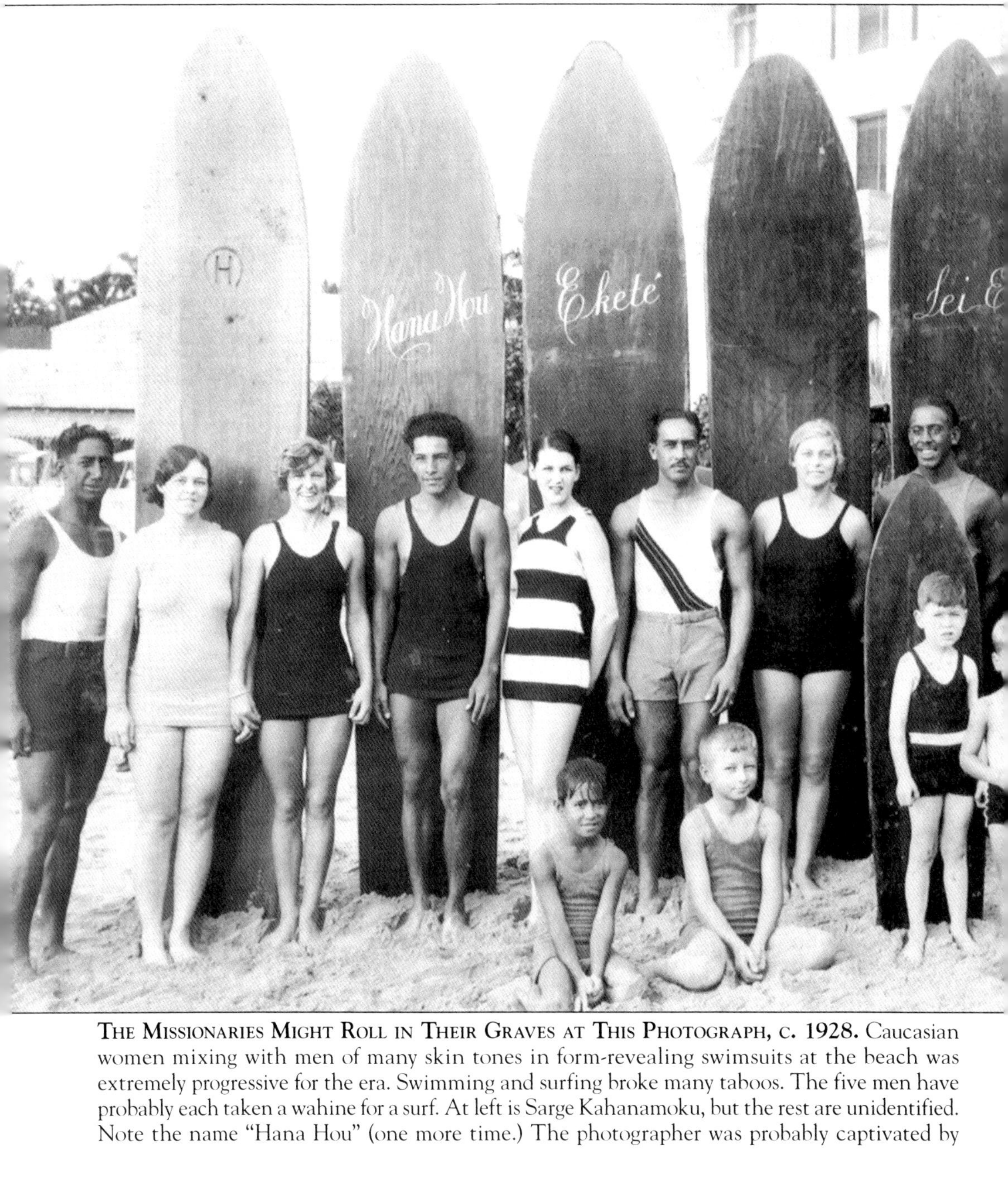

The Missionaries Might Roll in Their Graves at This Photograph, c. 1928. Caucasian women mixing with men of many skin tones in form-revealing swimsuits at the beach was extremely progressive for the era. Swimming and surfing broke many taboos. The five men have probably each taken a wahine for a surf. At left is Sarge Kahanamoku, but the rest are unidentified. Note the name "Hana Hou" (one more time.) The photographer was probably captivated by

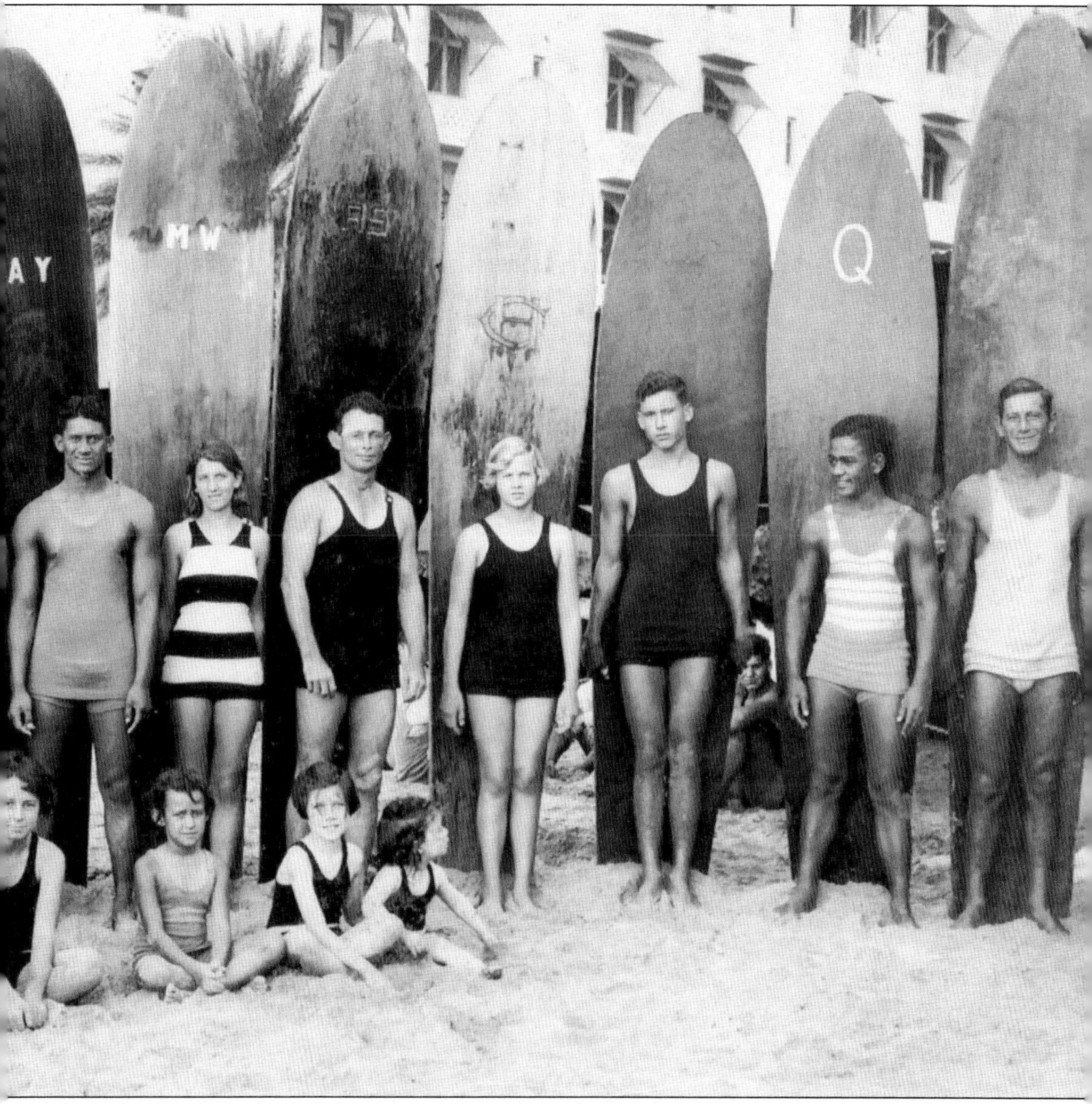

the little cherubs and asked them to pose as well on the beach at the Outrigger Canoe Club. In 1926, women were officially allowed to become members of the OCC, formally disbanding the Women's Auxiliary of the Outrigger Canoe Club. The women's auxiliary was replaced by the Uluniu Women's Swimming Club, presently known as the Uluniu Swimming Club. (Courtesy Outrigger Canoe Club.)

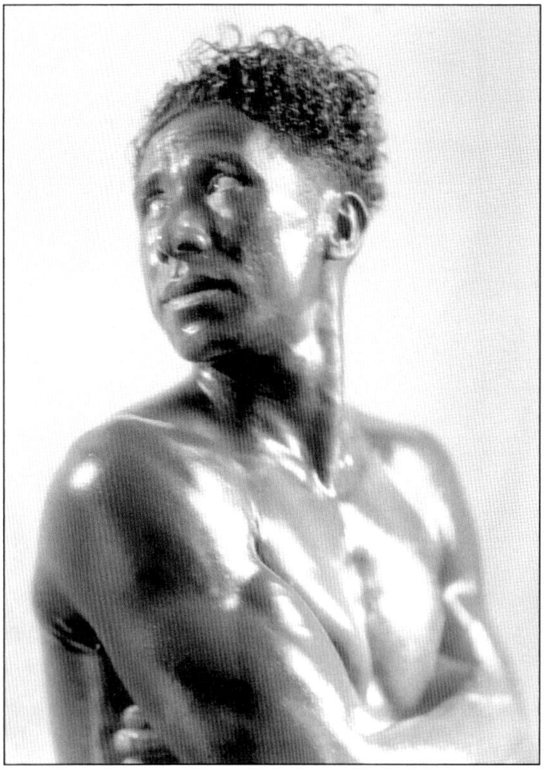

Chick Daniels, Beachboy, March 1927. Daniels was one of the most charismatic beachboys. He was head of beach services at the Royal Hawaiian and in many ways defined the beachboy era with his aloha, water skills, and fun-loving ways. He serenaded guests on the sand by day and performed at night with his band, the Royal Hawaiians. Chick was notorious for his "pants-dropping" hula. At the hula's conclusion, he would drop his pants, always wearing underwear, but one time he forgot he had none on. (Both photographs by Arthur Yarborough.)

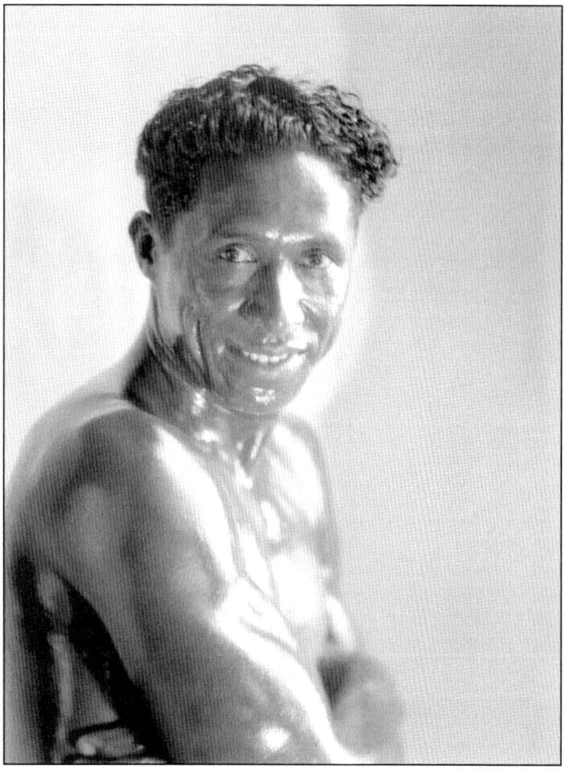

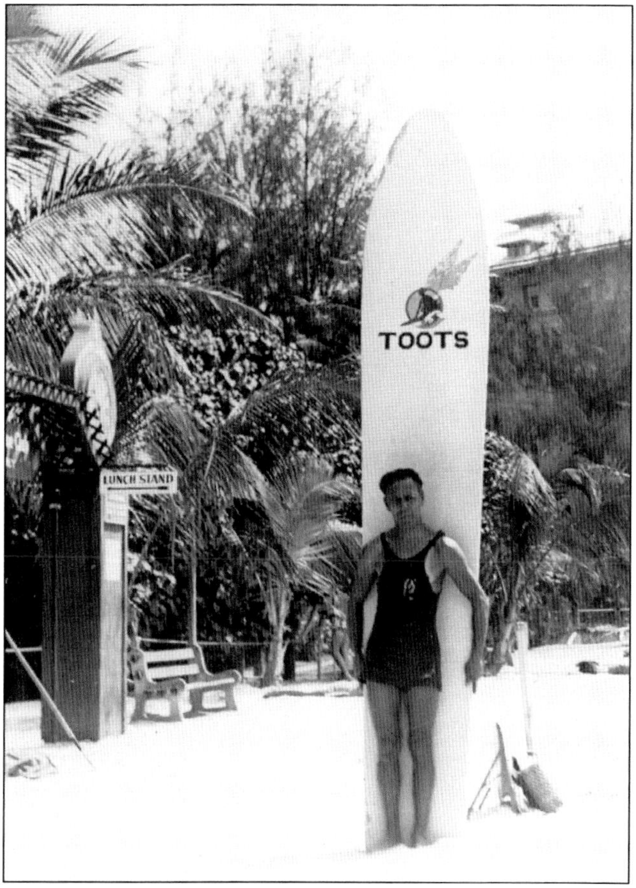

A.E. "Toots" Minveille. Colorado photographer Arthur Yarborough posed Toots in front of the Outrigger Club entrance in 1927 (right). Joseph Mattingly captured Toots surfing in 1928 (below). Hilo-born Minveille was the classic beachboy/waterman and the father of Hawai'ian outrigger canoe racing. He was a fine swimmer, joined the OCC at age 14, and there was coached by Dad Center. While surveying on Moloka'i, Minveille conceived the idea of an outrigger race across the 26-mile Kaiwi Channel from Moloka'i to Oahu. Toots formed the International Hawai'ian Canoe Racing Association, which established the grueling race in 1953, *the* premier event for outriggers. He is recognized for spreading the seeds of aloha and canoe paddling worldwide and is honored with a fine statue at Honolulu International Airport. (Below, courtesy Outrigger Canoe Club.)

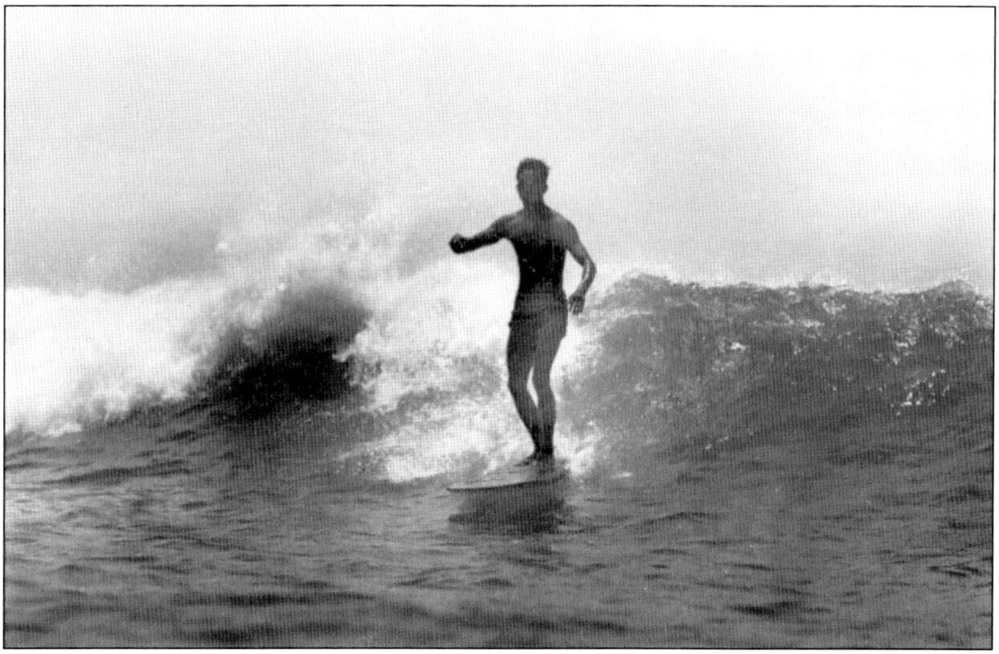

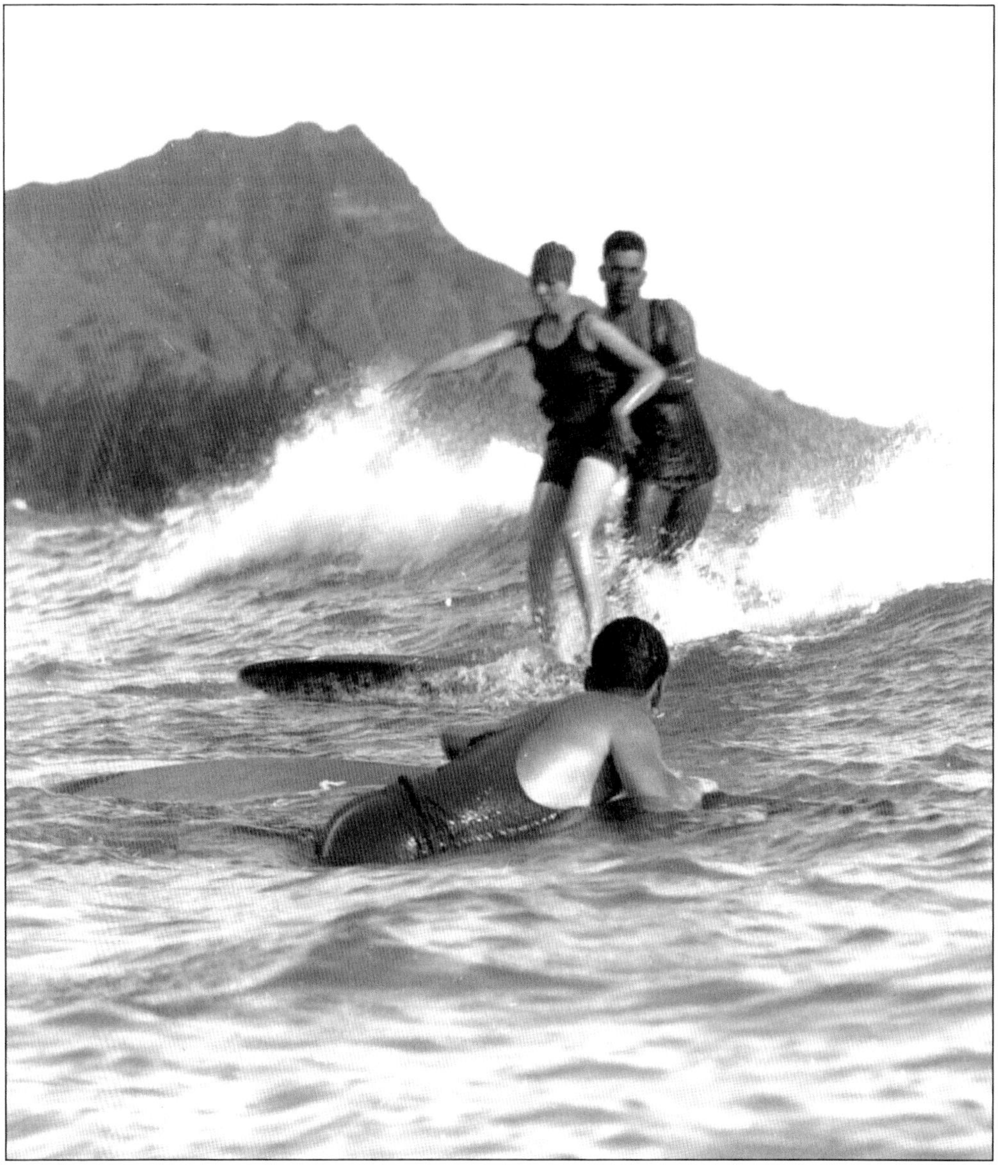

BEACHBOY TOOTS AND A FRIEND, 1928. Toots Minveille, although a college-educated professional, was also a classic beachboy/waterman. Much has yet to be written about Hawai'i's unique beachboys. The fact they were called "boys" when they were prime physical specimens whose domain was the ocean rather than the beach says that they are worthy of scrutiny. The fact is, they were always smiling and joking—even while prices for homes and land skyrocketed, and the influx of people made them fringe dwellers. They willingly shared their skills in teaching swimming, surfing, spearfishing, and squid-poking on the reefs at night with flaming torches. But above all, they shared their love for Hawai'i. It was a rare beachboy who could afford to live near the ocean or who became wealthy. Yet their sharing boomeranged; the beachboys helped keep the native Hawai'ian culture, anchored in aloha and hospitality, alive when they welcomed everyone to their beach and ocean playground. While the heyday of the beachboy was over in the 1930s, all oceangoers today have much to thank them for. (Photograph by Joseph Mattingly, courtesy Outrigger Canoe Club.)

BIBLIOGRAPHY

Blake, Tom. "Surfriding in Hawaii." *Paradise of the Pacific Magazine*. December 1931.

Brown, DeSoto. *Surfing: Historic Images from the Bishop Museum Archives*. Honolulu: Bishop Museum Press, 2006.

Clark, John R.K. *Hawaiian Surfing: Traditions from the Past*. Honolulu: University of Hawaii Press, 2011.

DeLaVega, Timothy Tovar. *200 Years of Surfing Literature, an Annotated Bibliography*. Hanapepe, Hawai'i: DeLaVega/Surfing Heritage Foundation, 2004.

Del Piano, Barbara. *Outrigger Canoe Club: The First Hundred Years, 1908–2008*. Honolulu: Outrigger Canoe Club, 2007.

Finney, Ben R., and James D. Houston. *Surfing, the Sport of Hawai'ian Kings*. Rutland, VT: Tuttle, 1966.

Hall, Sandra Kimberley, and Greg Ambrose. *Memories of Duke: The Legend Comes to Life*. Honolulu: Bess Press, 1995.

———. *Duke: A Great Hawai'ian*. Honolulu: Bess Press, 2004.

Kepelino, Zepherin. *Kepelino's Traditions of Hawai'i*. Honolulu: Bishop Museum Press, 2007.

Lueras, Leonard. *Surfing, the Ultimate Pleasure*. New York: Workman Publishing, 1984.

Malo, David. Hawai'ian antiquities. Honolulu: Bishop Museum Press, 1971.

Moser, Patrick. *Pacific Passages: An Anthology of Surf Writing*. Honolulu: University of Hawai'i Press, 2008.

Smith, Joel T. "Reinventing the Sport, Part II—Alexander Hume Ford," *The Surfer's Journal*. Spring, 2003.

Steiner, Keith. *Hawai'i's Early Territorial Days*. Honolulu: Mutual Publishing, 2001.

Timmons, Grady. *Waikiki Beachboy*. Honolulu: Editions Limited, 1989.

Consistent with our mission to preserve history on a local level, this book was printed in South Carolina on American-made paper and manufactured entirely in the United States. Products carrying the accredited Forest Stewardship Council (FSC) label are printed on 100 percent FSC-certified paper.

MADE IN THE USA